D1359212

The Four Seasons

by Bob Ryan

MASTERS PRESS

A Division of Howard W. Sams & Company

Published by Masters Press
A Division of Howard W. Sams & Company
2647 Waterfront Pkwy E Dr Suite 100
Indianapolis, IN 46214

© 1997 Bob Ryan
All rights reserved. Published 1997

Printed in the United States of America.

No part of this publication may be reproduced, stored in a retrieval system, or transmitted, in any form or by any means, electronic, mechanical, photocopying, recording, or otherwise, without the prior permission of Masters Press.

97 98 99 00 01 02   10 9 8 7 6 5 4 3 2 1

Library of Congress
Cataloging in Publication Information

Ryan, Bob, 1946-
  The four seasons / by Bob Ryan.
      p. cm.
  ISBN 1-57028-127-0

Information Pending

Dedication

To Elaine:
When she goes to games even when you're out of town,
you know you've found the right one.

Credits

Cover Photos©Tom Miller (Larry Bird,Celtics; Dave Meggett, Patriots), Dick Raphael (Carl Yastrzemski, Red Sox), London Life - Portnoy/Hockey Hall of Fame (Bobby Orr, Bruins)

Inside Photos©as credited

Edited by Kim Heusel

Cover Design by Suzanne Lincoln

Text Layout by Kim Heusel

Table of Contents

Introduction

Boston is not The Best Sports Town In America.

This simple statement of fact will come as a shock to the brain-washed Boston sports-loving public, which has been assured for the better part of three decades that it is in possession of a specialized blend of interest, knowledge and pure passion for sport that somehow exceeds that of any other city in the land.

Sorry, Bostonians, but it just isn't true. It's not true because there is no Best Sports Town In America. There are good sports towns and there are even great sports towns, Boston among them, but to single out one as somehow being superior to all the others is preposterous.

Such a city would be mad about baseball, football, basketball and hockey. Such a city — or, more specifically, such a region — would support an annual tennis tournament. People would turn out by the many thousands each year to patronize the PGA, the LPGA and the Senior Tours. There would be interest in the NASCAR circuit. They would make professional soccer a meaningful spectating experience. They would follow college football and basketball with great interest. High school, or, in certain areas, "Preps," would have a certain cachet. The locals might even demonstrate support for track and field.

Winning and losing would be inconsequential acts. Love of the particular sport would be paramount. Spectators would not be mere "fans," but would, instead, be patrons of the art. The professional sports franchises and the local big-time college programs would not be subject to the crass business of winning, as opposed to losing. Attendance would never vary.

The fans would be astonishingly knowledgeable. Local sports radio would rival the BBC in erudition. Letters to the editor in the sports page would reveal the readers to be encyclopedic, witty, insightful and compassionate. Team announcers would be chosen on the basis of wit, charm and their ability to interrelate sport and literature.

Everyone involved would have a sound historical perspective. The past would be cherished and respected, but it would never be allowed to be suffocating.

There is, of course, no such place. Every American metropolis has some demonstrated interest in organized sport. There are no exceptions. From Seattle to Miami, from Boston to San Diego, this is unquestionably a sports-obsessed society. But no one municipality loves *everything*, all the time. Team fortunes change. Sports rise and fall in popularity according to any number of factors, beginning with the venue in which the sport was played. Only a decade ago Atlanta and Cleveland were two of the more moribund baseball sites in America, but in 1997 both the Braves and Indians played to completely sold-out houses for the entire season. Improved play on the field is one reason. New fan-friendly ballparks is another.

No one will ever know if the Cleveland followers would have flocked to see their team were it still performing in the charmless, cavernous monster that was Municipal Stadium, as opposed to the cozy, lively, inviting structure that is Jacobs Field. All we know is that the Indians were the Ottoman Empire of the American League for many years, and that they moved into their new stadium in 1994, which happened to be the very season a well-planned youth movement began to bear fruit. The Indians had not been involved in a pennant race since 1959, when they finished five games behind the fifth-place Chicago White Sox, which means that at least two generations of fans had grown up knowing only ineptitude and irrelevance on the diamond. Combine that with a mausoleum of a stadium, whose sheer size (80,000-plus) eliminated the need to purchase a ticket in advance, and it was a recipe for box office disaster, which the Indians were for many long years. So now that Cleveland has a better team and a great ballpark, is Cleveland a certified Baseball Town?

Perhaps. But only perhaps. Let's see if the fans continue to fill the park when the Indians, as will inevitably happen, recede in the standings. Then we'll see how much of a Baseball Town Cleveland really is, as opposed to a Winning Baseball Town.

But does game attendance alone make a municipality a great sports town? Can a town care without actually flocking to the ballpark, stadium or arena at a given point in town? Suppose a franchise is being poorly run. Suppose a good team has been stripped bare by a foolish owner? Have not the fans a right to send some sort of a message by simply staying away? Case in point: Buffalo had, for a very short time, a vibrant franchise in the National Basketball Association. With exciting players such as three-time NBA scoring champion Bob McAdoo, all-time NBA consecutive game leader Randy Smith and passing wizard Ernie DeGregorio, the Buffalo Braves were one of the more exciting stops on the NBA circuit from 1972-76. Sellout crowds of 18,000 made the ancient Memorial Auditorium (known locally as "The Aud") rock on a continual basis. Then owner Paul Snyder systematically dismantled the team. Fans stayed away in logical protest. By 1978 the Buffalo Braves were the San Diego Clippers. You never hear anyone in authority discuss the city of Buffalo as a possible NBA location anymore. But I am here to tell you that, even though Buffalo is now regarded as the NBA's answer to Pompei, the Queen City was most certainly a Basketball Town 25 years ago. Conceivably, it could become one again, if given the chance.

People can love a sport without loving the current edition of the local team. They may, rightly or wrongly, hate the owner (Exhibit A: The Chicago White Sox fans and Jerry Reinsdorf). The stadium or arena may be forbidding. People can exhibit great interest in a team by listening to its games or watching on TV, or by following it closely through the newspapers. During the many barren Cleveland summers between 1959 and 1994, there were many who insisted that Cleveland still had a healthy interest in the fortunes of the Indians, the minuscule attendances notwithstanding. I, for one, was always impressed by both the volume and the quality of the letters to the editor of the Cleveland papers on the subject of the Indians.

Those people swore that Cleveland really was a baseball town, that the same passion which brought out a then major-league record 2,620,627 fans to Municipal Stadium in 1948 and a then major-league record gathering of 86,288 for a World Series game that autumn, could be rekindled, given the right circumstances. Given what we've seen in Cleveland over the past four years, we must conclude that those people were correct. Given the opportunity to back a contending team, and given a comfortable venue in which to do so, it is 1948 all over again in Cleveland, and perhaps even better.

You would say, without hesitation, that New York is a great sports town. After all, New York is, well, *New York*. Never forget, however, that neither local professional football franchise actually plays in New York. The Giants and Jets each play their games across the Hudson in New Jersey. People have gotten used to the idea by now, but it remains something of a stain on the city of New York. And before too much longer, the unthinkable might become reality. George Steinbrenner may very well join them early in the 21st century. If New York is such a Great Sports Town, shouldn't it at least be able to house its own teams?

And how about this: suppose someone had told you 10 years ago that by 1996 there would be no professional football franchise in Greater Los Angeles? Think you would have believed *that* one? How could this be? The Rams had made the NFL America's first truly national major sports league by relocating from Cleveland following the 1945 season. The Rams had given the world Norm Van Brocklin, Bob Waterfield, Elroy (Crazy Legs) Hirsch, Tom Fears, Dick Bass, Jaguar Jon Arnett, the Fearsome Foursome and Eric Dickerson. There was always a strong dose of romanticism attached to the franchise. The Rams had those wonderful helmets. The Rams beat the Dodgers to L.A. by 12 years and the Lakers by 13. They were the indigenous big-league franchise in town. But first they moved to Anaheim, which was half out of sight and out of mind, and then they did the impossible by moving out altogether, taking their history, and, worse yet, their nickname, to St. Louis in time for the 1996 football season. With the Raiders already having moved back to Oakland, the great city and county of Los Angeles was left without a pro football team. If put on paper at the dawn of the decade, it would have been dismissed as science fiction. But it is all too real.

So is pigskin-deprived Los Angeles a poor sports town? Or is it even fair to describe L.A. as being pigskin-deprived? On Saturday, September 6, 1997, a combined total of 135,402 turned out to see a pair of college football games played in local stadia located some 15 miles apart. UCLA and Tennessee played before 62,619 in the Rose Bowl up in Pasadena at noon, while 4½ hours later Southern Cal and Florida State performed before 72,783 in the Coliseum. You could rightfully assume that the people of Southern California were finding a way to get their football Jones satisfied, even if it were more of the semipro variety.

Being a good sports town involves swallowing myth. I am quite sure that people in Philadelphia consider themselves as constituting a Great Sports Town. Philadelphia offers all the staples. There has been major-league baseball for more than a century. The Philadelphia Eagles have belonged to the NFL since 1933. There has been a professional basketball team in Philly for 51 of the past 52 years. The Flyers were part of the original NHL six-team expansion in 1967. There is a tremendous heritage of college basketball, featuring the so-called "Big Five" of Pennsylvania, Villanova, Temple, St. Joseph's and LaSalle. Philadelphia might also have the greatest rowing legacy in America.

Philadelphia is clearly an important sports town. Its teams are well-covered by both the *Philadelphia Inquirer* and the feisty *Philadelphia Daily News*. There is a rip-roaring, take-no-prisoners talk radio station, WIP. Sports matter in Philadelphia.

But Philadelphia is not without its misconceptions, the most prominent of which is that Philly is a great Basketball Town. It is not.

It *was*, I should say, but it's not. People thereabouts rhapsodize about the Good Old Days of the Warriors, with Paul Arizin, Neil Johnston, George Senesky, Jack George & Co., when owner-coach Eddie Gottlieb ran the franchise out of his inside coat pocket. They might further rhapsodize about the Wilt Chamberlain era. They might continue on about Julius Erving. They might bring tears to your eyes spinning tales of the glorious Palestra doubleheaders, when, after a local team had dispatched some uppity national power in the first game of a doubleheader before a raucous crowd unified in its hatred of the infidel invader, the patrons would engage in pure fratricide during the Big Five clash to follow.

But that is all past history. Once Dr. J. retired in 1987, he took any 76er/NBA mystique with him. The Big Five, meanwhile, was destroyed when the ambitions of Rollie Massimino at Villanova and John Chaney at Temple assumed precedence over the good of the whole collegiate basketball community. The basketball pilot light is currently very, very low in Philadelphia. If Philadelphia is anything from November to March, it is a hockey town.

Presumably, this is all subject to change. Should Allen Iverson and Jerry Stackhouse, or Whomever, lead the 76ers back to NBA prominence, the new Core States Spectrum will (finally) reverberate with the sound of happy basketball fans. Winning almost always eradicates all perceived ills.

Everywhere you look there are cities who swing back and forth, first adoring this team and that sport, and then adoring that team and that sport, most of them supporting franchises through thick and thick. And why not? That's just plain human nature, isn't it? Aren't we all front runners at heart?

It is never wise to assume anything long range, in either direction. You could not give away a Braves ticket in Atlanta 10 years ago. There is no one more chic in the '90s than the Chicago Bulls. Old-timers well recall gatherings of 3,000 in the stinky Ampitheatre in the Bulls' early days. Not-so-old-timers remember rattling around the 20,000-seat Chicago Stadium in the company of no more than 5,000 in the late '70s, several years B.M. (Before Michael). Some local experts say that Chicago still isn't really a Pro Basketball Town, as opposed to a Bulls Town, or, more to the point, a Jordan Town. When number 23 retires, will the Bulls continue to matter more than Life or Death? Or will people decide they've seen the best they'll ever see in the world of basketball and move on to something else? It's hardly inconceivable.

The South is supposed to be official Football Country, but someone had better tell the people in Atlanta, who have reacted to the Falcons with spectacular indifference these past few years. Atlanta is within driving distance of a great deal of college football, and perhaps that is sufficient for Atlantans to placate any football cravings, at least until the Falcons present them with a truly competitive team.

Atlanta certainly isn't a Basketball Town. The Hawks have been there since 1968 without ever really ingratiating themselves into the hearts of the community for any prolonged period of time. Hockey came and went. The new king is NASCAR. Auto Racing is, in fact, the fastest-growing sport of them all, and Atlanta is in the forefront of the movement. But traditional thinkers (Yes, that's my hand you see waving quietly in the back of the room) regard the spectacle of noisy cars revolving in ovals as proof the Apocalypse will soon be upon us, rather than anything good or wholesome. Or interesting. In fact, I'd go so far as to say that the greater the local interest in auto racing, the smaller the legitimate claim a city has of being a Great Sports Town. So much, I suppose, for Charlotte and Jacksonville.

If you go strictly by the depth and breadth of newspaper coverage, you'd have to conclude that the honor of being the Greatest Sports Town In America belongs to Dallas. The *Dallas Morning News* survived a brutal circulation and advertising war with the late, lamented *Dallas Times-Herald*, and emerged to become the greatest devourer of small forests in the land, at least in terms of newsprint devoted to the world of sport. If there is a ball of some sort involved, or if someone is running, jumping, floating, sailing, tumbling, riding an animal, tossing an object, driving a conveyance of some sort at a high rate of speed or directing a punch at a fellow human being, the *Dallas Morning News* will be there to report it. Whether or not there is demonstrated interest in the sport appears to be of only minor concern. If it exists, the *Morning News* will provide the summary and the latest standings.

But anyone who lives there will tell you that only one thing really matters. It's not baseball. It's not basketball. It's not hockey. It's not skateboarding, either. It's really not even football, *per se*, as much as it's the Dallas Cowboys, specifically. The Cowboys were somewhat larger than life right from their inception, but in their latest incarnation they have become something else entirely. They are a living, breathing soap opera, except that the principals are honest-to-God real people. Their comings, their goings, their ups, their downs, their idiosyncracies, their foibles, their quirks and even their occasional good works are all the subject of enormous interest in Dallas.

They've got a nice new baseball park to help get them through the blistering summers and they have had their winter flings with the likes of the NBA Mavericks and NHL Stars and they always have both college and high school football to fall back on, but you could blow up The Ballpark and Reunion Arena and start making the college guys start going to class without disrupting the equilibrium of the local sports fanatic to any large degree. The Cowboys are a 12-months-a-year proposition in Dallas. They may not even sell out all the time, but that's not the point. They are the Cowboys, and they *matter*. Dallas is legitimately one dimensional. And so, despite the dedicated attention to all things sport as reflected by the splendid coverage offered by the *Dallas Morning News*, Dallas is not — I repeat, N-O-T — truly a Great Sports Town.

It is often very difficult to differentiate between the passions of Town X and Town Y. I have long believed, for example, that for the sake of a general argument, there is a certain homogeneity attached to the population of the entire 600-mile long megalopolis which runs from Boston southward to Washington, D.C. There is a certain sameness to the sporting, musical and culinary tastes and there is clearly a similarity in life tempo. Above Boston and below Washington, OK, all bets are off. You know when you're in Portland, Maine, some two hours north of downtown Boston, that you are in a kinder, gentler, *slower* world. I believe you would detect the same difference if you happened to find yourself in Richmond, Virginia, some 90 miles south of the nation's capital. And north of Portland and south of Richmond, are you kidding? Life is substantially different.

But the Boston-Washington corridor is essentially monolithic. Sure, you've got your crab cakes in Baltimore and your Tastykakes in Philly and your pastrami-on-ryes in New York and your frappes (not milkshakes) in Boston, and therein lies the fun. They talk funny to the Boston ear in Philly and even funnier in Baltimore, and everyone agrees that both the New York and Boston accents are downright impenetrable to everyone else, but that, too, doesn't obscure the fact that, when you scrape away the layers on top what you will find underneath is a fast-talking, meat-and-potatoes sports nut who loves his rock 'n roll and his sub sandwiches, by whatever name (they are, for example, "hoagies" in Philadelphia).

There have been great fan rivalries among these cities down through the years, but what most residents of these municipalities haven't realized is that they are far more alike in spirit and sensibility than they are different. They have far more in common with each other than they have with anyone in L.A., San Francisco, Seattle,

Phoenix, Houston, Denver, Minneapolis, Cleveland or Miami; that's for sure. Their closest kindred spirits reside in Greater Chicago.

The toughest place in this megalopolis for the truly well-rounded sports fan to find himself or herself for any prolonged period of time would be Washington, because sporting consciousness in the District of Columbia is dominated by thoughts of the Washington Redskins, the oversized gorilla of Washington sports. Much of what I said about the relationship between the city of Dallas and the Cowboys is replicated in Washington, where the Redskins have occupied a disproportionate place in the town's affairs since the George Allen days. Not having a baseball team for the past quarter-century might have something to do with it, but, given the tattered history of the Senators (both editions), it can probably be argued that the people of Washington *never* had a baseball team.

Washington being such a professionally transient city, the Redskins have become a strangely unifying force. Jack Kent Cooke was a wonderful out-sized personality who constantly stirred the pot, and now that he has gone to that Great Entrepreneur's Home In The Sky, it will be interesting to see if the Redskins will be able to retain the same social standing they had when first Edward Bennett Williams, and then Mr. Cooke, made invitations to Redskin games the Sunday afternoon equivalents of invites to chic Georgetown gatherings.

But while a prolonged stay in Washington might get on a broad-based sports fan's nerves, a Baltimorean transplanted to New York or a Philadelphian relocated to Boston would survive very nicely, the language barrier aside. There is a recognizable intensity level up and down the corridor. Indeed, there are astonishing pockets of frightening sports interest, such as in the New Jersey state capitol of Trenton, the seat of a mini-metropolitan area of perhaps a quarter million people. Trenton is the smallest municipality in America served by competing daily newspapers, and when I say "competing," I mean go-for-the-jugular enemies of the Serb-Croatian mentality.

The broadsheet *Trenton Times* and the tabloid *Trentonian* are mortal enemies, much to the benefit of the community, and, specifically, the sports fan. Trenton is interestingly situated, some 40 miles northeast of Philadelphia and approximately 60 miles southwest of New York City. Reporters from Trenton routinely cover the Phillies,

Eagles, Flyers, 76ers, Yankees, Mets, Giants, Jets, Nets and Devils, in addition to such colleges as Princeton and Rutgers. There is voluminous coverage given over to the many area high schools. It is an altogether extraordinary journalistic circumstance, and these two papers take full advantage of their opportunity.

Long before there was any such thing as cable television, or even before there was much fuss about the UHF portion of the TV dial, you could make a claim for Trenton being the television capital of America. Back in the '50s and '60s, Trenton residents were privileged to get every channel on the VHF dial between 2 and 13 with the exception of 8. Trenton got everything both New York and Philly had to offer, and this was especially bountiful when it came to sports. In an era when many millions of Americans were lucky to get three channels on their Philcos and Admirals, people in 1950s Trenton were fed an unrelenting diet of Phillies, Yankees, Giants and Dodgers games.

Radio? Same thing. They got everything New York got and everything Philly got, in addition to their own programming. Trenton was also 35 miles west of Asbury Park, and anywhere from a one- to two-hour drive from anywhere on the Jersey coast, a circumstance which rendered certain of those beach communities (most notably Seaside Heights), "Little Trentons" in the summer. Trenton was an astonishing microcosm of the entire East Coast, and it is amazing to me that the same sort of sociologists who invaded Muncie, Indiana, in the '40s failed to see the rich possibilities of exploring Trenton as a reflection of East Coast America a decade later.

Disclosure time: I grew up in Trenton.

When you grow up in Trenton, and you are raised a certain way, you come to know Philadelphia and you come to know New York and that is why when you get to Boston the sports fan in you has no trouble feeling at home. They may talk funny, and what you call a traffic circle they may call a "rotary," and what you may call a rubber band they may call an "elastic," but a ball is a ball and a strike is a strike and a jumper is a jumper and a first down is a first down and you learn that they are into all of it. And when you go to school in Boston you encounter kids from all over the Eastern half of the country and you inevitably compare notes, only to learn that you have much more in common with the kid from Greater Washington, Greater

Baltimore, Greater Wilmington, Greater Philadelphia, Greater New York, Greater New Haven and Greater Springfield than you ever imagined.

But you also learn that there really is something different about Boston. Hockey, for one thing. Most of the rest of the country grows up knowing less than nothing about hockey. The NHL is all over America now, but if you talk to the average fan you discover that he or she wasn't really introduced to the sport until he or she was into his or her 20s, or beyond. I must admit that in Silver Springs, Trenton and New Rochelle they don't know from MDC rinks. But in Boston *everyone* was taken to an MDC rink as soon as he or she could walk. And if you didn't go to an MDC rink, it was because there was a frozen pond at the end of your street. So right away we're light years away from that Scottsdale or Ft. Lauderdale experience.

There's more. In Boston there is history, probably too much of it. In Boston there is angst. In Boston there is always a sense of foreboding, a feeling that if something bad hasn't happened today, then it will surely happen tomorrow. In Boston there is always a "Yeah, but..." In Boston there is a sense that the world is going all to hell because they no longer do it the way *we* do it, which, as any sane person knows, is the one right and proper way to do it.

Boston is not the Greatest Sports Town In America, because there is no such thing. What it all comes down to is that Boston is a *unique* sports town. This I do not surmise. This I know.

The Bruins

1971-72 Boston Bruins, winners of the Stanley Cup. (Photo©Hockey Hall of Fame)

1

The Hockey Capital
of America

Boston has no equal as a true hockey town.

Boston truly is the Hockey Capital of America. Yes, there is great residual hockey interest in Minnesota (where the high school tournament is a major event) and in Denver and in a few other areas where it is deemed necessary to crank up the car heater soon after Labor Day. When it comes to a historical hockey narrative, however, Boston is America's home office.

What's indisputable is the fact that Boston is the certified home of major-league hockey. The Boston Bruins were the first American entry in the National Hockey League, and you can look it up.

The story begins with a New England businessman named Charles F. Adams. Long a hockey enthusiast, a dedicated backer of local amateur teams, he became completely infatuated with the sport when he journeyed north of the border to see what was taking place in the 1924 Stanley Cup Finals, then a round-robin affair featuring representatives of the NHL, the Pacific Coast Hockey League (PCHL) and the Western Canada Hockey League (WCHL). Adams found the competition so skilled and spirited that he simply had to get involved.

Thus were born the Boston Bruins, who set up shop in the heretofore All-Canadian National Hockey League for the 1924-25 season. While in Canada, Adams had made the acquaintance of a man named Art Ross, and it was to Art Ross that Mr. Adams entrusted the task of securing players for his new team and then coaching them. If that name rings some sort of vague and distant bell in the head of the generic sports fan, it is because each season the NHL scoring champion is named winner of the Art Ross Trophy.

And well they should, because Art Ross was one of the most important figures in the history of the sport. Start with the puck. That's right, the puck.

The NHL plays with the "Art Ross Puck." The puck, you see, wasn't always the simple hard rubber disc we all know today. Once upon a time, the puck actually had dangersouly sharp edges. Sooner or later, someone had to come up with a better idea, and that someone was Art Ross, who reasoned that a puck with bevelled edges made more sense.

And how about the net? That's another Art Ross creation. Before Art Ross attacked the problem, nets had sloping flat rear sections. Pucks frequently bounced out, causing confusion for players and officials alike. The Ross solution was a double half-moon interior which, 99.999 percent of the time, keeps the puck in the net once it enters the scoring area.

But Art Ross was more than just a mad hockey scientist. He was also a shrewd judge of talent and an inspired coach. He might not necessarily have been the life of the party, given that just about every printed reference to him portrays him as "crusty, sour Scot," but he knew his business and his business was hockey.

4

When Art Ross crossed paths with Charles Adams, he was 38 years old, just the age to have the perfect combination of accumulated knowledge and both physical and mental energy to tackle the formidable task of making the Boston Bruins competitive with the Canadian teams, all of whom had a huge head start on the American entry.

Having found the man capable of running his organization, Adams needed a nickname for his new team. He approached this task in very diligent fashion, even going so far as to set down guidelines.

The color scheme would be brown with yellow trim. These were the colors of Brookside Stores, whose president was — take a guess — Charles F. Adams. (Cross-promotion didn't come into being thanks to Disney). And the nickname must pertain to, in Mr. Adams' own words, "an untamed animal whose name was synonymous with size, strength, agility, ferocity and cunning," and which, of course, would also have to be brown.

So right away to say it was clear they would not become the Zebras, Pachyderms or Chihuahas. Adams entertained dozens of names, but none suited him. In the end he heeded the suggestion of a secretary of his at a sporting goods store he ran in Montreal. "Why not 'Bruins?' " she inquired. *Voila!* Bruins they were, and Bruins they remain.

Ross' acumen could only take the Bruins so far. They were something less than an immediate success, finishing sixth and last behind the Montreal Maroons, Ottawa Senators, Montreal Canadiens, Toronto Maple Leafs and Hamilton Tigers with a sorry 6-24 record.

The team improved significantly in its second season, advancing to fourth while winning more games than it lost, but Charles Adams knew the team was still several players short of the championship level. He had money and he had drive. He was definitely a big thinker. He cast his eyes westward, and what he saw was a Pacific Coast Hockey League in disarray. There was a player auction going on, and Mr. Adams was at the ready with his paddle and his checkbook. He plunked down $50,000 to purchase seven players, one of whom would become a Franchise Player in the truest sense.

That player was the mercurial Eddie Shore.

Charles Adams founded the Bruins, but it was Eddie Shore who institutionalized them. He was known as the "Edmonton Express" for his swashbuckling style of play, and for 14 glorious seasons he was the embodiment of the team. In a game where roughness is a given and extreme toughness revered, Eddie Shore was, without argument, the Toughest Man Of Them All. He came to Boston skating hard and hitting even harder and he became an instant hit with the fans.

By his second year with the Bruins Shore even had a new place to play. Adams had reached into his pocket once again, this time coming up with $500,000 to help fund a new indoor arena that would be constructed atop North Station in downtown Boston. The arena had originally been the brainchild of famed New York promoter Tex Rickard, who had built the third Madison Square Garden at 50th Street and 8th Avenue in midtown Manhattan. Rickard envisioned a string of Madison Square Gardens from coast to coast, but the only one which went up before his premature death was the one in Boston.

Boston Garden would be the home of the Bruins from 1927 through 1995, and it would become the most famous hockey venue in the United States. It was constructed with hockey, boxing and indoor track in mind, and its sightlines for hockey were magnificent. No building will ever be built that could come close to replicating the wondrous balcony seats, which hung out over the ice and afforded lucky occupants a spectacular view of the action. Located on both sides of the ice were additional balconies, known as the "second balconies," which, while lofty, were nevertheless desirable. These seats were done away with in the late '70s when the building was reconfigured to accommodate the construction of the loathsome "luxury boxes" which have become the *raison d'etre* of modern arena and stadium construction.

The first superstar to call Boston Garden home was Eddie Shore, who introduced the hockey fans of Boston to the taste of blood, if you will, and for the past 60-plus years they have passed on this appreciation of barely controlled aggression from generation to generation. The Boston fan does appreciate the nuances of the game as much as anyone, and more than most, but he simply cannot tolerate any player he or she perceives to be pacifistic in any way. The typical Bruins fan has long believed that it is somewhat palatable to have lost the game if the home team has at least won the fight. This way of thinking traces back to Eddie Shore, who first came to Boston when Calvin Coolidge was president.

But Eddie Shore was more than just some madman on skates. He was a rare combination of skill and moxie. He was an offensive-minded defenseman not unlike Bobby Orr, but it must be understood that the general concept of the game, not to mention the rules, was far different then. Someone might look at his career scoring totals of 103 goals and 176 assists compiled in 543 games over 14 seasons and say, "So?" But these totals were carved out in the context of times vastly different than ours. In Eddie Shore's day, a 20-goal scorer was a very formidable offensive weapon for any team to possess.

For those privileged to see him play Eddie Shore had an unforgettable presence. I was fortunate to make the acquaintance of a delightful man named Albert Minowitz, who was an all-around sports fan of the highest degree. He had been a Boston Garden two-sport regular for close to 60 years, and he once told me that he had seen Milt Schmidt, Frankie Brimsek, Bob Cousy, Bill Russell, Bobby Orr, Phil Esposito, Larry Bird and every other great or near-great ever to wear either a Bruins or Celtics uniform, and that the greatest recurrent moment in the history of the storied building were those times when Eddie Shore, the "Edmonton Express," would gather the puck behind his own net and set out on a patented end-to-end excursion toward the net at the far end of the ice. What higher praise could there be?

By 1928 Ross had enough support for Shore to make the Bruins contenders. He had a standout goalie in Tiny Thompson, solid defense from Lionel Hitchman and George Owen and a formidable offensive trio in the "Dynamite Line," which consisted of Dit Clapper, Cooney Weiland and Dutch Gainor. (Could a script writer have come up with better names for linemates than Dit, Cooney and Dutch?) Weiland became better known to future generations as the longtime head coach at Harvard, but the fact is that he was a high-scoring center who pumped in an extraordinary 43 goals in 44 games during the '28-29 season. Clapper played 20 distinguished and productive seasons for the Bruins.

Hitchman's number 3 and Clapper's number 5 are among the Bruins' eight retired numbers. Shore's vaunted number 2 likewise flies from the Fleet Center ceiling.

In their fourth season of existence the Bruins won the Stanley Cup, winning five consecutive taut games from the Montreal Canadiens and New York Rangers. Can you imagine the relentless tension as the Bruins became champions for the first time by scores of 1-0, 1-0, 3-2, 2-0 (What a beating!) and 2-1? But, close games and all, it was almost too easy. No doubt owner, coach, players and fans alike thought the Bruins would be dominating the NHL. There would be a 10-year wait for a second title.

The Bruins didn't win any more titles until the close of the next decade, but they did cement their fan following, in large measure due to the extraordinary play of Shore, a theatrical player who had no problem recognizing that sport and entertainment were, at the very least, first cousins.

But the Shore emphasis was always much more on the games and the competition than the yuks. And no one in the Boston Garden left in a festive mood on the night of December 12, 1933, for that was the night when Eddie Shore came very close to killing Irwin Wallace "Ace" Bailey.

The smooth-skating Bailey was busy killing off a Toronto penalty with his customary *elan* when Shore was tripped by the legendary Frank "King" Clancy. Shore, apparently believing somehow that the offending party had been Bailey, set out in pursuit of the Toronto winger. Bailey had his back to Shore when the latter delivered a fearsome blow to the kidneys. Bailey went head over heels, his head striking the ice with terrific force.

Two brain operations later, Bailey was again a functioning human being, but his professional hockey career was over. Shore had been suspended immediately by the NHL, but after a month of deliberation the governors exonerated him, citing the fact that, as rugged a performer as he had been during his six-year NHL career, he had not once received a match penalty for injuring an opponent. He and Bailey would have a *rapprochement* of sorts by shaking hands at a benefit being thrown for Bailey. The astonishingly conciliatory Bailey refused to demonize Shore for the gratification of the outraged

Toronto populace, simply saying, "We didn't see each other coming." Bailey later became a familiar sight at Maple Leafs home games as one of the so-called "minor officials."

Among the spectators present in the Boston Garden on the night when Ace Bailey nearly met his maker, courtesy of Eddie Shore, was a 14-year-old named Roger Naples. He is among the very few still around with first-hand memory of that night. "What I still remember was Red Horner going after Shore after he decked Ace Bailey," Naples recalls.

George "Red" Horner was a pugnacious Toronto defenseman who definitely rivaled Shore on the Toughman scale. He, too, was afraid of no man, and he reacted to Shore's attack on his teammate by nailing Shore with a right uppercut to the jaw, an act which drew a suspension, but which also satisfied an ancient hockey code.

Naples was an all-around sports fan, but it was hockey that really got his pulse racing. He and his buddies became fierce Bruins fans, attending as many games as they could over the next few years.

"Those were still the days of what they called the 'rush' seats," he explains. "You'd go into the Garden at 2 o'clock for an 8:30 game. This was a little aggravating, and we were about to boycott the place when we went to the people at the Bruins and asked about getting the first two rows of the Garden second balcony reserved. They said OK, and now we could be like everyone else and get to the game five minutes before they dropped the puck."

This was the birth of a great American sporting institution — the Gallery Gods. Roger Naples, was, and is, their president.

"We've got about 780 people who pay their dues," he says. The dues are to help fund the Gallery Gods' various charitable endeavors, which include dinners and such. "But we've had a lot of people drop out. People can no longer go to the games because of the prices.

Some have kept going by getting together and splitting the tickets four ways. It's the only way they can afford it."

When Roger Naples formed the Gallery Gods in 1937, the per-game price for his second-balcony seat in section 118, row A, seat 13 was 40 cents. The price for the behind-the-net balcony seats he and his fellow Gallery Gods paid for a single-game ticket in the 1997-98 season is $24, and that's because they are season ticket holders. The single game seats for Joe Fan are $29.

Roger Naples did well enough in his long career as a recreation department worker in the city of Revere to keep paying for each increase in season tickets, but I suspect that even if he really couldn't afford the seats he would have found a way to keep going because he simply loved both the game of hockey and the Boston Bruins too much to stay away.

In those days there were no barriers between players and fans. You might find yourself riding to a Bruins game on the streetcar next to one of the players. They weren't making that much more money than anyone else, and they didn't consider themselves to be a separate breed. There were no agents, handlers or middlemen of any kind. If you wished to engage a player in conversation all that was necessary was to amble up and say "Hi."

So it was that when 18-year-old Milt Schmidt arrived in Boston as a center of some promise in the fall of 1936 it was no big deal for young Roger Naples to make his acquaintance. The two have been friends for the past 60 years.

"Milt Schmidt has been my role model," declares Roger Naples. "I remember the day he came up and I remember the day he retired." And, I am sure, a few thousand days in between Schmidt's arrival in 1936 and his retirement in 1955. "On the ice, it was 'Look out, get the hell out of my way,' but off the ice he was a perfect gentleman. He is a true humanitarian, just a great guy.

"I went to games on the road," Naples continues, "and when he'd see me in the lobby he'd say, 'Need any money?' That's the kind of guy Milt Schmidt is."

If Roger Naples, or anyone else, for that matter, wanted to find Milt Schmidt away from the ice he was not difficult to find. It was hardly a state secret that Schmidt and some of his teammates lived in a rooming house in Brookline, Mass., run by a lady known as Ma Snow. "The house was at 2 Coolidge Street," says Naples. "I drove by it not long ago. Still looked pretty good."

Art Ross placed Schmidt between right wing Bobby Bauer and left wing Woody Dumart, and in so doing made hockey history by inventing the "Kraut Line," a handle which would never fly in these decidedly politically correct times, but which had no trouble passing societal mustard in 1937.

"That's one line I'll never forget as long as I live," Naples says. "They really knew what it was all about."

Ross was reloading. He still had Shore, he had the Kraut Line and he had a dazzling playmaker in the gifted Bill Cowley, a player who was so clever with the puck that he remains the standard by which all future Bruin stickhandlers are measured. Cowley relied on finesse, whereas Schmidt was a more rugged player. Cowley fans always maintained that were their hero placed on the Kraut Line he would have gained everlasting immortality rather than polite local acclaim.

After a disappointing three-game sweep by Toronto in the 1938 playoffs, the Bruins looked ahead to the 1938-39 season with great anticipation. They had finished first during the previous regular season, and they felt they were now poised to make an even bigger splash in the NHL pool.

Ross himself was in general agreement, but he had one last project in his mind. Though veteran goalkeeper Tiny Thompson was still quite viable, having won the 1938 Vezina Trophy given to the goaltender on the team allowing the fewest goals, Ross thought he could improve the situation.

Ross had his eye on an American-born goaltender playing down the road in Providence. His name was Frankie Brimsek.

Scouts liked him, but there were reservations. An *American*? One thing everyone agreed on was that, however popular the game was becoming in the States, the game itself belonged to the Canadians. But Art Ross didn't care about that. When he looked at Brimsek he saw a great, not merely a good, goaltender. He was aware that the Detroit Red Wings shared his judgment and were prepared to offer Providence the staggering sum of $15,000 for his services. Three weeks into the season, Ross made his move. He sold Tiny Thompson to the Red Wings and he purchased the contract of Frankie Brimsek.

The veterans were apoplectic. The fans were outraged. "I thought he was cuckoo," admits Roger Naples. "I really thought the man was insane."

In Frankie Brimsek's first seven games he allowed two enemy goals. He broke into the NHL with six shutouts in the first three weeks. He shut out Chicago twice. He shut out Montreal twice. He shut out the New York Rangers. And he shut out the Detroit Red Wings.

And he had a new and everlasting nickname: Mr. Zero.

"What a glove hand," says Roger Naples. "It didn't take him long to get everyone on his side."

The Bruins of 1938-39 were nothing if not decisive. They only played two ties during that 48-game season. What they did, most often, was win. They finished first in the regular season and this time they finished the job, defeating the Rangers in seven games and the Maple Leafs in five to bring the Stanley Cup to Boston for the second time.

The 1939 Stanley Cup Finals marked the emergence of a new hero, Mel (Sudden Death) Hill. The Bruins won Games 1, 2 and 7 in overtime, and in each case the winning goal was supplied by Mel Hill, a relatively nondescript player who had only scored 10 goals during the regular season. These Stanley Cup heroics gave Mel Hill a nickname he would carry through the remainder of his 10-season, three-team NHL career.

The Bruins finished first for the third consecutive season the following year, but they were beaten in the playoffs by the Rangers. Little did anyone in New York know that it would be another 54 years before they would see anyone skating around Madison Square Garden — by then in its fourth incarnation — with the Stanley Cup held aloft.

The season was not without controversy, and, of course, at the center of it all was Eddie Shore. Actually, he was only the party of the second part. The party of the first part was Art Ross.

By 1939 Shore had given the Bruins 13 good years and the distinctly unsentimental Mr. Ross reasoned he didn't have many more to give. He let it be known that he would consider parting with the team's cornerstone player, and he was delighted to learn that the New York Americans might be willing to go as high as $25,000 in order to add a legend to their roster.

This, however, was Eddie Shore, and he was a step ahead of the game. Unbeknownst to Ross, he had been taking steps to fulfill a long-standing ambition. He was making plans to spend $42,000 to purchase the Springfield franchise of the American Hockey League, for whom he planned on becoming a player-owner.

When Ross learned this, he called for a summit, and the men agreed on a novel proposal. Yes, Shore would be allowed to move 100 miles west in order to manage and play for the Springfield team, but in the case of "emergency," he would still be available to the Bruins, as well, any time after December 15, 1939. Ross immediately tried to alter the deal by declaring an emergency in advance of December 15, 1939.

Ross therefore pressured Shore into playing three games. Shore scored his final goal as a Bruin on December 5, 1939, whereupon he said that was it, that he was through playing games with Ross.

Ross harrumphed for a month before declaring that he would allow Shore to fulfill his Springfield obligations. Two weeks later he traded Shore to the New York Americans for Eddie Wiseman.

Roger Naples ran into Shore just after the trade. "Kid," he said, "it's just like being a priest. Here today, gone tomorrow."

Shore finished out the season with the Americans. After that, he belonged to Springfield, where he spent the next four decades enhancing the Shore legend as owner of the Springfield hockey team (first the Kings and then the Indians) and as operator of the Eastern States Exposition, where his team played its games, and from which Shore ran every aspect of hockey in that Western Massachusetts city. Suffice it to say that during his time in Springfield he gave new, deeper meanings to such words as "cantankerous" and "penurious."

Case in point: if a local high school hockey team rented Shore's building for a one-hour practice from, say, 5 to 6 in the afternoon that did not mean 4:53 to 6:07. It meant 5 to 6. If you weren't off the ice, showered and dressed at 6, off went the water and out went the lights. Good-bye. Keep in mind that Eddie Shore was a man who never really apologized for almost killing Ace Bailey. He was the One and Only Eddie Shore.

The 1940-41 season was another glorious Bruins year. Finishing first once again (this time doing it by tying a whopping 13 times), the Bruins won Stanley Cup number three by outlasting Toronto in seven games and blowing away Detroit in four. They won this title for Cooney Weiland, who had replaced Ross following the 1939 title when Ross decided he would stick to general managing for a while.

Then came World War II.

The Boston Bruins were hardly the only sporting enterprise severely affected by the war. There were Great Imponderables by the hundreds. In Boston, for example, how many millions of words have been written on the subject of Ted Williams, and what numbers he would have fashioned had he not lost three full seasons to the war at the peak of his physical powers? The story can be repeated in city after city and team after team where World War II was a fact of life.

Consider, for a moment, the Boston Bruins in 1941. Frankie Brimsek was 26 years old. Milt Schmidt was not yet 24. Bobby Bauer was 26. Woody Dumart was 25. Bill Cowley was 29. The Bruins may very well have been on the verge of constructing a dynasty.

The war changed all that. In a move so emblematic of the times, the Kraut Line enlisted in the Royal Canadian Air Force together. Such a move today would be derided by cynics as pathetic grandstanding, but in that sweeter, far more innocent era it seemed perfectly appropriate to one and all.

The Bruins' remnants did make it to the Stanley Cup Finals in 1943, losing four straight to Detroit after disposing of the Montreal Canadiens in five games. No one thought there was anything dramatic about that. It was the fourth time the Bruins had played the Canadiens in Stanley Cup competition and it evened the all-time series ledger at 2-2.

Hah!

The next time a Bruins team would defeat a Canadiens team in Stanley Cup competition would be nine American presidents, two new states and 14 Bruins coaches later.

The Bruins made it back to the Finals in 1946, losing to Montreal — file that away — but after that they finished out the '40s as a harmless, middle-of-the-pack kind of team.

They never finished first during the '50s, but that's not the issue in the National Hockey League. It's what you do in the postseason that counts, and the Bruins roused themselves sufficiently to reach the Cup Finals in 1953, 1957 and 1958. There was one common denominator. In each case the Bruins lost the big series to the Montreal Canadiens. By this time a rather serious pattern was emerging.

- 1946: Montreal 4, Boston 1
- 1947: Montreal 4, Boston 1
- 1952: Montreal 4, Boston 3
- 1953: Montreal 4, Boston 1
- 1954: Montreal 4, Boston 0
- 1955: Montreal 4, Boston 1
- 1957: Montreal 4, Boston 1
- 1958: Montreal 4, Boston 2

And the torture wasn't even half done!

We can throw out the '57 and '58 results. In those days *nobody*, nobody could beat the Canadiens when it mattered. This was the middle of Montreal's phenomenal strangulation of the NHL. It was a team replete with star after star, and it was in the midst of winning five consecutive Stanley Cup championships. The names are all part of hockey history: Richard, Beliveau, Plante, Harvey, Moore, Johnson, and that's just the beginning. This team needed its own wing in the Hockey Hall of Fame. It was a team of larger-than-life players, and it was superbly coached by Hector (Toe) Blake. You can forgive the Bruins for losing to this team.

But as the years went on, it didn't seem to matter how good the teams really were, or who was hurt and who was healthy. No matter how often it may have seemed that the Bruins had an equal, if not better, team, Montreal would find a way to win. Generations (plural) of dedicated Boston hockey fans would see their hair whiten, their skin wrinkle, their teeth loosen and their dispositions sour while waiting for the almost unimaginable day when the Bruins would defeat the Canadiens in Stanley Cup competition.

It almost became the defining reason for being a Bruins fan. It gave people reason to root for the team, reason, in some cases to *live*. Just as people maintain they simply *must* hang on long enough to see their beloved Red Sox actually win the World Series, so, too, were Bruins fans turning into Montreal-obsessed people. And whereas the Red Sox situation made it mandatory to focus energy on all teams, because any of them could be the nemesis in a given year, the Bruins' fans could place all their focus and all their mental energy on a fascinating love-hate relationship with the Montreal Canadiens.

And there was, if not love, then surely genuine admiration, because the Canadiens were eternally pretty to watch. Oh, they had their goons along the way (the name John Ferguson was, for many years, positively Hitlerian in nature to Boston fans), the essence of the Canadiens was (seemingly) effortless skating and the capacity to make dazzling plays. Bruins fans could not help but admire the team which consistently taught their own heroes just how beautiful this game could be.

But what Bruins fan could possibly have believed it if, the day after Montreal's series-clinching 5-4 victory on March 30, 1943, someone had walked up and said, "That child of yours who was born today has an excellent chance of becoming a grandparent before either of you will ever see another Boston team win a Stanley Cup series from the Montreal Canadiens again?"

But that was the case, and it wouldn't have necessitated any Loretta Lynn, grandmother-at-31 deal, either. A child born on March 30, 1943, would be 45 years of age when the Bruins would next win a playoff series from Montreal.

Incroyable!

The Bruins fell down a dark hole in sort of Alice In Wonderland fashion in 1959-60. After finishing a respectable second, and losing a hard-fought seven-game series to the Maple Leafs the previous spring, the Bruins fell to fifth. That was bad enough, but the following season was even worse. The Bruins secured for themselves a nice long-term lease on the National Hockey League basement.

For the next seven years the Boston Bruins were, indisputably, the worst team in the National Hockey League and were a serious candidate as the most inept team in all of North American major-league sport. There was neither a spin nor a message that could be put on the record. The Bruins finished sixth (in other words, last), sixth, sixth, sixth and sixth from 1960-61 through 1964-65. They rose to the apparently dizzying height of fifth the following year, but the effort must have been far too taxing, because the following season they were sixth and last again.

They were landlords at the Boston Garden and they were paired off in the public mind against their own primary tenants. For while the Bruins were establishing new standards of incompetency in their sport, the Boston Celtics were likewise establishing new standards of excellence in theirs. Matched up against the Bruins during an almost incomprehensible stretch of eight years in which the Bruins could not manage to make even one playoff appearance in a six-team league, the Boston Celtics won championships in 1960, 1961, 1962, 1963, 1964, 1965 and 1966, to go along with titles in 1957 and 1959. The Celtics finally lost the title in 1967 when the Philadelphia 76ers had a miracle year in which they won a then-record 69 games. The Celtics did not exactly suffer through an off-year, winning 60 games, but 1966-67 was simply destined to be Philadelphia's year.

In this circumstance, any outsider — that is to say, anyone re-siding outside of New England — would have assumed that the Bru-ins would be standing on Causeway Street outside the Boston Garden begging people to come inside, while the Celtics would be finding it necessary to hire security police to prevent frustrated ticket buyers from storming a sold-out building. But that, as every good Bostonian knows, was not the case.

This era was the Golden Era of the Bruins fan, the time when he demonstrated that love of team and love of sport can indeed tran-scend the crass matter of winning and losing.

More often than not, you couldn't get a ticket to a Bruins game. People loved them, come hell, high water or five-minute major. The Celtics? Well, there was a hard-core fandom, but basketball simply wasn't a widespread Boston winter passion. The numbers are forever startling to contemplate. The Celtics were, without question, the greatest basketball team man had ever been privileged to see. They had Bill Russell, whom only Michael Jordan challenges as the greatest team sport athlete in American history. They had Bob Cousy. They had Bill Sharman. They had Tom Heinsohn. They had Sam Jones.

They had Frank Ramsey. They had K.C. Jones. They had John Havlicek. All are in the Hall of Fame. They were basketball artists of the highest degree. But the best they could do during those eight years in which they were kings of their world and the Bruins were infants in theirs was average 10,409 a game in 1966-67. Their eight-year average was slightly in excess of 8,000 a night, or not even 60 percent capacity.

One reason the Bruins continued to attract a steady paying clientele was their adherence to what we shall refer to as the Eddie Shore style of play. The Bruins might not have won many games during those eight Lost Years (149 out of 560), but there was many a night when the fans could exit the Boston Garden saying, "OK, we might have lost the war, but at least we won the fight."

And it wasn't just a matter of fisticuffs. The Bruins always had at least one or two truly entertaining players. Consider the reality of a six-team league. There were just over 100 jobs in the league, and the players in the NHL were the best players in the world. No one was about to question that. So even the worst players on the Bruins could play the game. And some, like Bronco Horvath and Leo Boivin, could *really* play.

Horvath moved over to the Bruins from the Canadiens in 1957 and proceeded to establish himself as one of the great scorers in the league. In 1959-60 he finished second in scoring to the great Bobby Hull. Along with Johnny Bucyk and Vic Stasiuk, he was part of the "Uke Line," so-called because each was supposed to be of Ukranian extraction. This wasn't exactly true, but, as the journalist said in *The Man Who Shot Liberty Valance*, when the truth conflicts with the legend, it's always best to print the legend. Bucyk, who came to the team from Detroit in a deal for troubled goaltending genius Terry Sawchuk in 1957, was able to stay around and enjoy the glory years of the early '70s.

Boivin lives in legend because of a singular skill. A defensive defenseman with typical '50s and '60s defensive scoring totals (47 goals and 164 assists in 717 games as a Bruin), he made a name for himself by becoming the most noted body checker of the day. Whereas checking in the modern game normally takes place along the boards, Boivin was a terror in the middle of the ice. He made the midice hip check an art form, and he was good enough at his specialty to become a member of the Hall of Fame.

Boivin personified the spirit of the Bruins in the eyes of people such as Roger Naples and his friends in the Gallery Gods. The team had precious few scorers, and the goaltending often scared people, but there was a nobility about Boivin which pleased these aficionados of the game. This, clearly, was a man who played the game in a manner Eddie Shore himself would have appreciated.

The fidelity of the Bruins' fans was truly amazing. Much would be made a decade or so later about the faithfulness of the New York Giants football fans. This was after Allie Sherman and pre-Bill Parcells, when the Giants labored through a prolonged period of ineptitude while playing before continually full stands, first at Yankee Stadium, next at Yale Bowl and, finally, at Giants Stadium in the North Jersey swamps. But to compare a football fan's trials and tribulations to that of a baseball, basketball or hockey fan's is preposterous. Football is not just a sport. It's an *event*. Once a week — actually once every *other* week — is, well, once every other week. Football is tailgating and socializing and betting. It doesn't require a major emotional, or, comparatively speaking, financial commitment.

But trooping back into the venue of a perpetually losing baseball team, basketball team or hockey team is another matter entirely. It is difficult to imagine that there ever was, or ever will be, a fandom whose loyalty will match that of the Boston Bruins fans who made the 13,909-seat Boston Garden a madhouse so often during the eight Lost Years. Did they sell out *every* night? No. But did they often dip below 11 or 12 thousand in that building which very nearly seated 14,000? Absolutely not. The Bruins were like a lovably incorrigible child. They might have been messy and unkempt. They might have been hard to discipline. But they belonged to the people of Boston, and thus they were loved.

19

There was one other thing which kept the Bruins coming back. There was strong evidence that a savior was on the way, that in the not-too-terribly-distant future there would be a payback available to all those nefarious Maple Leafs, Black Hawks, Red Wings, Rangers and, yes, Canadiens who had delighted in beating up on the Bruins throughout the many Lost Years.

Understand that 40 years ago the Dominion of Canada had a very relaxed attitude toward the care and feeding of its young hockey players. The National Hockey League was a revered institution, and it was allowed to conduct its affairs pretty much as it saw fit. Since the province of Quebec was extraordinarily proprietary toward its beloved Canadiens, it was a no-questions-asked rule of thumb that *les Habitants du Montreal*, (Habs for short) had first call on a young man born in the province. There was more. Players as young as 12 years of age could become property of a given team.

So it was that scouts began to descend upon a precocious youngster from the Ontario town of Parry Sound. His name was Robert Gordon Orr. Bobby Orr. He was first spotted playing a game in the Ontario town of Gananoque. There happened to be Bruins officials in attendance, and they decided there was no time to waste. They put his name on their negotiation list. Two years later, at the age of 14, he was signed to a professional contract and dispatched to play for the Oshawa Generals in the high-level Ontario Hockey Association. This was Junior A hockey, and it should have been pretty heady stuff for a lad of 14.

But this was no ordinary young man. Though not particularly big, he could skate, pass, shoot and, above all, think. He had an extraordinary instinct for the game, an ability to size up a situation and make unerring judgments about the next move of everyone on the ice. There are certain indefinable and unteachable aspects of every game. Even the garden variety Hall of Famer manages to rise to a high level without ever being discussed in terms of his almost extraterrestrial concept of the game. Bobby Orr was one of the Chosen, one of the very, very few who had it all.

Roger Naples had heard about Orr, and when he read that the Oshawa Generals were coming to the Garden to play an exhibition game he was very excited indeed. He went to the game, and he came away reaching for the cyanide pellets. About the only impressive thing the kid had done was get into a fight with a brash kid on the other team by the name of Derek Sanderson.

"I couldn't believe this was the kid I'd been hearing about," Naples chuckles. "To me, he looked like a statuette out there. Everybody was going around him."

Maybe it was something he ate. Maybe he was just too intimidated by the thought of playing in the hallowed Boston Garden.

But Naples came away feeling better when he spoke with his old friend Milt Schmidt, who was now the general manager. "Milt said not to worry, that the kid would be something special," Naples says. "And I also knew a Bruins player named Al (Junior) Langlois. He said to me, 'That kid is going to be one of the greatest things the game of hockey has ever seen.'" Al Langlois knew whereof he spoke, and today he can bask in the reflected glory of seeing his old number 4 hanging proudly from the Fleet Center ceiling. For he is the answer to one of Boston's hardy perennial trivia questions: Who wore number 4 before Bobby Orr?

Orr joined the team in 1966. He was 18. He was everything he was supposed to be, a complete revelation. He was an easy runaway winner of the Calder Trophy as the league's best rookie. But as good as he was, he wasn't enough to transform the Bruins all by himself. The Bruins actually dropped in the standings from fifth to sixth, winning four fewer games than they had the year before.

Milt Schmidt was a great player for the Bruins. His number 15 is retired and he has been a member of the Hockey Hall of Fame since 1961. He coached them with some distinction. But it is conceivable his greatest contribution to the organization came in 1967, when, in his capacity as the team's general manager, he traded the Bruins into two Stanley Cups.

There have been notable thefts in sports history, as Boston sports fans are only too painfully aware. This is the town which, never forget, lost Babe Ruth. But there have not been many multiplayer trades, in any sport, more beneficial to one team at the expense of another than the trade in which the Bruins shipped defenseman Gilles Marotte, forward Pit Martin and minor-league goaltender Al Norris to the Chicago Black Hawks in exchange for Phil Esposito, Ken Hodge and Fred Stanfield.

In retrospect you must ask, "What were the Black Hawks thinking of?" Well, Marotte was a strapping young defenseman, 22 years of age at the time of the trade. Big and strong, and a good hitter, he was a solid defenseman who would have been a fine addition to any team. He was an OK player. So, why not Marotte for Esposito? Or Marotte for Stanfield? All Schmidt obtained for the Bruins in that deal was a trio which would combine for 883 goals and 1,212 assists in Boston uniforms. Esposito won five scoring championships as a Bruin. Hodge would join him as part of one of the most productive lines in NHL history. Stanfield was the kind of reliable professional who comprises the backbone of championship teams in any sport.

It was a trade that completely transformed the Bruins, making them into a team to whom attention would now most certainly be paid. The club gained 40 points in the standings, moved from sixth to third, increased its goal-scoring output from a team record 259 (a total that would soon become throw-it-back-'cuz-it's-too-small material in a few years) and put a spring in the step of every fan who had suffered through the Lost Years. But the season ended, well, can't you guess how the season ended? Waiting for the Bruins in their first playoff appearance since 1959 were the dreaded Montreal Canadiens. Zip, zip, zip, zip. Four straight, over and out.

The Bruins were now among the league's elite. They increased their goal-scoring total to a dazzling 303 the following year, with Esposito crashing through the 100-point barrier by scoring an almost unimaginable 126 points. The Bruins moved up to second place. They won their first playoff series in 11 years by sweeping Toronto (pulverizing them by scores of 10-0 and 7-0 in Games 1 and 2). Then Guess Who was waiting. This time the Bruins extended Les Habs to six games. The Bruins were continuing to make progress.

Everything fell into place in the 1969-70 season. After suffering from knee problems for two years, Orr bounced back to play in each of the team's 76 games, and the league felt his full fury when he led the league in scoring with 120 points, a stupendous total for a defenseman. The Bruins were sound in goal with the savvy tandem of Eddie Johnston and Gerry Cheevers. (The local joke was "Will it be Eddie J or Cheesie between the pipes tonight?"). The Bruins again finished second, but when the Stanley Cup playoffs came they were ready.

I don't know how you would define "ready," but I would define it as rolling through the Stanley Cup playoffs with a 12-2 record, the only losses coming in Games 3 and 4 of the first-round series in New York. The real Stanley Cup Finals took place in the semifinal round, when the Bruins swept the Chicago Black Hawks, a fellow member of hockey's "Original 6" franchises. The last perfunctory chore was to defeat the expansion St. Louis Blues, the undeserving Finals participant in a playoff format which was quickly discarded as impractical and unfulfilling.

St. Louis had a great veteran goaltender in Hall of Famer Glenn Hall, and the Blues put up a fight in a desperate attempt not to get swept. Game 4, played on the afternoon of Sunday, May 10, went into overtime. It was Orr, of course, who ended it by taking a feed from behind the net and slipping the puck past Hall. An instant after shooting the puck, Orr was tripped by St. Louis' Noel Picard, which sent him airborne. Photographer Ray Lussier snapped Orr at the apex of his trip to the ceiling, the resultant photo becoming one of the most famous sports pictures in Boston history. People came to believe that Orr had actually scored the goal while in the air, and there is little sense in trying to change their minds. Again we turn to *The Man Who Shot Liberty Valance*. Go with the legend.

It was the first Stanley Cup championship for Boston since 1941, and the Bruins had won eight straight playoff games in order to get it done. No one wanted to dwell on the fact that the title had been won without the need to play You-Know-Who.

The Bruins were universal favorites to make it two straight, and why not? They were a well-rounded, experienced, swaggering champion. They had more good players than any team in the league. This was, clearly, their year.

But they would be doing it for a different coach. The man who had taken them to the title was Harry Sinden, a former minor-league defenseman who had been named head man back in 1966. After winning the title, he couldn't reach suitable contract terms with the Adams family, who were still in charge of the franchise. He quit the team in disgust and went into the modular home business.

The new coach was Hockey Hall of Fame defenseman Tom Johnson, a great player who had made his name with the vaunted

Canadiens teams of the '50s and '60s. He was a laissez faire type, a "good cop" type, and the team obviously responded to him because they made a mockery out of the competition during the 1970-71 regular season.

What else can you say about a team that scored a truly staggering 399 goals, gave up 207 and lost just 14 games, four of them in succession late in the season when Johnson decided it would be prudent to take the pedal off the metal and give his regulars some rest prior to the playoffs? The 1970-71 Bruins were one of the truly great one-season juggernauts the NHL had ever seen, and that most definitely included the best Canadien clubs.

Care to guess whom The Juggernaut drew as a first-round opponent?

By this time the Montreal playoff domination over the Bruins had been stretched to 10 series, covering 25 years. But this time the Bruins were so good, and the Canadiens were old and supposedly decrepit, that there wasn't going to be much of a contest. The Bruins were installed as 4½-1 favorites. They were two-goal favorites in Game 1, to be played at the Boston Garden. Some suggested that the only thing the Bruins had to fear was fear itself.

"My team is confident," said coach Johnson, "but not too confident."

The Bruins won Game 1, 3-1. Nature was apparently taking its inevitable course in Game 2 as the high-powered Bruins moved to a 5-1 lead with just over four minutes remaining in the second period. Then venerable Henri Richard stole the puck from Derek Sanderson and went in for a score on Eddie Johnston.

With rookie goaltender Ken Dryden stopping the Bruins, the Canadiens came roaring back, scoring five unanswered goals in the third period. The word "catastrophe" is inadequate to describe what this turn of events represented for the Boston Bruins, because now they had been reminded just who it was they were playing.

A shaken Johnson had no answer for the team's astonishing collapse in such an important home playoff game. "If I ever find the formula for stopping something like that or for shaking up a team, I'm sure as hell not going to release it," he said, adding that "this team can come off this as quickly as it went into it. But it was unbelievable."

The series lurched into a seventh game. Boston Garden or no Boston Garden, it didn't matter. The Canadiens were the Canadiens and the Bruins were the Bruins. The Boston team was the defending Stanley Cup champion, and it might have been undisputed heavyweight champion of the English-speaking hockey world. But no Bruins team had defeated a Montreal team in head-to-head competition since 1943, and this wasn't going to be any different.

Final: Montreal 4, Boston 2.

The painful postmortems dwelled on the gruesome turnaround in Game 2, and on the gangling rookie goaltender, Ken Dryden. He was no stranger to local hockey buffs, having displayed his magnificent talents in goal for Cornell University against the likes of Harvard, Boston University, Boston College and Northeastern for three years. As great as he was in goal, that's how grounded he was as an individual, however, and he was in no rush to become a professional athlete, choosing to attend McGill Law School full time while playing for the Canadian national team. He had spent the 1970-71 season splitting his time at law school, where he remained a full-time student, and the American Hockey League Nova Scotia Voyageurs before joining the Canadiens at the tail end of the season. When he slipped onto the ice in Game 2 of the playoffs, he was a veteran of six Stanley Cup games.

And he turned out to be the difference, starting with his performance in Game 2. "The big thing," said Derek Sanderson, "was that Dryden didn't die. Most goalies would have quit right then (when his team was trailing, 5-1). He didn't. He stayed right in there and shut us out in that period. He's some kid — and what a glove!"

Canadiens coach Al MacNeil agreed with Sanderson. "I don't know what Dryden's goaltending did to the Bruins in that game," he said, "but I know it gave us a big lift. Every time we needed a big save in the series he came up with the big save."

Ken Dryden and his mates knocked all the swagger out of the Bruins in that fateful Game 2. Boston managed to get the series to a seventh game, but the Bruins were clearly on life support for the remainder of the series, culminating in a lifeless performance before a shocked home crowd in the seventh and deciding game, which the Canadiens dominated from start to finish.

Wrote the estimable Tom Fitzgerald of the *Boston Globe*, "It was a flat Bruins team, outskated and beaten to just about every move in skating, passing and shooting."

The Bruins entered the series as the highest-scoring team in history, particularly deadly on the power play, where they had scored 80 of their 399 goals. Their power play haul in Game 7: 0-for-3.

"They deserved to win," said Esposito. "We didn't. And if there's a blame for it, blame the team. We didn't play hockey."

Most of the Bruins were in a stupor. They had been completely convinced this was the year when they could feel sorry for Montreal, rather than the other way around.

"How can you accept it?" moaned Ken Hodge. "Now you have to go around making excuses."

The Canadiens never made excuses, of course. If they lost, they lost. And if they won, well, wasn't that the natural order of things? According to 35-year-old Henri Richard, however, some wins were definitely sweeter than others. "That's the greatest series victory of my career," he enthused. "The greatest ever."

Hart Trophy winner (MVP, in other words) Bobby Orr did not have a Bobby Orr series, and the Canadiens believed they should be given the credit. "I want to tell you," said Richard, the famed "Pocket Rocket, "we did a good job on Orr. We kept him from penetrating. We kept him from controlling."

Orr, always a stand-up guy, was ready to accept his share of the blame. His main concern was making sure people didn't jump on the coach, a natural target because of his easygoing demeanor. "I suppose they'll be taking shots at Tommy," Orr said. "They shouldn't, because he's a damned good coach. We lost because we didn't play hockey, not because of coaching."

It had been a group effort, all right. All those regular-season victories and all those goals seemed pretty irrelevant to the Bruins on the night of April 18, 1971.

"Somehow," mused defenseman Don Awrey, "the beer doesn't taste quite as good."

2

The Greatest
Year of All

Did everyone in Boston casually forgive and forget?

Not quite.

No Boston Bruins team was ever placed under more microscopic scrutiny in training camp than the 1971-72 Boston Bruins. The team which stormed through the 1970-71 regular season, breaking upwards of two dozen records, and which then disintegrated in the playoffs was the highest-paid team in the league. It had entered the playoffs as prohibitive favorites and then proceeded to lose to a third-place team.

Veteran *Boston Globe* columnist Jerry Nason, who had seen them all, from Shore to Orr, as it were, greeted the team a few days prior to the season opener with this observation: "Everything looks just peachy — but forget it. There may never have been a pro team more under the gun than the Boston Bruins ice hockey team this season. The Bruins are on the spot. You may not see it, but it's there, just under the surface. People step carefully around it, pretending it isn't there, but the fact is the Bruins last spring authored one of the classic collapses in the history of pro sport . . . It was also a preposterous waste of talent — an assembly of remarkably skilled and coordinated athletes who went into a multiple seance where it counted, the playdowns."

The loss to Montreal looked even worse in retrospect the following autumn than it did the night it was finalized. The Bruins had managed to lose to a team that itself was in disarray. The Habs were old, fragmented and, as it turned out, damn near rudderless. Management response to winning (yawn) yet another Stanley Cup was to fire coach Al MacNeil.

"Canadiens won the Cup and fired the coach," continued Nason. "Bruins blew the Cup and rehired the coach. Thus in both instances the players were fingered as solely responsible for the results by the front offices."

There were mixed reviews during the exhibition season. Coach Johnson started out with his usual relaxed approach, rarely keeping his team on the ice for more than an hour during the early lazy, hazy days of late summer in London, Ontario.

"If they go all out for an hour," he said, "they're not going to get much more good out of another 30 minutes." But when the team put together a string of sloppy preseason performances, the mentor found it necessary to get tough as the season drew near. Practices got longer, and he even took the startling step of calling for a multiple practice encounter only four days before the season's opener at home against New York.

The Bruins were professionals, true, but there was also a lot of adolescence in them, as everyone knew. It was part of their endearing collective charm and it went a long way toward explaining the unconditional love affair between themselves and their fans.

Most of the primary name players would take a drink. It was no secret. And when they did, it was generally in a pack. The Bruins were very much into a One-for-All-and-All-for-One posture, and this would remain their trademark, right to the present day. The Bruins played hard on the ice and they often played even harder off the ice. Far from objecting to this, fans thought it was great. It played into their idea of what it *should* be like to be a professional athlete, especially in Boston. What could be more romantic? Blow someone out of the rink and then close the bar. That's living!

Whoever was coaching the Bruins at any given point in time had to know how to look the other way on occasion. The Bruins weren't going to change, but every once in a while they needed to be reminded that work had to come before play. There can be little doubt that Tom Johnson was making a statement about getting priorities straight when he decided there would be a double session so close to the first game of the regular season.

At least one of the more noted revelers claimed that he was trying to mend his ways somewhat. "I've lost something like 10, 12, 15 pounds (since last season)," explained goaltender Gerry Cheevers. "I did it by just giving up beer. I haven't had one in three months."

Johnson rewarded him with a start against the Rangers on Opening Night.

And his team rewarded the coach by stinking up the joint. The Rangers beat the Bruins by a 4-1 score and it was pretty ugly.

Throughout the preseason, Johnson had done his best to put on a happy face. Like everyone else who watched and/or participated in the team's 3-6-1 exhibition campaign, he kept saying "We'll be all right when they ring the bell." But the shoddy Bruins' performance on Opening Night proved that the coach was on to something when he decided to become a bit more of a taskmaster in the days leading up to that first game.

One game was all he needed to see. The Bruins were going to get serious, or else...

The day after losing to the Rangers, Tom Johnson made a decision, and a very interesting one, at that. Effective immediately, a freeze was being placed on the Bruins' outside activities.

It wasn't the drinking and general partying, but the appearances, which so concerned the coach. The Bruins had become larger than life during the past few years. Every organization, particularly on Boston's hockey-oriented North Shore (where everyone lived and socialized), wanted a Bruin for this function or that. The coach was just going to have to take a stand, somewhere, somehow. He needed to get their attention.

"I have talked to them for 10 days, trying to wake them up," he explained, "but that's all talk. From now on, I want the concentration to be on hockey. At this point, the appearances are limited. Players with advertised commitments through next week will be permitted to fulfill them, and after that it will be strictly hockey."

In the context of 1971 this was a big step. While the Orrs and Espositos were making serious money for the day, the rank and file were not. The extra bucks a Mike Walton or Don Awrey or Johnny McKenzie could pick up for saying a few words at Joe Schmo's new store opening was welcome income.

What all this added up to was that one game into the new season the Bruins were facing a certified Big Game. For Game 2 happened to be a trip to Madison Square Garden for a rematch.

Talk about instant gratification: Boston 6, New York 1.

The coach looked like a true genius, not only because had he cracked the ol' whip with the ban on outside appearances (a move which, predictably, aroused the ire of Players Association chief Alan Eagleson), but also because he had made a strategic move by placing veteran Eddie Westfall back at right wing prior to the game. Westfall picked up two goals, while suds-deprived (or so he said) goalie Gerry Cheevers kicked out 34 New York shots in a scintillating goaltending display.

Buffalo was next, and the Bruins' performance, said coach Punch Imlach, confirmed his judgment. "Let's be realistic," he said. "The Bruins are still the best. I don't care about the bad exhibition record or the slow start in that first game. Some of the rest will have to prove something to me before I change that opinion."

Hours later the Bruins bombarded his Sabres, 6-2. Esposito had a pair of goals and three assists. Orr racked up his first goal of the year on a 65-foot mortar. Serenity had returned to Bruins country.

The Bruins were now in a groove. There was a 2-2 tie at home against Toronto. Detroit fell. The team journeyed to Los Angeles and slapped the Kings around, 5-1. They beat Vancouver, as well, and now their unbeaten streak was up to six.

The next stop was Montreal.

Sacre bleu! Nothing had changed.

The Canadiens won it, 5-2, the key being a three-goal splurge by Pete Mahovlich, Henri Richard and Guy LaPointe in the span of 2:52. Guy Lafleur, a youngster of note, scored the first of many goals he would score against Boston.

The Bruins had once again been abused by the Habs, and they were unable to shake themselves out of their stupor. They returned home and were shut out by the California Golden Seals and Gilles Meloche. It was the first time the league's greatest goal-scoring machine had been blanked in the Garden in 84 games.

The Bruins didn't have a game scheduled for three more days, but that didn't mean there wasn't any hockey going on in the Garden. For by this time there was *another* professional team in town called the Boston Braves. This development was A-OK with the Bruins. They owned them.

Hockey Fever had gripped The Hub in a way it never has, before or since. So popular were the Bruins, and so dramatic was the spin-off effect on the sport, at every level, that the Bruins thought it would be foolish not to capitalize on it in every way possible.

The Bruins, like everyone else, needed a minor-league affiliate, correct? And, like everyone else, they wanted to maintain one in a locale where someone would come see them play. Well...

Boston?

This was unheard of. Major-league sport was major-league sport, and minor-league sport was minor-league sport, and never the twain shall meet. There were always going to be cities in which there would be major-league franchises in this sport or that sport and a minor-league franchise or two in other sports (think Indianapolis or Charlotte), but nobody had the audacity to place both a major-league franchise and its prime minor-league affiliate not only in the same general locale, but actually in the same *building*.

Gerry Cheevers protects the goal against the St. Louis Blues. (Photo©London Life-Portnoy/Hockey Hall of Fame)

The Bruins did. They created the Boston Braves and they gave them all the dates they needed in the Boston Garden. And then they hired extra help to count the money.

The Bruins fulfilled a need in the Boston sports community of the early '70s. It was hockey, and that was all that mattered. Since the Bruins were selling out regularly, and since there were so many people in Greater Boston who needed to satisfy a hockey fix, the Braves were an instant success. They were coached by a gruff long-ago Bruin named Armand (Bep) Guidolin, a real character who had made a wartime debut with the team while in his teens, and they had a huge crowd-pleasing star in Terry O'Reilly, a take-no-prisoners banger who would go on to become one of the most popular Bruins ever.

Boston management had hoped to attract 8,000 a night, which would have been an astonishing success by American Hockey League standards. Right from the start, they knew they had underestimated the local appetite for hockey. On the night of October 30, 1971, the Braves established a new AHL record when the home team shut out the Cincinnati Swords by a 5-0 score before an amazing 13,964 people.

There was no longer any remote doubt. Boston was no longer just the Hockey Capital of America. It was now making a serious bid to be the Hockey Capital of the World.

While the Boston Braves were a new local phenomenon, the parent club had an ample supply of existing phenomena. What made the Boston Bruins so downright intriguing was not simply their immense skill. This was a team of personalities, and none was more luminous than Derek Sanderson, the skilled center whose tentacles reached far beyond the playing surface.

Sanderson had come to Boston just when the Bruins were making the transition from bottom feeders to penthouse dwellers, and he was determined to enjoy as much of it as he could. On the ice, he was an interesting player, a crafty playmaker who could deliver a hit, if necessary, and who had a way-above-average capacity to kill penalties. Over the years he was as dangerous a player in penalty-killing situations as there was in the league.

He was also a very good face-off man who more than once scored chilling goals in those situations.

Off the ice, he was very much a man of his times. Long before Billy Crystal's Fernando Lamas opined on the circumstance, he believed it far better to look good than to feel good. He wore bell bottoms when people wore bell bottoms, only more so. He wore platform shoes. His hair was right off the Sgt. Pepper album cover. He was one of the first NHL players to cease scraping his razor over his upper lip. He hung out until closing time, and beyond. He had a faithful following of old-line hockey fans, who fed off the classical nature of his game and young fans who believed he was one of them. He did not lack for female companionship.

You know what the young Derek Sanderson was? Mod. Recall that word? He was Mod, and most guys in that league had no idea what the hell "Mod" was.

On a team which contained the best goal scorer in hockey, assorted other 100-point players, two excellent goalkeepers and a player who many thought was nothing less than the best player of all time, Derek Sanderson somehow managed to corral as much general attention as any of them. It was a classic study in self-promotion.

Writers and broadcasters alike knew that he was a perpetual loose cannon who was liable to say anything. He had no inhibitions. The governor which even the exceptionally candid players and coaches had on their tongue was noticeably missing from his.

Go back to the Bruins' trip to Montreal. The club arrived in town, picked up the morning English-language *Gazette*, and stared in quiet disbelief as some fairly interesting words from the mind and mouth of Derek Sanderson leaped off the page.

Among the Sanderson observations: "If you're not ahead 9-1 by the end of the first period, they're booing. They're expecting too much."

And: "I'm glad to be back in Canada. I'm a Canadian and I'm going to stay Canadian."

And: "What I'd like to do is buy some land out in Alberta, start a commune, raise some quarter horses and try to help the Indians. Nobody else is doing very much for them."

When questioned about all this, Sanderson had the standard celebrity excuse. He was, he said, misquoted, or, at the very least, misinterpreted.

"I was feeling lousy and down on just about everything," he explained. "I was just talking to the newspaper guy (reporter Tim Burke), just kind of rapping, and he didn't take any notes. Some of the stuff sounded worse than I intended."

He wasn't down on all the fans, he insisted. He *loved* the fans. "I don't think that way about most of the fans," he said. "Boston fans have been very good to me. I was really talking about the small percentage of loud ones who hand out all the criticism, which I think is unfair."

Sanderson had a point. Numbered among the Garden patrons were some awesomely acerbic folks. They knew their hockey, and they had no sacred cows. They were there to have a good time, and if the players couldn't take the needling, too bad.

I happened to be present at a game in the late '60s or early '70s when Bruins forward Wayne Cashman, known more for his ability to dig the puck out of the corner and his general feistiness than for any particular expertise as a goal scorer, wound up for a slap shot, only to make minimal contact with the puck, which meekly dribbled away.

Out from the balcony, a voice rang out. "What a blay-zah, Wayne!" he shrieked.

Many years later Cashman was nearing the end of his career. Gerry Cheevers was now the coach, and he was known to be loyal to the old guard. Cashman had been battling injury, and he hadn't shown very much that season, even when healthy. Now it was a playoff game, and with things not going particularly well for the Bruins, Cheevers sent Cashman out to the ice.

As Cashman lifted his leg over the dasher and before his skate could even make contact with the ice, a voice was heard.

"Chee-vahs! Have you lost yah mind?"

If I live to be 120, I'll swear it was the same guy.

Those were quintessential Boston Garden and Boston Bruins moments, and there were many more like them during the 68 years the Bruins spent playing atop the train station in Boston's North End. Sanderson might very well have been subject to that guy's barbs himself, and he was just going to have to learn to live with it.

As far as being down on the USA, Sanderson insisted he was completely misunderstood. "I don't know how that idea came out what I was saying," he said. "My home is really in the States. The country has really been good to me in giving me such a great living. As a matter of fact, I have been looking forward to taking out my U.S. citizenship papers."

The real problem was that Derek Sanderson just didn't feel very good. His first inclination was to link his rotten feeling to an ear infection he had come up with earlier in the year, but he was just guessing. "I don't know really what it is," he said. "I have to wonder if I might have mono. I just feel tired all the time."

In due time Derek Sanderson would find out what his problem was. He had colitis.

The Bruins' brass was not unlike any other set of upper management in sport. The men in the offices didn't like the rank and file rocking the boat, and they especially didn't like them casting aspersions on their most precious commodity — the fans. "I have some reactions," fumed general manager Milt Schmidt. "But I would really rather not give them to you right now. I'm afraid I'll blow my stack. I need a cooling-off period."

That flap occupied people's thoughts for a few days, and it helped get their minds off the fact that the Bruins, after going unbeaten for six games, had just lost two games in a row, and had actually been shut out in their own building. The next game would be at home against the Minnesota North Stars, and it was time the Bruins started playing their brand of hockey.

The final was 5-2, Boston, and guess who scored two goals? Yup, Derek Sanderson. The two goals were the 99th and 100th of his career. And people have the nerve to question which is more fascinating, truth or fiction?

Among those who played strong games were the members of the fourth line, which had been nicknamed the "Black Aces." Their names were Ivan Boldirev, Reggie Leach and — get this — Ace Bailey.

He was no relation to the Irwin Wallace "Ace" Bailey who had almost gone to meet his maker, courtesy of Eddie Shore, nearly 48 years earlier. His name was Garnet "Ace" Bailey, and, unlike the original Ace Bailey, he would not wind up being inducted into the Hall of Fame. This Ace Bailey spent five years with the Bruins, scoring 31 goals and 46 assists.

The Black Aces were aggressive kids, happy to be on board. Tom Johnson said they should have been called the "Incentive Line."

Leach scored two goals in a 6-1 conquest of St. Louis, a game in which longtime crowd favorite Ted Green made his first appearance of the season.

Ted Green was one of the '60s mainstays who was fortunate enough to be a functioning player when the juggernaut was flexing its muscles. But "fortunate" may be an inappropriate choice of words to describe a man who was very lucky to be alive.

Green was a 29-year-old, much-feared defenseman for the Bruins at the dawn of the 1969-70 season. Not for nothing was he known as "Terrible Ted." He was one of the league's premier tough guys, a marauder who delighted in separating sticks from pucks and teeth from jaws. This is a league where players cannot afford to be intimidated, but Ted Green truly intimidated people. He had elevated himself from pure "goon" status by 1969. He might not have been Orr or Esposito, but he was a valued member of the cast.

On the night of September 21, 1969, he became engaged in a frightening stick-swinging incident with Wayne Maki of the St. Louis Blues. In the course of the battle, Maki hit a helmetless Green on the top of the head. There were chips of skull embedded in his brain. The doctors performed two operations just to save his life. He was paralyzed on his left side. Playing hockey was hardly the issue.

Amazingly, he made it back to the ice for the '70-71 season. He was now wearing a helmet, and he was no longer quite the swashbuckler he had been prior to his injury, but he was a functioning NHL defenseman, and the Bruins were happy to have him back. Nonrelated injuries delayed his return to the lineup for the '71-72 season; hence, his late move onto the roster.

The Bruins had their overall record up to 8-3-1 as the Canadiens came to town. It just seemed that when these two got together, things were never simple and straightforward. This time a disputed call cost Sanderson and the Bruins a game-tying goal. The Canadiens managed a mere 19 shots on net, but in this game quality is more meaningful than quantity. Montreal won, 3-2, all Bruins protestations notwithstanding.

The issue was an apparently quick whistle by referee John Ashley during a scramble for the puck in front of Montreal goalkeeper Ken Dryden. Reggie Leachy and Ace Bailey were frantically whacking away at the puck, when Bailey finally freed it to Sanderson, who fired it by the octopus masquerading as a goalie in the Montreal net. But Ashley had blown the play dead, and that was that.

"Things have been going against us all year," fumed Johnson, who may have been exaggerating just a tad. "I never heard a whistle all night. It was a loose puck, but from what I see the officials are losing a lot of things."

Could it be that the mentor's frustration was racheted up a notch or two, based on the identity of the opponent?

The real bad news that night had nothing to do with a bad call. Reliable defenseman Don Awrey broke an ankle and would be sidelined for a minimum of eight weeks. It's a good thing Green was back.

37

Bulletin: On November 9, the Boston Braves increased the AHL record single-game attendance to 14,031 with a 3-0 whitewash of Providence.

One thing about these Montreal losses was that they put the Bruins in an apparent funk. For the second time in the season's first five weeks a Montreal loss led to a two-game losing streak. The Bruins lost a 3-1 decision to Chicago and the Brothers Hull (Bobby and Dennis) three nights later.

The Bruins were, nevertheless, off to a good start, if not necessarily a great one. They were engaged in a three-team race for first place with New York and the Canadiens. After 14 games the Bruins were 8-5-1. They were solid, but there was real room for improvement.

They ran all over the California Golden Seals by a 5-2 score on November 11. Nice. Encouraging. Then the Los Angeles Kings hit town.

November 14, 1971, may very well have been the actual Opening Night of the hockey season for the Boston Bruins. The exhibition season was basically a mess. The first 15 games were spotty, with the Bruins getting by strictly on talent, as opposed to the desired mixture of talent, intelligence and just plain dedicated hockey. But on this night the Bruins were not just a good team. They were a colossus. They completely trampled the Kings by an 11-2 score.

"They were skating and they were shooting," observed L.A. coach Fred Glover.

Orr was the First Star winner with three goals. Surprisingly, it was only the second hat trick of his brilliant career. Esposito and Mike (Shaky) Walton each had two goals, while Bucyk, Bailey, Westfall and defenseman Rick Smith had one goal apiece. It was the most goals anyone had scored in the league during the early season.

The Bruins were straightened out now, and for the remainder of the season there would be no serious doubts about either their ability or their character. They were determined to show the hockey world that they had learned whatever lessons there were to absorb from the Montreal playoff loss the previous spring.

The Bruins probably wished they could have played a double-header that night . Well, probably not. That would have delayed the postgame celebration. They had to be antsy waiting three more days for a game, but you'd never have known it. Orr scored two more goals and Cheevers stopped everything the Vancouver Canucks threw at him. It was a 5-0 final.

Johnson was blessed. He had two veteran goaltenders in Cheevers and Eddie Johnston. Each was at the top of his game. Cheevers was about to turn 32, while Johnston was 36. Cheevers was clearly the number one guy, he being the one with the reputation of being the "money" goaltender, but in the eyes of the Bruins they were 1 and 1A. That season Cheevers would finish with a record of 27-5-8, two shutouts and a goals-against average of 2.50. Johnston would finish with a record of 27-8-3, three shutouts and a goals-against average of 2.70. Each man loved the arrangement. Each was the other's biggest fan.

Tom Johnson could never go wrong. Cheesie, Eddie J, Eddie J, Cheesie. It was either going to be one unflappable, been-through-it-all veteran goalkeeper or another. Who said coaching is hard?

He threw Cheevers back out there in the wake of his shutout over Chicago and what he got was another outstanding performance. Eddie J was seen leading the cheers for Cheesie on the bench. The final score was 2-1, and, while there have been scores of 2-1 Bruins' victories in their history, there weren't many like *this* one. The Boston Bruins, known throughout hockey as "The Big, Bad Boston Bruins," had just skated 60 minutes without drawing a penalty. What would Eddie Shore think?

The Bruins were in cruise gear now. People were starting to re-think their analyses of this team. Though still noted for offense, the Bruins were now one of the premier defensive clubs in the league. When the Bruins went to Philadelphia for a 2-1 victory on November 24, they emerged with a goals-against average of 1.3 in their last eight games.

The Bruins won a rematch in Boston the following night, and in this game Bobby Orr demonstrated why his teammates revered him so. Orr had scored a goal which had been announced as unassisted. He had knocked down a clearing shot and then swatted away at the puck with his glove until he had gained sufficient control to deposit the disc into the net.

When Orr heard the public address announcement designating an unassisted goal, he began gesturing toward Ken Hodge, who had been in on the play. Hodge had nailed Philadelphia's Barry Ashbee with a stinging check to knock the Flyers' defenders off the play. He then kept Ashbee blocked off as Orr began to make his move. It had not been a good evening for Hodge, who had become something of a fan scapegoat for any perceived Bruins' failings. The ruling stood, but the Bruins' players knew, as if they needed to be reminded, that the best player in the game cared about more than himself.

Tom Johnson's postgame comment: "Eddie J won it for us."

Along about this time *Globe* scribe Tom Fitzgerald, a renowned hockey scholar, discovered an interesting tidbit. In their first 10 games, the Bruins had scored 13 goals in the first periods of those games, 13 in the second period and 9 in the third. In their 11 most recent games, they had scored 10 in the first period, 13 in the second and 23 in the third. They were outscoring their opponents by a 32-8 margin in the season's third periods. The Fitzgerald conclusion was that the Bruins were the biggest team in the league and therefore needed more time to get into peak shape.

Bulletin: The Boston Braves had now increased the AHL record for single-game attendance to 14,995.

The Bruins had a run of seven straight victories snapped by a 6-6 tie against St. Louis, but that was just a minor bump in the road. Toronto fell when the Bruins hit them with four goals in the first period. They beat the Pittsburgh Penguins, 5-3, but Cheevers wasn't very happy. "Blame me for all three goals," he said. The Bruins hit the West Coast and started off by stopping L.A., 5-3. Their unbeaten streak was up to 11. New York was still in first place with 39 points. The Bruins and Canadiens each had 38. Life was good. There was no hotter team in the league than the Boston Bruins, who believed to a man that taking over first place on a permanent basis was merely a matter of time.

The caravan moved up the coast and out of the country to scenic Vancouver. Esposito popped in a pair, his 21st and 22nd, as the Bruins cruised, 6-2.

That was it for the unbeaten string. They moved back down to the Oakland Coliseum, where the Golden Seals were ready. The final was 4-2, California, despite Esposito's 300th career goal.

Phil Esposito had, by this point in time, become a unique figure in hockey. He had redefined what a center could do. He had practically invented a whole new position.

The classical goal scorers had always been men who swooped down upon goaltenders. Espo didn't swoop. He camped. He came into the goalie's view with his suitcase and he just made himself at home.

Phil Esposito was a big man. He was in the 6-2, 6-3 range and he weighed a solid 215, 220, 2 whatever. He had quick wrists and great instincts. His forte was making something out of nothing, or, at least, very little. He redirected shots. He converted quick passes. He didn't need much room in which to work.

He was an immovable object once he set up shop. In the National Basketball Association he would have been called for three-second violations, but there is no such thing in hockey. He made his living right in front of the net, and in his prime nobody could do a God's blessed thing about it.

Here is the description, written by Kevin Walsh of the *Boston Globe*, of that 300th goal on the night of December 11, 1971:

"In case you missed Phil Esposito's 300th regular-season NHL goal last night in Oakland we'll paint you a mental picture. Put the big center in the slot area, 15 or 20 feet in front of the California Seals' net. Have him facing Johnny Bucyk, who's alone in the left corner. Chief (Bucyk) makes the play as he outmuscles the Seals' defense in the battle for the puck and slides a pass along the ice in Phil's direction. The rest is simple. Phil pulls the trigger on what he calls his "snap" shot and gains another milestone."

Notice that Esposito said "snap" shot, not "slap" shot.

"I feel the snap shot is the most underrated thing in hockey," Esposito said. It's something I picked up when I was playing with Bobby Hull in Chicago. It's a great shot, because it's quick. I usually catch the goaltenders moving the wrong way. It's somewhere between a wrist shot and a slap shot and has really helped me be a top scorer."

41

Phil Esposito had a knack for "making something out of nothing, or, at least, very little." (Photo©Frank Prazak/Hockey Hall of Fame)

Whatever's Chicago's reservations about Esposito, the big guy with the snap shot had established himself as one of the handful of greatest players in Bruins history. A quarter-century later there has never been anyone who could come close to duplicating his expertise in the slot.

The Bruins had something to look forward to as they flew back home following their trip to the Left Coast. Their first game back would be against the New York Rangers, a team they hadn't seen since playing them in the first two games of the season. The Bruins had not forgotten the empty feeling of losing the season's opener at home to the New Yorkers. Even though they had bounced back with a triumph, and a big one (6-1), three nights later, there was still a feeling that payback was necessary.

Fred Stanfield summed it up for everyone. "You're up automatically," he admitted. "You're thinking of the Rangers. You *have* to be thinking of them, because no one will ever let you forget them. That's all you hear. We have to be up. We have to be physical."

So how does 8-1 sound? Is that "up" enough for you?

"That was as complete a team effort as we've had all year," said Cheevers. "We really got back to that old Stanley Cup feeling."

The Bruins came out flying, scoring four goals in the first period. Orr opened up the scoring with a classic bit of legerdemain, beating Jim Neilsen with a soft backhander after appearing to make the puck sing the national anthem and order dinner at the same time. The night was so bad for New York that Bruins defenseman Dallas Smith even got a goal when Ranger defenseman Dale Rolfe swept the puck past Neilsen with his glove.

The game having been settled in the first period, the boys came off with the gloves. Before the evening was over, the referee had handed out 114 minutes in penalties.

Cheevers had 38 saves, but he wasn't impressed with himself, declaring that his season's Rembrandt had been submitted in Chicago. "There weren't as many tough ones this time," he said. "There were at least a half dozen in that game."

In the course of seemingly endless baseball, basketball and hockey seasons, few games have true meaning when detached from the whole. This was one of those games. The Bruins had planted the very real thought in the minds of the New York Rangers that they were simply superior, and should the two chance to meet the following spring in the Stanley Cup playoffs, there would be no doubt as to the outcome.

This, despite the fact that when the game started the Bruins were five standings points in arrears. A loss would have dropped them seven points behind, while a win would have advanced them to minus-three. In NHL parlance, this is known as a "four-point game."

What pleased the Bruins most about themselves was their overall on-ice demeanor. They had come out skating, and, equally im-

43

portant, hitting. It was a game reminiscent of the style that had brought them a Stanley Cup in 1970. The Bruins had come to realize that they had gotten a bit too fancy while racking up those 399 goals the year previous.

"For about four years we were the Big, Bad Bruins and we were intimidating people," said Eddie Westfall. "Last year we weren't that way because we were winning so easily, and look what happened. We are best when we are taking charge and this time we took charge solidly. If we keep that up, well, it can be great. But don't run down the Rangers. That's a good team, a damned good team."

Maybe so, but in the last two head-to-head confrontations, the Bruins had outscored the Broadway Blueshirts, 14-2.

There was a nice strategic subplot. Coach Johnson had been confronted with the question as to whether or not it would make good sense to match up his first line of Esposito, Cashman and Hodge against the famed New York GAG (Goal-A-Game) line of Jean Ratelle, Rod Gilbert and Vic Hadfield.

The answer was yes, and the battle was strictly No Contest. Esposito himself had a goal and three assists, while the GAG boys were held scoreless for only the fourth time all season.

"It was a good move by Tom," confirmed Esposito, "and we played the way we did two years ago. I can't say it was a real physical game for me, because that's not my style. But the other guys were checking, checking good."

The Bruins took care not to pour any petrol on the conflagration with ill-chosen words. They made the Rangers sound like the reincarnation of the 1958 Canadiens. "We handled them tonight," said Esposito. "They might do the same to us next time. You don't count on anything that."

Those were diplomatic words, ideal for public consumption. Behind closed doors, the Bruins could think salivating private thoughts. They simply knew they were now substantially better than the New York Rangers.

"It might have been the turning point," prophesied the *Globe's* sagacious John Ahern. "It could have been the game that set the course to the Stanley Cup."

The wins, and occasional ties, continued rolling off the assembly line. Losing no longer appeared to be a viable option. What motivated the Bruins now were milepost games, and the next one was scheduled for the 29th of December in the Chicago Stadium.

The Bruins had not won in this wonderful old palace since March 22, 1969. Their winless streak in Chicago had reached nine. On the bus ride over, Orr, not ordinarily given to the rah-rah stuff, cleared his throat and uttered a simple sentence. "Don't forget, guys," he said. "This is a big one."

The Blackhawks were working on a home ice stretch of 15 wins and two ties, during which no opponent had scored more than three goals. So what must they have been thinking when Walton Bucyk, Esposito and Johnny MacKenzie poured in goals during the game's first nine minutes?

The star of stars, however, was Orr, who had a goal, three assists and a superb defensive evening. Said Tom Fitzgerald, "On this night, Robert O was close to his best, if there is any measure for such an evaluation."

What pleased the mentor was his team's attention to defensive detail. Having scored those four quick goals, the Bruins did not then decide it would be a fun idea to score 10 or 12. They instead fell into a defensive mode. "You don't often find us with five men at the blue line," Johnson said. "But we did it in this one. We'll do it again, too, with the same result."

The point of all this was that the Bruins had clearly learned something from the notorious proceedings in Game 2 of the '71 Stanley Cup series with Montreal, when, after leading 5-1 late in the second period, they got greedy and then they subsequently got stung.

A 2-2 tie in Minnesota and another routine dispatch of the Rangers (4-1) extended their roll to one loss in 22 games. On second thought, this victory was anything but routine, since the stat man insisted that the Bruins had scored four goals on 15 shots while the Rangers had managed just one goal in 41. Cheevers was in command all evening, and he was even feeling rambunctious enough to pick up a roughing penalty for blasting Ted Irvine. "He bumped me," Cheevers shrugged. "I pushed him back."

"I don't know whether it was his best, or even how you figure these things," said Johnson. "Just say the guy's fantastic, and let it go at that."

He could have said the same thing about Orr, who had scored a highlight goal during which he first broke up a play at the defensive end, took a return pass from Hodge at the other end, fired a shot that hit the right goalpost, hustled to pick up the carom off the backboard near the face-off circle, spun around and whipped a shot into the near side of the net.

"One of the most beautiful shots I've ever seen," gushed Johnson, for neither the first nor the last time.

Goaltending expertise was a nightly topic of discussion, and Johnston did nothing to diminish the story by shutting out Toronto in the Maple Leaf Gardens. The Bruins were now 26-6-5 and a dazzling 15-3-3 on the road.

But they were still not in first place. Montreal had fallen back, but the Rangers were still doing fine — as long as they did not have to play the rampaging Bruins. It wasn't until Game 38, on January 6, that the Bruins assumed solitary control of first place by defeating Buffalo, 5-1.

There were three power play goals in this one, but when it was over they were talking about just one of the five goals, the second. Again allow Mr. Tom Fitzgerald, whose nightly chore was to summon up new ways of describing the indescribable, to rhapsodize about young Robert Gordon Orr.

"And if you are one of those people who think you have seen everything in that wonder boy's repertory, you should add this to your collection.

"Robert got a pass from Rick Smith, another fine defenseman, and as he moved in, the defenseman on his side, Chris Evans, was wiped out in a collision with teammate Randy Wyrozub.

"Orr swirled past them and fired. His shot was turned aside with a long reach of the stick by Roger Crozier. It looked like the finish of the play, but Orr gave it another effort.

"Continuing far to the left, Bobby picked up the puck on his backhand, and while he was a little off balance and definitely on a bad angle he put it into the upper part of the net."

Night after night, year after year, Bobby Orr did things veteran hockey people had never seen before. Or since.

What separated the Bruins from not only all their NHL brethren, but also their counterparts in baseball and basketball, was that their exploits were regularly available for perusal on home television. In an era when televised accounts of regular-season games were not the routine events they are now, the Bruins, and channel 38 in Boston were pioneers. "*Everybody* got to see those games," recalls Nate Greenberg, currently carrying the title of Senior Assistant to the President. "The Bruins were televising just about everything but the West Coast games even then. Lots of clubs weren't televising *any*."

It is still a fact that the backward thinking management of the Chicago Blackhawks still refuses to televise any home games at all. The Bruins would be the first to explain to Blackhawks owner Bill Wirtz that the more exposure you give your product, the greater the chance of making yourself a fan who will not only purchase an occasional ticket but who will likewise purchase a hat, T-shirt, sweatshirt, or even a key chain with your team's logo.

Boston had always been a hockey town, but now there was a phenomenal explosion of interest. The Braves were a perfect reflection of just how ga-ga Boston had gone over the sport.

Greenberg was a member of the Fourth Estate that first Braves season. But by the '72-73 season he had joined the Bruins' organization, and his special province was the AHL club playing in the varsity's very own building.

"It was the trickle-down effect of the big club, certainly," Greenberg reflects. "But the Braves really had their *own* following. The prices were more affordable, of course, and so what happened was that young people really made the Braves *their* team."

The Braves were so big even some of *their* games were on TV. People just couldn't get enough hockey in Boston.

Just when the Bruins were perhaps beginning to swagger a bit *too* much, expansion teams swiftly brought them back to *terra firma*.

Fresh from that scintillating triumph in Buffalo, and with the pleasant memories of authoritative road victories in New York and

Chicago pleasantly rolling around their minds, they stumbled badly against St. Louis (5-3 loss), Pittsburgh (2-2 tie) and Los Angeles (1-1) amid whines pertaining to fatigue, unconscious enemy goalkeeping and teams playing them here in January as if it were the Stanley Cup Finals.

Given the opportunity to pick up six nice 'n easy points in the standings, and thus gain significant ground on the still first-place Rangers, the Bruins had only come up with two. This was clearly not acceptable.

"I don't know what it is, and neither can anyone else," said Eddie Johnston after the L.A. deadlock. "We're lax. There's no doubt about that. Probably we're tired. Maybe we've been too long on the road. But it's life and death with these expansions. Look 'em over."

The most likely explanation was that the Bruins were playing to the level of the competition, a malady which inflicts superior teams in just about all high-level team sport competition at some point in time.

"I don't know," said coach Johnson. "I wish I did."

"I can't say that," said Fred Stanfield. "I haven't studied it out. But it does appear that way lately."

This was no minor matter. The Bruins were engaged in life-and-death competition with New York in a season when added emphasis was being placed on finishing first in a division. Rising up to squash contenders and then squandering gimme points against expansion teams was, frankly, immature.

Against this backdrop the Chicago Blackhawks came into the Garden, the memory of that 5-1 pounding in their own rink very much in their minds.

"I hope it's the kind of competition we thrive on," said the mentor.

It was surely the kind of competition Phil Esposito thrived on, especially since the Chicago goaltender was none other than brother Tony, 14 months his junior. With the score tied at 2-2, and five minutes remaining, the game was suddenly reduced to a backyard pond skirmish back in Sault Ste. Marie, Ontario (or, as Espo himself would call it, "The Soo"). First Espo stole the puck from defenseman Phil White and whipped a low 25-footer past Tony's right skate. Not too much later he came swooping in, a la Orr, juking his kid brother before flipping a sweet backhander by him. This is what stars are paid to do.

The Bruins liked the feel of that victory so much they came out the very next night and treated the Detroit Red Wings like some sort of backwater Junior A team. The final was 9-2. Sanderson, obviously having regained at least some of his old fire, registered his third career hat track. The crowd-pleasing highlight of this one came when Eddie Johnston picked up an assist on a goal by Ken Hodge.

There was a basic day off after that one, with the rink available for volunteers. The Bruins call it an "optional skate." And guess who exercised his option?

"I put in a good hour because I figured I needed the work," said Phil Esposito, who was leading the league with 76 points in 43 games and who routinely logged double shifts in addition to duty on both the power play and the penalty-killing unit. "I didn't think I was getting my shot away quickly enough."

With the Rangers in a minor slide, the Bruins had pulled into first place before the next game with St. Louis, which had beaten the Bruins 10 days earlier in their building. This game was the artistic flip side of the Detroit romp. Cheevers was the story, turning in his first shutout of the season as the Bruins won a tense game by a 2-0 score. Esposito's extra work apparently paid off, as he knocked in his 38th goal. Then again, with him, how could you tell? *He* was the only one who even knew there was a problem.

There was no general problem when the Bruins journeyed to Montreal four days later. After trailing 2-0, the Bruins whipped in five quickies during the second period. The victory ended a 22-game (19-0-3) Canadiens' home ice unbeaten string, but there was something of an asterisk attached. A big guy wearing Ken Dryden's jersey was in the Montreal goal, but he was there in name only. It was only Dryden's second game back in action after missing three weeks due to a back ailment, and someone forgot to bring along the Rustoleum.

The Bruins settled back into the championship groove. The next game of note was a 5-2 victory over St. Louis, a game which was broken open by a pair of startling short-handed goals off the sticks of Orr and Sanderson within 35 seconds of each other.

Now here's a stunner: the Orr goal was a thing of beauty.

Again, allow Mr. Fitzgerald of the *Globe* to describe:

"Orr swung down the left, striding away from (Gary) Unger. Then, angling toward the net, he looked like a pro fullback busting for first down yardage as he went by Larry Hornung and Mike Murphy.

"As he veered close, Orr got the puck off the backhand to beat Wayne Stephenson, the amateur goaltender who was filling in for St. Louis."

"After Bobby's goal," explained Sanderson, "they were pressing and it was a good break for me. I got the puck away from Hornung, and, when I went in, I delayed just a little. The goalie started down, and I just got the puck over him."

"We get a break," sighed Barclay Plager of the Blues. "This is when we cash in. Then it's all over. There's nothing left. Call off the game and let us go home. Now you know about the Bruins. Power. More power. More power. They kill everybody."

As for Orr, Plager had a wish. "I hope the new league (the fledgling World Hockey Association) offers him millions to go with them."

Plager was on to something, as it turned out. The WHA would turn out to have a seriously deleterious effect on the Bruins, but the targets would be Cheevers and Sanderson, not the Bruins' nonpareil *wunderkind*.

It was time for another trip to New York, and this time the Bruins were in a very defensive mode. "Cheevers came up with the game of his life, or at least this season," opined Fitzgerald. Yes, it was season shutout number two for the crafty goaltender. Esposito (number 44) and Orr (23) supplied the necessary offense, their goals coming two minutes and 45 seconds apart in the third period of a well-played game. With that victory, the Bruins moved up by eight points in the standings (78-70). Since that opening night loss in Boston, the Bruins had knocked off the Rangers four straight times.

There was something about taking care of New York that seemed to energize the Bruins, who returned to Boston the next evening to

Ken Hodge missed eight weeks of the 1971-72 season after breaking his ankle in a game against Minnesota. (Photo©Graphic Artists/Hockey Hall of Fame)

pulverize Minnesota, 6-1. This time there was no weeping and no gnashing of teeth over any inability to concentrate when the opponent was one of the six new teams created for the 1967-68 season. The Bruins had a devastating 47-16 shot advantage, and, for once, that stat reflected the true difference between the clubs on this occasion. "They can think of every trophy there is," said Minnesota mentor Jack Gordon. "That club's got everything."

As proof of Boston's top-to-bottom efficiency, check out Esposito's point total in this easy dispatch: 0-0-0.

But there was bad news coming out of this one. Hodge, who had, admittedly, been having an up-and-down season, fractured his right ankle and would be out for approximately eight weeks.

Buffalo took care of an important chore on February 6. The Sabres administered a needed dose of humility to the Bruins, blasting them by the savage score of 8-2 in the Memorial Auditorium. These are the kinds of games which coaches in Johnson's exalted position really don't mind in the long run. You know you're not going to win them *all*.

Your eye is always on the Big Prize and what it will take to get there. Experience told Johnson that his very talented team would react well when chastened and humbled. The Montreal playoff scenario was easy to summon.

As scheduling luck would have it, there was a rematch scheduled for the coming weekend. "We'll be ready on Saturday," Johnson promised.

But first there was a warm-up against Vancouver. This one turned out to be nothing but target practice. Stanfield led the onslaught as Boston demolished the Canucks, 9-1. Cheevers ran his personal unbeaten streak to 20 games. Esposito, who had been in an uncharacteristic goal-scoring slump, ended a drought of 207 minutes and 29 seconds by putting one past Vancouver goaltender George Gardner.

Bulletin: The Boston Braves were now projecting a season's attendance in excess of 420,000. They were averaging 11,000 a night.

With the division race now becoming more and more abstract, with the Canadiens absolutely out of it and the Rangers slipping more and more by the day, the Bruins were now playing against themselves and against perfection. What they relished were challenges, and playing a Buffalo team that had humiliated them so badly in Buffalo one week earlier was precisely the kind of challenge the Bruins thrived on.

The emotional leader was Johnny McKenzie, whose energy seemed to jump-start the Bruins as they cruised to a 5-1 mauling of the Sabres.

"Don't think we forgot that," McKenzie said. "We couldn't have forgotten if we wanted to. We lose three times in 39 games, but everybody in the street last week only wanted to remind us of that one loss."

That's life, of course, and that was life in 1972 Boston if you happened to be a Boston Bruin. The Bruins really *did* walk the streets, and they certainly were recognized. And because they were all such regular guys, people had no compunction about saying anything at all to them. The fans regarded the Bruins as the kind of guys who you have a drink or two with, and the fans were right.

Johnny (Pie) McKenzie was one type of athlete who exists in every sport. Simply put, with these people there are no in-betweens. If one of them is on the opposing team, you despise every corpuscle in his miserable body. You want nothing more than for the toughest guy on your team to tear out his heart and serve it to you on a platter with a nice glass of chianti. You don't have enough time in the week, month or year to annotate all the ways in which this guy irritates you. You become like Robert DeNiro's Al Capone in *The Untouchables*. You want him dead, dead, dead, and it wouldn't bother you at all if you also get his family while you're at it.

Ah, but if he is on *your team*, that is a different matter entirely. Entirely. Then you regard him as a master of gamesmanship. You delight in seeing him torment blustering opponents.

Johnny McKenzie was in the 5-9, 5-10 range and he was not exactly robust. But he was sneaky and clever and very handy with the stick. He was a consummate agitator. He would spear or use the butt end of his stick on a foe and know how to get away with it. Though he could fight if he had to, he worked better when he started something and let one of his big buddies take care of it.

But none of this would be enough to justify his presence in a lineup as talented as Boston's if he honestly couldn't bring something more to the table than an attitude. Johnny McKenzie was a good finisher. He knew how to score goals. He was the perfect guy to put on a good team's second or third line. During his seven years and 453 regular-season games as a Bruin McKenzie scored 169 goals while racking up 700 penalty minutes on the nose.

He was a very good locker room guy, as they say, fitting in perfectly with these fun-loving guys. Johnny Pie was a central figure in the mix, and respectful opponents had a much higher regard for him than enemy fans did.

"He gives that team something the way he goes out there," said Montreal backup goalkeeper Phil Myre. "There's a guy every team would love to have."

The Bruins were almost frenzied in this one. They forced exhausted Buffalo goalie Roger Crozier to come up with 50 saves, as they seemed to have possession of the puck 75 percent of the time. In those days no one was able to keep track of such a football-oriented stat as "time of possession," (today, they can if they want to), but this had to be as overwhelming an advantage in this category as one NHL opponent had over another NHL foe all season.

It was all so easy it was almost surrealistic. It wasn't the way hockey used to be, or, according to the keepers of the NHL flame, the way it should be. But expansion was a fact of life. The days of the six-team league when the NHL was an incredibly exclusive fraternity of 108 men were memory. There were very few times when diehards would see the kind of hockey they had been weaned on.

The very next night after that Buffalo wipeout, they got to see one. The Bruins and Canadiens went up and down all night, only to finish in a 2-2 tie, and no one felt frustrated or cheated because he had seen a real, honest-to-God hockey game.

"I'm exhausted," said Cheevers. "Maybe I only had 17 shots, but I was in the game for 60 minutes. Against those expansion teams, it's hard to stay in a game for the whole game, even if there are twice as many shots. Against a Montreal, a New York or a Chicago, you're tired even if you have three shots against you every period."

"When you come here to play," chimed in Dryden, "you are ready to play. "You might not be very emotional or charged up the night before or the morning before, but when you get in here and see the people and hear the noise, you get charged up very easily."

Both sides took time to look at the Big Picture. The Canadiens knew the Bruins had a better team than they had the year before, while the Bruins knew that in the 6-foot-4 Dryden they had a formidable foe who would be a major obstacle for years to come. "He's the best tall goalie I've ever seen," said Cheevers, who knew something about the art of goaltending. "He has tremendous poise or attitude or philosophy or whatever it is. I'd probably have it, too, if I were a doctor or a lawyer, but I have to do this for a living. This is all I've got."

After a routine 6-3 home dispatch of California, the Bruins headed out on the highways and byways of America for six games. It was, and is, an annual February trek, because February is when the operators of Boston's major indoor sports arena, be it the venerable Boston Garden or the new Fleet Center welcome the annual ice show. The Bruins and Celtics routinely vacate the premises for the better part of two weeks, and there is never any point in either the players or coaches of both teams complaining about it. Eddie Shore had to put up with it. Milt Schmidt had to put up with it. Bob Cousy had to put up with it. Bill Russell had to put up with it. Bobby Orr and Phil Esposito had to put up with it. Larry Bird would put up with it. And Raymond Bourque *still* puts up with it.

If the team is shaky in general, or just not going well, February is a nightmare. But if the team is a great team, as the Bruins had become, the February trip can be a joy. These prolonged trips are bonding experiences.

The mark of a mature, successful team is full appreciation of the enjoyment which comes from winning on the road. To these people, there is nothing sweeter in sport than the sound of silence you hear when you have defeated a top team in its own building, or on its own field, as the case may be. For every perceived disadvantage there can be an advantage. A player on the road does not have to concern himself with the mundane details of daily family life. He doesn't have to change diapers, take out the garbage or pick little Chauncey up at school and take him for his violin lesson. He is free to concentrate on his sport. He can get into an orderly, pleasurable routine.

The Bruins established their routine by slapping around the Philadelphia Flyers, 4-1, as Esposito had a (yawn) hat trick. It was his 19th career three-goal game and it increased his league-leading point total to 99 in the season's 58th game. The caravan moved on to Minnesota, where Sanderson and Orr reprised their bang-bang short-handed goal routine as Cheevers increased his unbeaten streak to 23. Chicago was next on the docket. Esposito punched in with goals 50 and 51 as the Bruins prevailed, 3-1.

The real excitement on the trip came in Vancouver when the Bruins discovered that management was not above tinkering with the product. It may seem risky to alter the chemistry of a winning team, but general manager Harry Sinden felt he could not pass on the opportunity to upgrade the talent level. The California Golden Seals were offering slick defenseman Carol Vadnais, a perennial Western Conference All-Star. The price to obtain Vadnais and Dan O'Donoghue was high, at least in the opinion of emotional Bruins fans, who had grown very attached to Rick Smith, Reggie Leach and Bob Stewart, the three players California obtained in return.

Bruins fans, perhaps more than Red Sox, Celtics and Patriots combined, have a tendency to either fall in love with, or out of love with, particular players. They had clearly fallen in love with Smith and Leach, in particular, and with the team winning so regularly the faithful could not understand why any change was necessary.

But if you happened to be Milt Schmidt, and you couldn't be certain that the injured Don Awrey would return from his injury at anything close to 100 percent, and you had the opportunity to obtain a player of Vadnais' caliber, you would arrive at the conclusion that you would be an idiot to pass up such a deal.

Vancouver fell easily enough, but California was a bit more stubborn. The Seals got off to a great start, going up by as many as five goals. If ever there was an opportunity for the Bruins to take a night off.

Uh-uh. Winning on the road was just too much fun. The Bruins pulled it out, 8-6. That left one more game, and the sluggish Bruins did what they had to do, squeaking one out over the stubborn Kings, 5-4.

12 points available: 12 points in the bank.

And yet, this had not really been a dazzling trip. As far as the mentor was concerned, the six victories were more a case of superior talent asserting itself just often enough than it was of a dedicated hockey team playing something near its best every evening.

"We played pretty well before we went to the Coast," analyzed Johnson. "On the Coast we had some fair moments and we had some awful ones. When we came from five goals down against Oakland, it had to be the best comeback I've ever made. Saturday night (against L.A.), we played some poor hockey and survived. When you can play like that and win, things are all right."

Understand that it isn't all that simple for an Eastern team to hit California and play its best hockey in the middle of the winter.

I discovered that myself two years later when I happened to be with the Bruins as they toured Vancouver, Oakland and Los Angeles in February. Vancouver was no problem. All it did was rain. It rained as hard as I've ever seen it rain anywhere, any time in my life. The Bruins won, 4-2.

Oakland was no problem, either. Northern California in February is pleasant, but hardly tropical. The Bruins won, 5-2.

But L.A. definitely presented a problem. We hit L.A. on one of those positively gorgeous days Southern California delights in dispensing during the months of February and March. It had to be between 85 and 90 in bright sunshine as the Bruins alighted from the team bus approximately two hours before the game. At the Forum the players walk down a ramp at one end of the building in order to reach the locker room area. As we strolled down the ramp, Esposito bellowed, "We're supposed to play hockey in *this*?"

Summoning great resolve, the Bruins won, 5-2.

Playing so-so, or even poorly, and still winning is yet another mark of a superior team. The Bruins were amused with themselves for having gotten the maximum 12 points out of the trip, if only because they assumed that New York coach Emile (Cat) Francis had quite naturally assumed that the long Boston trip away from the Boston Garden was a splendid opportunity for his own team to gain some precious ground in the standings.

"He knew we'd stumble on our faces," chuckled Eddie Westfall. "And then the race would be pretty close again. I hate to laugh, but what else can you do?"

Such a frank admission would seldom be heard anywhere in sports today. Players are too programmed. The Bruins were refreshingly normal. They reflected normal human emotions. They really *were* just like the guy next door, only in their case they skated and shot better and were always ready to knock you into the boards.

Eddie Johnston couldn't help thinking about a sputtering Cat down there in The Apple. "Emile was telling everybody to wait until we had our long trip. He was telling them that there was the difference. Of course, he had a right to think that way. A lot of people claim if you break even on the road you're ahead of the game, and I think he thought we might break even while the Rangers were winning. It has to be a great shock."

The Bruins now stood at 101 points, to 92 for New York and 84 for Montreal.

Cheevers was now up to 25 straight without losing, and Johnson was waxing more and more enthusiastic about his 32-year-old netminder by the day. Much of the discussion focused on the Cheevers style, which, according to the ex-Canadien star, was a variation on a theme originally composed and executed by the legendary Jacques Plante. "He (Plante) changed the theory of goaltending," explained Johnson. "It used to be the goalie stayed in his crease, played in the net. Then along came Jacques. He came out and handled the puck, passed it wisely and in such a way that made it easier for his team to get the puck out of the zone. He showed us how important skating was to a goaltender."

And Cheevers was probably the best-skating goalie of his time. Cheevers had actually been a part-time forward during his time in Junior A hockey, a circumstance verified by Westfall. "It's true," he said. "I know. I played against him a couple of times in the juniors."

With but 15 games remaining in the regular season, the Bruins were in a position to indulge in some self-analysis. Barring a monumental collapse, they were going to win the division. It was obvious that this was a better team than the one which had been starched by Montreal the previous spring. And there was a strong belief that it was a more talented team than the none which had taken home the Stanley Cup in 1970. But until this club matched that achievement, this contention was mired strictly in the realm of conversation.

"We're better defensively," asserted Cheevers. "We always get that man back this year. That helps."

GM Schmidt had an interesting take. He really thought the team had matured, and this even included veterans such as Esposito, McKenzie, Stanfield, Cheevers, Johnston, etc. "They had to live with that awful collapse of a year ago," Schmidt pointed out. "You get sick and tired of answering questions about it. You're embarrassed. They've got a lot of points to prove.

"But here's one that's hard to explain," he said. "How does a veteran 'mature,' especially a veteran in his 30s? You have to laugh at the thought of it, but some of them not only have matured but they also have a better attitude, as well."

"It does sound kind of funny," agreed coach Johnson. "A veteran maturing. It's true, though. That loss in the playoffs brought maturity and new thinking. You can see the difference."

That all having been said, the Bruins ran their record to 47-8-9 by flattening Vancouver, 7-3. Esposito had his third hat trick of the season. Orr had three points to go over 100 points for the third straight season. Remember that in Eddie Shore's day a 50-point defenseman would have been regarded as a visitor from another planet. Eddie Johnston supplied a nice notebook filler by submitting a record-tying fourth assist in the '71-72 season.

Cheevers ran his personal unbeaten string to 26 with a 5-4 victory over Detroit, prompting Johnson to wonder why his goalie's achievement wasn't attracting more national attention. "It has to be the greatest goaltending achievement ever," he declared. "But nothing is being made of it. It's hard for me to say anything because we have *two* fine goaltenders who have played great hockey, and I wouldn't want to be praising one over the other. But, let's face it. Who should be the all-star goaltender? How could you do any better than 26 games without losing?"

Cheevers knew there was more to his streak than just a good glove hand and a friendly goalpost or two. "I know better than anyone else I have this streak because of this team," he said. "I think there were about eight games in there that I might have lost with a lesser team. It helps when you play on a club that scores the way we can."

Amid all the talk about maturity and keeping concentration, the Bruins knew the regular-season race was over and they began to play accordingly. That is to say, for the remainder of the regular season, some nights they had it, and some nights they didn't.

A scheduling quirk sent them all the way to Los Angeles for one game on March 16, and instead of acting petulant they put on a show for the Forum crowd, burying the local darlings by an 8-3 score. Johnson had expressed some pregame concern about the whereabouts of his team's powers of concentration, but he felt a whole lot better after watching them pop in five goals in the game's first 30 minutes.

"I was really pleased with the way the guys played," he said. "That's the best hockey we've played in two weeks."

"We've got to play this type of hockey the rest of the way," said Esposito. "The playoffs are coming up, and this is the kind of hockey that you have to play in the playoffs."

The eight goals were by eight different people.

One game remaining on the regular-season schedule had everyone's attention. The Bruins had grown exceedingly fond of the good feeling generated by a good old-fashioned butt-kicking of the hated Rangers, whom they had ruled all season after dropping the first game of the season to the Broadway Blues at home. They couldn't get enough of it, and there was one regular-season game left with New York. Just in case the two should be matched up in the Stanley Cup playoffs, the Bruins wished the Rangers to realize the futility in store.

The mission was accomplished.

The Bruins won convincingly. The final was 4-1, and it didn't even matter that Esposito got himself thrown out by referee Bruce Hood in the aftermath of a tussle with New York's Brad Park.

Cheevers was once again majestic in the nets, his streak now swollen to an almost unbelievable 31. He had also beaten the Rangers four straight, allowing just three goals.

"They've got it," said Emile The Cat, alluding to first place. "They beat us good tonight. We played our best. They were too much for us. A good, strong, fast team. And they were missing some men. They came to us and beat us. They are a team."

Eddie Westfall, who answered to the name "Steady Eddie," appreciated the Cat's words of praise. "We *are* self-disciplined and we have reached a spot we want to be in. We know that we are powerful and we know that we can win if each one of us does his best. That's all we ask of ourselves, and it's reasonable. Montreal has always been a team. The old Yankees were teams in the true sense."

Those were the words of a prudent 32-year-old. It was left for Derek Sanderson to utter the words of a brash 26-year-old born without a governor on the tongue.

"I would think we have that team psyched out about now," he smirked "I don't think they'll be looking forward to playing us in a seven-game final after the way we've played against them this season."

The actual division-clinching, anticlimax that it was, came on March 26 with a 5-4 victory in the Boston Garden over Montreal. The victory wasn't even necessary, since New York had already eliminated itself with a loss even before the Boston game began.

"This was our first objective," said coach Johnson. "Now we'll look to the other objective."

One decision had already been made. There would be no wholesale resting of primary personnel. Johnson had tried that the year previous, and 'nuff said.

The players understood. "We've got all summer to loaf," reasoned McKenzie.

"The only one who gets to rest now is Milt Schmidt," said Milt Schmidt.

The Bruins weren't the only people in the NHL capable of playing with words. Montreal coach Scott Bowman, his team several light years astern of the Bruins in the standings, seized the occasion of this defeat to issue a playoff warning. "In playoffs," he preached, "it all comes down to goaltending and conditioning. You have to have the strength, not muscle, to play four games in five days. We (Canadiens) have it. I'm not sure they (Bruins) do."

The Bruins finished out the season with three losses (the only time all year they lost three in succession) and a victory in Game 78 against Toronto. Esposito won the Art Ross Trophy as the league's premier scorer with 133 points. Orr was second with 117, including a rather dazzling pre-Gretzky/Lemieux total of 90 assists. Bucyk, the ageless team captain universally known as the Chief, had 83, while Stanfield, McKenzie, Sanderson, Walton, Hodge and Cashman all had more than 50 points.

They maintained their reputation as a high-scoring team with 35 performances in excess of five goals, 19 over six, nine over seven and seven over eight, to go with three over nine and an 11-goal game. More to the point in terms of regaining the Stanley Cup, they held opponents to two goals or fewer 43 times, or 55 percent of their games.

They had the sharp memory of that horrifying collapse against Montreal the previous spring frozen in their minds. There could not possibly be an excuse. They were the best team in the league. *Everyone* knew it. They had also been the Best Team In Hockey entering the 1971 playoffs. But in order to win the Stanley Cup it is necessary to be better somewhere than in your own mind. Their task was to win 12 more hockey games in order to make it all official.

3

The Stanley Cup Playoffs

The first playoff opponent was going to be Toronto, a team which might not have known it had already performed a great service to the Bruins simply by showing up for the final game of the regular season.

Tom Johnson had not been particularly pleased going into that game, the 78th and last of the long, long regular season. Games 75, 76 and 77 had been something far less than satisfactory, the Bruins having lost in Detroit, Toronto and Montreal. He wanted to see a little more pizazz in Game 78, and he got it as the Bruins survived the absence of messrs. Orr, Esposito and Vadnais to come away with a needed 6-4 victory.

The available Bruins, infused with youthful energy supplied by Braves' call-ups Terry O'Reilly and Ron Jones, skated with fury and purpose, much to the mentor's delight. Sanderson summed it all up best.

"They woke the sleeping giant," he observed.

Toronto was a middlin' team no one seriously expected to give the Bruins much trouble in Round One. There was nothing approaching the Bruins' phobia in the Montreal Forum. The Maple Leaf Gardens was a comfortable, respectable place, and if it was known for anything, it was for housing the most polite and sedate fans in all of North American sport. The Leafs' followers were known for their almost British reserve, although that restraint did not seep down to the bench, where truly legendary (as opposed to mere legendary) Frank (King) Clancy was in charge.

By that time the 69-year-old Clancy had been a member of the Hockey Hall of Fame for 14 years. He could have been selected for his 17-year playing career with the Maple Leafs and Ottawa Senators. He could have been selected for his 12-year officiating career. He could have been selected for his coaching expertise. Or he could simply have been selected because he was the one and only King Clancy and it was impossible to imagine a National Hockey League without him. In fact, there had never actually been a National Hockey League without him.

Clancy was only coaching because the regular Toronto mentor, John McLellan, had taken sick. And when anything needed to be done in Toronto, they knew the King would be ready to step in. "John's a good friend," Clancy shrugged.

Clancy promised one thing prior to the series. "We'll play a good, rough game, but not dirty," he said. Given that Bobby Orr was even then pencilled in for his third knee operation, the Bruins could only hope that Clancy could be taken at his word. Rough, they could handle. Dirty was another matter.

The Bruins were a little concerned about health. Orr, Esposito and Stanfield had all been dealing with balky knees. Carol Vadnais had a hand problem. Hodge was still struggling with his ankle. Sanderson had, by this time, been diagnosed as having colitis. King Clancy was unmoved. You think maybe the ol' King just fell off the boat, or what? "They're kidding old Francis Michael Clancy with that injury stuff," he growled. "When the whistle blows, all of them — Orr, Esposito, Vadnais, Stanfield, Hodge and Sanderson — will all be on deck. I know my hockey players — and these men are hockey players."

Where, oh where have all the characters gone, anyway?

The King knew whereof he spoke. They all played, and most of them played well. The Bruins spanked the Maple Leafs, 5-0, with Cheevers posting his fourth career playoff shutout. But already the spectre of Montreal loomed large. No one in the Boston locker room got very excited.

"Not until it's all over and we have the top money," said Ace Bailey. "Then we'll all get excited."

Esposito slipped two by the venerable Jacques Plante in the span of 2:17 of the second period, but the man drawing comparable raves was Cashman, who had put the puck on Espo's stick.

The King, God bless 'im, was full of I-told-ya-sos. "All I heard about was the injuries," he snorted. "Esposito's got a bad knee...Orr's got a bad knee...Hodge has a cranky ankle...Sanderson's got stomach problems. Well, if any of these guys are sick or hurting, I'm the first Chinaman named Clancy."

At least one member of the vanquished Leafs displayed the kind of moxie that would make The King proud.

"The Bruins aren't in shape," sneered veteran Bobby Baun. "That's how the Canadiens beat them last year, by outskating them. We'll do the same."

He did look prescient when the Leafs evened the series with an overtime victory in Game 2 on a goal by Jimmy Harrison. "The only thing that really got hurt tonight was our pride," said Westfall.

The Bruins regained control in Game 3 when Eddie Johnston came up with a clutch goaltending effort and Orr and Walton scored the goals in a 2-0 victory. The Bruins went up, 3-1 with a four-goal barrage in the third period of a 5-4 triumph. The Bruins had trailed 3-1 and 4-2. Hodge had two goals. Westfall had a shorthanded goal.

The series came to a merciful conclusion back in Boston when a third-period Hodge goal provided the Bruins with a 3-2 decision.

The goal culminated a strong series for Hodge, who had become the whipping boy for the Boston crowd and who didn't like it one little bit.

The series now tucked safely away into the record books, The King could say what he *really* thought about the Boston Bruins. "You're a good team," he said while making a congratulatory visit to the Boston dressing room. "Hope you go all the way. Never mind what I said before. I like you all. Now go all the way."

One foe down, two remaining. The next opponents were the St. Louis Blues, the team Boston had conquered in order to win the Stanley Cup in 1970. That series was a four-game sweep, and there was no reason to think this one wouldn't be, either.

It was.

The first two in Boston were ugly. The first one in St. Louis was similarly uncompetitive. Only the last game in St. Louis was competitive and interesting, but the results were all the same. The Bruins simply gave St. Louis the backs of their hands.

There had been some question before Game 1 about the effects on the Bruins of a weeklong layoff following the Toronto clinching. Excuse me? Stanfield had a hat trick as the Bruins won Game 1, 6-1. Curt Bennett of the Blues denounced the Bruins as "arrogant," saying "They push you and shove you around and expect you to take it." Well, yeah, Curt. What was the point?

Game 2 was frightening. This time it was Bucyk's turn to get himself a playoff hat trick. The final was 10-2.

Bucyk was everybody's friend. This was his 16th season as a Bruin and his 18th in the league. He was strong and tough, but in possession of such a soothing temperament that he would retire as a two-time winner of the Lady Byng Award for gentlemanly play.

The nickname carried real weight. He was the unquestioned team leader. The team bus left when The Chief said it left. The charter plane took off when The Chief said it took off. He was the one who made sure everyone was fed and taken care of on trips. He was just an amazingly decent man who could really play some hockey.

St. Louis coach Al Arbour spoke bluntly after Game 2. "We're in a trance," he said. "Maybe our guys can't believe they're on the same

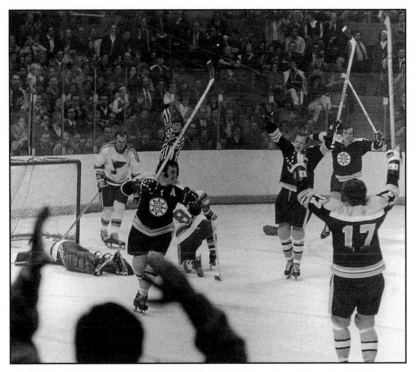

The Bruins whoop it up after a goal against St. Louis. (Photo©London Life-Portnoy/ Hockey Hall of Fame)

ice with the Bruins. We were running around all over the place, and an experienced team like Boston will capitalize on your every mistake."

Things got no better for the Blues on their home ice. The Bruins smacked them around, 7-2. Westfall had another one of those Bruins' staples — a shorthanded goal.

"You have to look at them and size them up and you have to admit it's one of the greatest teams in hockey," said Arbour. "One of the all-time best. They've got so much depth, so much power. They go to the bench and they come up with players who could start for anybody else."

St. Louis salvaged some pride in Game 4, but two goals by Esposito and two goals by Bucyk propelled the Bruins to a 5-2 victory. Thus ended one of the great bombardments of all time. The Bruins had outscored the Blues, 28-8.

"Look at them," marveled veteran Barclay Plager. "They have everything. They manhandled us. Not physically, because it wasn't a skating series. They skated over us, around us and through us. Look at Bucyk at his age (37). He still plays like a kid. But it's not one line. It's all four and the way Johnson works them there *are* four lines."

This, of course, is unimaginable in today's expansion-ravaged hockey. Teams who can put together two potent lines consider themselves fortunate. That's why contemporary fans with long memories laugh when fans in newly minted hockey locales start boasting about how good their team is. Someone unfamiliar with hockey as played a quarter-century ago cannot be faulted for failing to understand what it was like to have a team like the '71-72 Bruins available for perusal every night. That fan would simply have no comprehension.

Nor would the modern fan have any idea what it was like to be watching Robert Gordon Orr every night. Said Al Arbour, "They have balance, they have magnificent goaltending and then, when everything else seems to run out on them, they've got Bobby Orr, the greatest thing that ever showed up on ice."

Orr was anxious to wrap things up. Though he had a dazzling 15 assists in the St. Louis series, he wasn't quite himself, and it was all due to his battered left knee. "I know Orr isn't right," said Plager. "We sat down on the ice one time and we just looked at each other and I said, 'Are you hurting?' and he said 'Yes.' No matter what, if he had only one leg, he'd still be the greatest thing out there."

How great was this? The Bruins were going to face New York in the Stanley Cup Finals.

The Rangers? Oh, wow. New York had beaten the Bruins by a convincing 4-1 score on Opening Night, but that was the end of it. The Bruins won the remaining games between the two by scores of 8-1 and 4-1 in Boston and 6-1, 4-1 and 2-0 in Madison Square Garden. That's 24-4, but who was counting?

The Bruins felt there was no way they could lose, if only because they had one thing no one else did. "Orr is the difference, no doubt," said Esposito, who wasn't bad himself. "But he's the difference against any club."

The series opened in Boston and it was a terrific game. Hodge had a hat trick, one of which was a shorthander (Sanderson matched that one), while Ace Bailey provided the winner late in the third period. It wasn't the Bruins' best night, starting in goal, where the ever-candid Cheevers admitted he was "daydreaming" on one Bruce MacGregor goal. The final was 6-5.

Game 2 was an old-fashioned, tight-checking playoff game, one that Eddie Shore and King Clancy undoubtedly would have liked. Hodge got the game-winner on a third-period power play goal scored just three seconds before the expiration of a 5-on-3 situation. Johnston was the winning goaltender.

Back home in New York the Broadway Blues *had* to have a victory, and they came away with a 5-2 triumph behind two Brad Park goals.

Game 4 was an Orr showpiece. The Bruins beat New York, 3-2, as Orr scored twice while manufacturing a personal highlight film. "Even though the miseries in his celebrated left knee were aggravated during the course of the proceedings," wrote Tom Fitzgerald, "the world's best hockey player left his unmistakable stamp on the 3-2 victory the Bruins wrested from the Rangers in a very physical encounter."

Orr also sparred with Brad Park in a game spiced by 104 minutes of penalties. The Rangers must have been conferring with King Clancy. "Orr didn't play like someone with a sore knee," said Ranger goalie Ed Giacomin. "He was flying out there." But the truth is that Orr had missed more than 10 minutes of action while receiving treatment on his very sore left knee.

All Orr would admit to was being "a little sore."

One game away from elimination, the Rangers came up with a big game, stopping the Bruins by a 3-2 score, and doing it in Boston. Bobby Rousseau scored twice for the Blueshirts. "We were tight all the way," said a somewhat perplexed Johnson.

Said Eddie Johnston, "We were getting in each other's way."

The Bruins would rather have won at home, as they had in 1970, but they were hardly afraid of a road game. They had done some of their best work away from the Garden.

"All we have to do is go back to the game we played Sunday. It's as simple as that. Then we hit everything that moved. Tuesday night we didn't even skate across their shadows."

Bobby Orr was the name on the lips of all of Boston's opponents during the Bruins' run to the 1972 Stanley Cup. (Photo©London Life-Portnoy/Hockey Hall of Fame)

All season long Gerry Cheevers had come up with big games. This was just one more on the list. The Bruins regained the Stanley Cup which they had handed away the year before by shutting out the Rangers, 3-0. Cashman scored twice and Orr scored once, and nothing more was needed.

And there it was. The Bruins had been the best team from start to finish, and this time it was official.

And once again, the primary name on the lips of the opposition was Bobby Orr.

"We played them pretty even, except they had Bobby Orr," said Ranger captain Vic Hadfield.

The final punctuation on the season was supplied by Boston mayor Kevin White. The impish Johnny Pie had put himself in most of the headlines back in 1970 by pouring beer on hizzoner's head during the official City Hall celebration of the Stanley Cup triumph. The Mayor had been waiting for two years, but he did get his revenge, dumping some beer on the cranium of the feisty winger. The mayor also presented McKenzie with a special medallion citing him for his "spirit, enthusiasm and energy."

That designation could have been applied to the entire team. The town is still waiting to see another one like it.

No one thing brought down the Bruins, but the World Hockey Association was a good beginning. The new league eventually made off with both Cheevers and Sanderson. The Bruins reached the Finals for the third time in five years in 1974, but the Broad Street Bullies of Philadelphia took them out in six games.

Little by little, the great Bruins team disintegrated. General manager Harry Sinden stunned the hockey world with a huge trade in 1976, trading Esposito and Vadnais to the Rangers for Brad Park and smooth playmaker Jean Ratelle. Orr, his knees all but shot before the age of 30, was allowed to depart to Chicago for a brief run later that year. There are people who *still* haven't forgiven the Bruins' organization for that one.

Bombastic Don Cherry took over as coach in 1974, and the Bruins settled into a long run of basic contention, reaching the Finals in 1978. The flash point came in 1979 when the Bruins had — all together now — Too Many Men On The Ice.

The great Raymond Bourque showed up in 1979, thus guaranteeing the Bruins the nightly presence of a superstar till 1997 and, who knows? Cam Neely, a true goal-scoring machine, arrived on board via a great trade with Vancouver in 1986 and he, along with Bourque, got the Bruins into the Stanley Cup Finals in both 1988 and 1990. There was a great civic embarrassment in 1988 when a transformer failure in the North End caused a blackout in the Garden and subsequent halt of a 3-3 hockey game which was resumed two nights later in Edmonton. The Oilers won the game to complete the sweep. The teams met two years later and the Bruins were fortunate to win a single game.

That made them 1-8 in two Stanley Cup appearances against Edmonton, but few in Boston were complaining. These were the great Edmonton teams anchored by Wayne Gretzky and Mark Messier, and no rational being believed the Bruins were going to defeat *that* team.

71

The Bruins have not seriously contended since. But Boston remains a staunch hockey town. There is no greater urban market for college hockey. The high school hockey tournament is an annual Event. And always there are the Boston Bruins.

People are not especially pleased with the Fleet Center as a hockey venue, at least not when compared to their beloved Boston Garden. But if they're old enough, what they really miss is the brand of hockey they got to see when giants named Orr, Esposito and Cheevers roamed the earth.

"You couldn't even *think* of assembling a team like that again," says the Bruins' Nate Greenberg. "No one could afford it in these times. What balance. Every facet of the game. Line after line, they all brought something to the table. It was sad, because it was far too short a run. It was a bitter disappointment losing to Philadelphia in '74. There was no way we should have lost that."

But no one appreciated what was taking place on that Garden ice in those wonderful days more than Roger Naples and his friends in the Gallery Gods. They keep the vigil even now, hoping that Sergei Samsomov and Joe Thornton might be the heirs to the Orrs and Espositos.

Well, not quite.

"These kids might be good," he sighs, "But another Orr? I doubt it. Those were such great years. What I wouldn't do to live through all that again."

The Celtics

1986 NBA championship game at Boston Garden. (Photo©Tom Miller)

4

More Than an Afterthought

I began covering the Boston Celtics for the *Boston Globe* in the fall of 1969. I was 23.

What's wrong with that picture?

The Celtics were coming off their 11th championship in 13 years. Next to the Harlem Globetrotters, they were the most famous basketball team in the world. They ranked with the New York Yankees, Green Bay Packers and Montreal Canadiens as one of the most successful franchises in North American sports history.

So it would stand to reason that sportswriters would be lining up outside the boss' office door, begging for the opportunity to cover this wonderful team, correct?

Not so. Not at all. When Bob Sales, who had been covering the team for several years, left the sports department in favor of the city room, there was no heir apparent for the job, no one lusting for the job. Sports editor Fran Rosa turned to The Kid and said, "Cover the Celts' opener against Cincinnati."

The team's coverage was then entrusted for the first couple of months of the 1969-70 season to not just one, but two kids — myself and Peter Gammons, a University of North Carolina grad. After a while, the rest sort of became mine, no questions asked. Gammons didn't mind. He liked basketball well enough, but his heart was, and is, in baseball. He has gone on to become one of the most influential journalists in baseball history, both as a writer for the *Globe* and *Sports Illustrated*, and as a broadcast analyst for ESPN.

But how could it possibly come to pass that the job of covering an 11-time NBA champion be handed over to a 23-year-old kid?

To understand this, it is necessary to go back to the beginning. It is necessary to go back to 1946 and the Commodore Hotel in New York City and the meeting in which the Basketball Association of America was born. It is necessary to realize that Boston Garden president Walter Brown was giving the city of Boston something it had neither wanted nor asked for when he walked out of that meeting of arena owners with a basketball franchise.

The BAA came into existence at that point in time because these arena folk were looking for a way to fill some open dates in their buildings and they hoped that a professional basketball league would serve that purpose. It wasn't any deeper than that. There was little pure basketball passion involved. This was business, pure and simple.

Basketball was a popular sport, but professional basketball was a shoestring, fly-by-night affair. People had been playing for pay as far back as 1896, but no league had ever achieved true national prominence. Professional basketball, under any guise, had no presence in either the Far West or the South. It was strictly an Eastern and Midwestern concern.

When you thought of basketball in the mid-40s, you thought of New York City, first and foremost. You thought of Chicago. You thought of Indiana. One place you did not think of was Boston, and for very good reason. The city had dropped basketball from the high schools in 1925. An entire generation of Bostonians had grown up with no knowledge or feel for the sport. The winters had been completely given over to hockey. There was basketball in the suburbs, but this was an era in which cities, not suburbs, reigned supreme in American life. Core city populations were enormous. Cities set the social tone. And in Boston there was simply no such thing as basketball if you resided within the city limits.

In this barren basketball environment Walter Brown invented the Boston Celtics.

Given the reality of basketball interest in Boston at the time, I am continually struck by the actual attendance figures. Splitting their home games between the Boston Garden and the much smaller (by more than half) Boston Arena, the Celtics averaged 3,608 that first year. In the circumstances, that's actually pretty good, I'd say.

The first coach was John (Honey) Russell, a knowledgeable veteran of the basketball wars whose proud boast at the time was that he had participated in more professional games of all types than any man in history. He began playing professionally at age 18 and accepted his final paycheck 28 years later.

Honey lasted two years before giving way to Alvin (Doggie) Julian. Honey's teams weren't very good, and neither were Doggie's. But Honey's were good for more laughs, if only because Honey had one Kevin (Chuck) Connors, and Doggie didn't.

Chuck Connors would later become famous as television's *Rifleman*, but in his youth he was a tremendous athlete, good enough to play both professional basketball and professional baseball (Dodgers and Cubs). He was also a certified nut case (OK, eccentric), a born clown and showman. He was showing off on Opening Night in 1946 by slapping the glass backboard at the Arena (not, as folklore would have it, by dunking), and in so doing the glass shattered and the game was held up for about an hour and a half while team publicist Howie McHugh went over to the Garden for a replacement.

The Garden backboards were stacked behind Brahma bull pens, rodeos being a regular Garden feature, and it was necessary to displace some confused and angry animals before the backboard could be retrieved. According to Honey's son and biographer, John Russell, what had once been a large house had dwindled substantially by the time the game began. The Celtics wound up losing to the Chicago Stags by two. "Every ballplayer has probably at some point cost his team a game," wrote the younger Russell in *Honey Russell...Between Games, Between Halves*, "Not many could match Connors in costing a new franchise its opening-night audience."

The Celtics were relentlessly uninspiring during the first four years of their existence, churning out records of 22-38, 20-38, 25-35 and 22-46. This did include a 1948 playoff appearance in which they were beaten, 2-1, by the Stags.

At this point the Celtics were 89-147 and Brown and his investors (some would say his fellow masochists) were roughly a half million dollars in debt. The NBA was hardly a stable venture. After the third season, the league merged with the midwest-based National Basketball League to form what we now know as the National Basketball Association. That resulted in a completely unwieldy three-division, 17-team league.

The story of those early Celtics is, ultimately, the story of Walter Brown. This hockey man had, against all better personal judgment, fallen in love with the entity known as the Boston Celtics. In all I have ever read about this man, I have never seen any kind of rational explanation for this phenomenon. But the team, and, I suppose, the sport, stirred something deep in his soul. The Boston Celtics were no longer just a fascinating business proposition for Walter Brown. They had become a crusade, and, as such were a phenomenal strain on both his nervous system and his bank account.

Julian resigned after the '49-50 season, and needed a coach. Just to underscore the extent to which those were far more carefree and innocent days, Brown's methodology for hiring a new coach included calling for a meeting of newspaper people. He figured they knew the league and basketball better than he did and could give him a hint or two on just exactly whom he should hire to coach his basketball team.

The recommendation: Arnold (Red) Auerbach, a 32-year-old Brooklyn-bred character who had been a charter league mentor with the Washington Capitols and who gave new and deeper meaning to such words as "brash," "arrogant," "pushy" and "demanding." That he knew his basketball was pretty much beyond dispute. He knew talent and he was a born leader of men. He was available only because he had been fired from the Tri-Cities franchise by Ben Kerner, a man whose ego and abrasiveness were quite the equal of Auerbach's.

If the story of the early Celtics was the story of Walter Brown, the story of the next 40-odd years of Celtics history was the story of Red Auerbach. And if you were to pick one man who embodies the entire NBA experience, there is only a massive tie for second place. Red Auerbach is Mr. NBA, the most important and influential man in the history of the World's Greatest Basketball League.

Auerbach's first season in Boston was a vitally important one for several reasons, starting with the fact that he himself represented true purpose and vitality for the organization. It was also the year in which Bob Cousy and Easy Ed Macauley became Celtics. Finally, that was the season in which the Celtics took a serious stand for social justice, signing Duquesne star Chuck Cooper, who just happened to be an American Negro.

Over the six-year period from 1950-56, the Celtics were, to borrow the words of historian Clinton Rossiter, a "first-class, second-class team." High-scoring and endlessly entertaining with a fast-break style of play Auerbach had learned from Bill Reinhart during his college days at George Washington (a school to which he has remained zealously devoted for the past 56 years), the Celtics were unable to advance more than one round in the playoffs because they lacked the rebounding and defense necessary to become a champion.

Bill Sharman, one of the consummate middle-distance shooters of all time, joined the team in 1951 and teamed with Cousy to form the definitive backcourt of the '50s. Sharman was also a baseball player who had the distinction of being thrown out of a major-league game without ever having participated in one. Called up by the Brooklyn Dodgers in September of 1951 after a successful season at St. Paul, he was minding his own business one day when an umpire, unable to identify just which leather-lung had been harassing him, summarily cleared the entire bench. The Dodgers were even then in the process of being overtaken by the Giants, whom they had once led by 13½ games, and manager Charlie Dressen never did get him into a game. But he can tell his grandchildren he was in the

Brooklyn dugout on October 3, when Bobby Thomson hit The Shot Heard 'Round The World.

Cousy, Sharman and the slender 6-foot, 8-inch Macauley combined to average a combined total of 54 points a game from '51-52 through '55-56. But the Celtics were never tough enough to get past New York or Syracuse in order to get to the finals against the Western Conference champs.

While the Bruins were generally playing before full houses at the Boston Garden, the Celtics had to rely on a staunch cult following, the bulk of which were Jewish clientele from Brookline, a wealthy town which, geographically speaking, is to Boston what San Marino is to Rome. Jewish or otherwise, however, the average Celtic fan had one major obsession — the inimitable Bob Cousy.

Cousy was Boston's, and Auerbach's, greatest lucky accident. The story about how he became a Celtic against Auerbach's will has been told and retold, but it remains endlessly fascinating. Simply speaking, Cousy's name was chosen out of a hat.

We now live in an era of $30-million players, state-of-the-art arenas such as The Rose Garden in Portland and an NBA with regional offices all over the globe. We've got a commissioner telling me that "we've got to beef up our operation in Kuala Lumpur." But in 1950 you had the Chicago team folding — ponder *that* one as you watch yet another championship banner go up in the United Center — and a player dispersal held. You had the players being picked off until there were only three names left, and three teams (New York, Philadelphia and Boston) arguing over them.

The players in question:

1. Max Zaslofsky. A true NBA star of the day. A shooting guard who could conceivably have enormous appeal to any city with a large Jewish clientele; that is to say, any one of the cities involved.

2. Andy Phillip. A former Illinois All-American and one of the reigning playmakers in the league.

3. Bob Cousy. A great college star at Holy Cross. A tricky passer. Also a rookie who had already been dismissed by Auerbach as a guy whose style wasn't right for the pro game.

It was decided that the three names would be placed into a hat supplied by Syracuse owner Danny Biasone (father of the 24-second clock, and thus one of the most important figures in league history). Walter Brown, ever the gentleman, told New York's Ned Irish to pick first. Auerbach, ever the competitor, was furious. Philadelphia's Eddie Gottlieb went second. What transpired was Auerbach's worst nightmare. New York got Zaslofsky. Philly got Phillip. He was stuck with Cousy.

The rest, as they say, was blissful history. Long after Zaslofsky and Phillip were retired, Bob Cousy was making passes and scoring points for championship Boston Celtic teams. He played until 1963, retiring with his reputation secure as the greatest passer the game has ever seen. He remains the standard by which all floor leaders and so-called "playmakers," as opposed to mindless penetrators, are judged.

When Auerbach came to Boston in 1950, Boston was still getting used to the idea of professional basketball. The college game was very popular, thanks to the great success enjoyed by Holy Cross after the war. The Crusaders had won the NCAA tournament in 1947, when Cousy was a freshman substitute. Over the next three years, Holy Cross owned not only Worcester, but also Boston, by virtue of its constant presence in Boston Garden college basketball doubleheaders. But Boston being relatively unsophisticated in the realm of basketball, there was some confusion in the mind of the public. Red came to work in a town which actually believed the college team 35 miles away could beat the professionals.

Red preached the basketball gospel as best he could, but this was Boston and there was only so much he could do. There were a few writers, such as Jack Barry of the *Globe*, Sam Cohen, sports editor of the *Boston Record* and Joe Looney of the *Evening Traveler*, who knew and understood the game properly, but for most members of the press, being assigned to the Celtics was more of an insult than a reward. The team was very often covered by people, who, as the saying went "didn't know whether it was blown up or stuffed." And nobody knew this better, or resented it more, than Auerbach.

Those who did catch on to what was happening were passionate about it.

"I was there," says Jack Craig, who grew up in the city and who would go on to a distinguished career at the *Boston Globe* as a radio-

TV sports critic. "My friends and I went to a lot of games. You could always walk up and get a ticket. We'd ride the MTA (As in "Charley and..."). Nobody drove. Nobody. Most people didn't have a car, anyway, and there was nowhere to park, anyway. You rode to the Garden on either the Green or Orange line. It was the only way to get there. Only later did parking become an issue."

The Celtics teams of the early and mid-50s were winning more than they were losing, but not enough to make any kind of a secular saint out of Auerbach. "As a coach," maintains Craig, "Red was considered quite mediocre. He hadn't really won anything (after compiling the league's best record in the inaugural season of 1946-47, his Washington club had been eliminated in the playoffs). He was considered to be a loudmouth. A (Bill) Parcells, without the winning."

Auerbach was indeed an easy target for the anti-basketball set. Feisty and argumentative, he was almost incapable of getting through a game without getting into at least one major, time-consuming argument with an official. Boston newspaper archives are replete with photos of Auerbach, rolled-up program in hand, jaw to jaw with an NBA official, most often Sid Borgia, a bombastic sort who, like Auerbach himself, was both vertically and follically challenged.

The game was likewise doing itself very little favor with the preferred style of play. There was no time clock, and teams with clever ball handlers were able to freeze the ball away in the last quarter, often as customers streamed toward the exits in disgust. The quintessential game of the day took place on March 21, 1953, when the Celtics defeated Syracuse in a four-overtime playoff game by the score of 111-105. As tense as it was, much of the overtime was spent dribbling and shooting free throws. Cousy scored 50 points, with 30 of them coming at the foul line.

Though Cousy was one of the prime beneficiaries of the old style since he was the consummate dribbler, the advent of the 24-second shot clock in the 1954-55 season actually enhanced his game, since it encouraged more up-and-down play. Cousy proved himself to be even more damaging to opponents running fast break after fast break than he had ever been doing his Marques Haynes imitation at the end of 64-62 games.

Auerbach, who was the team's de facto general manager, traveling secretary and player personnel director, as well as its coach, ran local clinics and tried to act, in his own condescending way, as some sort of basketball ambassador, but the man who kept the sport afloat in Boston during this time was Cousy. Even if not all that many people in Boston realized how good he was, the rest of the world did. He was, along with George Mikan, one of the two great stars of the league's first decade, and he was especially well-loved and appreciated in his home town — New York. Born on the East Side and raised in Queens, he was embraced by the knowledgeable basketball scribes in New York as, among other things, "The Houdini of the Hardwood." His appearances in New York were regarded as events.

Cousy brought a new flair and elegance to the game. For Auerbach, it had not exactly been a case of love at first sight. Red was openly skeptical of Cousy's ability after watching him play for Holy Cross, a team which, due in large measure to Cousy's brand of basketball, had been dubbed the "Fancy Pants A.C." He would have much preferred Max Zaslofsky or Andy Phillip.

But it did not take Red very long to realize that he had completely misjudged this kid. Red came to understand very quickly that Cousy was something new and different and efficient, not something new and different and useless. Once he saw that more of Cousy's unorthodox passes were finding the target than were missing them, he signed onto the experiment.

Within a couple of years, Auerbach was Cousy's biggest fan and his unofficial press agent. Long after Cousy had retired, Red would bristle whenever there would be some new backcourt hotshot and references would be made to the kid perhaps being "another Cousy." To Red, those were fightin' words that were not merely inaccurate, but which were also downright offensive.

Red remains proprietary about the Cousy image and reputation to this day. And there really haven't been many players worth discussing in the same breath as Robert Joseph Cousy if you're talking about the combination of awareness and flair. Pistol Pete Maravich was certainly one. Ernie DeGregorio, a playmaking comet who flashed briefly across the sky before he was done in by injury, was another.

Magic Johnson was naught but a modern 6-9 Cousy. And now there is John Stockton, an easy call as the Cousy of the '90s.

They didn't take fan surveys in those days, so there is no way of knowing for sure how many people would have come to Celtics games if Cousy had not been there. It has often been suggested that Cousy personally kept the team afloat until Bill Russell arrived. Craig, a great Cousy admirer, won't go that far. "I don't think there was any indication they would have folded and gone out of business without Cousy," he maintains.

What we do know is that Walter Brown was completely dedicated to the proposition that there was going to be a Boston Celtics. Attendance had improved to the point where the Celtics were averaging almost half a house in the 13,909-seat Boston Garden, but it's not as if Walter Brown was making any money out of his team. One season he did not have the money for the players' playoff shares. He just didn't have it. Everyone understood. He asked them to be patient, that when he came up with it they would get it. They were, and he did.

As I said, these were different times.

If Red Auerbach did nothing else for the Boston Celtics, he got them Bill Russell. Now we are entering into a very tricky area. How much credit does Bill Russell get for being Bill Russell? How much credit does Red Auerbach get for being Red Auerbach? What would be the Red Auerbach legacy had Bill Russell never come along? Does anyone really know whether or not Bill Russell would have been as valuable an NBA player performing for any other coach? Does it really matter who gets the credit, since the end result was that the Auerbach-Russell marriage resulted in the greatest concentrated stretch of dominance in league history.

It is so difficult for people weaned on the modern game to understand what a risk Auerbach was taking when he tried to move heaven and earth in order to make Bill Russell a Celtic in 1956. Even though Russell was the foundation of a University of San Francisco team that won back-to-back NCAA championships in 1955-56, there was considerable doubt among learned NBA scholars concerning the degree to which his style of play would translate to the NBA. The better centers in the NBA of 1956 were scorers first and everything else second, and Russell, despite averaging 21 points a game during his college career, was not regarded as having much scoring potential in the professional ranks.

His strengths were rebounding, defense and making the outlet pass on the fast break. Auerbach did not need more scoring. He had Cousy and Sharman and a rookie named Tom Heinsohn to do that. (He also had a still-viable Macauley and Cliff Hagan coming out of the Army, but they would wind up being the trade bait for the rights St. Louis held to Russell). All in all, Red believed he had enough people to put the ball in the basket. What he needed was the basketball. I will always believe that was his primary thought.

Russell was a new kind of explosive, quick-to-the-ball, rebounder.

I think the effects of defense, and especially the shot-blocking, were underestimated by everyone, Auerbach included. Russell was just too revolutionary in this regard. There was simply no frame of reference. I suspect that even Auerbach reasoned that Russell would not be able to transfer his shot-blocking skill to the NBA because, well, it was the NBA, and these were the best players in the world. No kid was going to enter the NBA and change the entire game. No kid was going to come into the NBA and ruin individual careers.

Bill Russell did.

It's all a matter of record now, but none of this could possibly have been foreseen in 1956. Auerbach just knew that he wanted and needed Russell. The two teams standing in his way were Rochester and St. Louis. Rochester stepped aside when Walter Brown was able to promise Rochester owner Lester Harrison he could swing some Ice Capades dates his way (have I mentioned it was a vastly different world?). St. Louis really didn't want Russell all that badly, first because it was a prisoner of the old-line thinking process and therefore couldn't really grasp the value of this strange new player; secondly because Russell, as a Negro, was rumored to be getting himself into a bidding war with the NBA on one side and the Harlem Globetrotters on the other; and, finally, because he was a Negro and there was some question as to whether this town, often described as the "northernmost Southern city," was ready for that. Auerbach, meanwhile, had an attractive package to trade, because Macauley, then only 28 years of age, was a local guy who had starred at Saint Louis University, and because the 6-4 Hagan was clearly going to be a terrific player.

There was, of course, the Walter Brown factor. Walter always aimed to please, and everything with him was always very personal. He would never have authorized a Macauley trade if Easy Ed weren't willing to go. But Macauley had a sick child and was very happy to return home.

So Auerbach got Russell and a basketball dynasty was born.

Auerbach and Brown received instant dividends. The Celtics won the 1957 NBA championship, first knocking off longtime play-off nemesis Syracuse in three straight and then outlasting stubborn St. Louis in a thrilling seven-game championship series. You couldn't ask for much more in the way of drama, for St. Louis was the team, after all, from whom Auerbach had obtained the rights to Russell.

The series was oddly book-ended with 125-123 games. St. Louis won the opener by that score in overtime and the Celtics won the title two weeks later by the same score, this time in two bladder-stretching overtimes.

The Celtics have been engaged in more memorable playoff games than the rest of the league put together, and there are some who believe that none have topped Game 7 in 1957 for sheer get-me-the-cardiac-specialist excitement. St. Louis guard Jack Coleman, for example, was sailing in for what appeared to be an unmolested sneakaway layup that would have put the visiting Hawks ahead by three points in the final minute of regulation when Russell made what in subsequent years would be universally referred to in basketball as a pure "Russell play." This means he mysteriously materialized after seeming to be out of the play in time to block Coleman's shot. He then sprinted back the other way to score a go-ahead basket.

Russell was magnificent throughout, as expected, but the man who time and again made big plays was fellow rookie Tom Heinsohn, whom the Celtics were able to draft, as was the custom of the day, as a so-called "territorial" draft pick. Russell fouled out during the first overtime, but Heinsohn was relentless, eventually finishing with 37 points and 23 rebounds.

A free throw by (Jungle) Jim Loscutoff with one second remaining in the second OT made it 125-123, Celtics. But Alex Hannum, the ever-resourceful player-coach of the Hawks, had a plan. He took the ball and threw it the length of the court, striking the backboard.

Bob Pettit caught the carom and attempted to steer the ball back into the basket. The ball rolled off the rim, and the Celtics were world champions for the first time.

St. Louis fans and players don't want to hear this, but you don't need a Ph.D. in Hoopology to know that if Bill Russell hadn't gotten hurt the Celtics would have defended their title the next season. But the game's greatest player *did* injure his ankle during the third game of the Finals, and he was essentially useless for the remainder of the series. Even then, it took a spectacular 50-point performance by the great Bob Pettit in Game 6 to topple the Celtics.

They would not lose another playoff series for nine years.

The sports world in general, and the NBA in particular, had entered into the era of Bill Russell, the unquestioned greatest team sport American athlete this country had ever produced. Here was a man who was not about statistics. Bill Russell was about one thing, and one thing only — winning. He influenced other people — "made them better," people said — but that was only half the story. For even as he was making his own teammates more efficient, he was also making opposing players less efficient. Certain pet moves and tendencies which had been, and which would continue to be, useful against everyone else were of no value against Bill Russell.

It is vitally important for the modern fan unfortunate enough to have been born too late to see this man play, and who has never had the opportunity to see his legacy preserved on video, that he was simply a superior athlete in every way, physically and mentally. Be assured that he was not merely somewhat better than his contemporaries. Be assured that were Bill Russell, just as he was in 1956, dropped into the NBA of today, that careers would again be threatened, just as they were in the mid-50s.

Bill Russell changed the game by glamorizing the blocked shot and by making defense in general a vital part of the game. He also triggered the greatest fast break the game had yet seen by thinking about making an instant transition from defense to offense with every defensive rebound and by then executing the quickest, most accurate outlet passes the game had ever seen.

He was playing for the one man on this earth best geared to coach him, and Russell has never failed to acknowledge this. "I could not have become the player I was in the NBA under any other coach," Russell says, and that is no mere hyperbole, for what Auerbach brought to the partnership transcended basketball technicalities.

Bill Russell was a handful. A proud, intelligent African-American, he had very well-developed ideas about both the game and life. Auerbach appreciated him for the sensitive individual he was as much as he did for the superior athlete he was. Though to this day his ex-players joke in public that Auerbach, much like Vince Lombardi, "treated us all the same way — rotten", that was far from the truth. Auerbach treated each of them in a specific way. There were generic whipping boys, Tom Heinsohn being the prime example, whom Auerbach used to score points with the group as a whole, and there were others, Cousy and Russell being examples, whom Auerbach would absolutely, positively, never *ever* criticize harshly, publicly or privately.

But do not discount the technical aspect. Auerbach put Russell's mind at ease from the beginning by assuring him there would be no pressure on him to score. He never presumed to spoil Russell's fun by telling him *not* to score, but he made it clear that his primary responsibilities were to rebound, play defense as he knew how and make those exquisite outlet passes. The points, he assured him, would fall his way. And they did. Russell finished his career having scored a solid 15.1 points per game.

What became evident from the outset of Russell's career was that while he might not have been a skilled shotmaker, he was a great offensive basketball player. He set great picks, for example, and he was a master of salvaging the broken play. If taken for granted by an opponent, he could make someone look very foolish by executing the counter option on one of Auerbach's legendary, and unstoppable, six offensive plays. He always knew where each of the other nine men on the floor were, and he could project future happenings instantly. He was an above-average passer. Cousy was the master chef out there, and he always regarded Russell as the main ingredient. The Boston Celtics' offense was run through Bill Russell.

The Celtics survived a major threat from a sadly forgotten, but quite potent, Syracuse team in 1959. Game 7 of the division finals was a wild, up-and-down affair, during which each team thought it had delivered the other a knockout blow. The Celtics prevailed, 130-

125, and then obliterated the Minneapolis Lakers in the first four-game sweep of the Finals the NBA had ever seen.

With that, the Celtics spent the next seven years playing against two things: Themselves and Excellence. Spurred by Auerbach and always anchored by Russell, who had established himself as the most threatening and majestic force in all of sport, they won regular-season titles in 1960, 1961, 1962, 1963, 1964 and 1965 before Philadelphia ended the run with a one-game victory in the 1965-66 season. Nowadays, the instant a team wins a championship speculation begins that the number one impediment to winning another the following season is motivation. Looking at a somewhat cracked mirror in history, people simply cannot fathom how the Celtics — how *Auerbach* — did it. But they did. Each year they came to training camp knowing there was a giant bull's eye on their collective backs, and each year they went out and proved themselves all over again.

The intriguing question was "Did anybody care?" They had managed to draw an average of 10,517 a game for 25 Garden dates in the first championship season of 1956-57. By 1961-62, four championships in hand, the per-game attendance for 28 Garden dates fell to 6,852 a game, even as the perennial basement-occupying Bruins were attracting nightly sellouts. The Celtics were prophets only partially honored in their own home town.

Playoff games were regular sellouts, true, but didn't the Celtics deserve more? Was Boston *that* ignorant a basketball town? Where were all those people who regularly filled the Garden from 1947-50 to see Cousy's Holy Cross teams? Did they believe that playoff basketball was much more interesting than regular-season basketball (the Celtics usually got the appropriate 13,909 for playoff games)? What could possibly make them think, if indeed this was what they did think, that the college basketball they had seen in the late '40s was more entertaining than the professional basketball being provided for them now? It was all a great mystery.

Jonathan Schwartz would have been to *all* those games, if only he weren't residing at 139 East 94th Street in Manhattan. But though geographically separated from the Boston Celtics, he was 100 percent emotionally connected. If those saps in Boston didn't fully appreciate what the Celtics were doing, Jonathan Schwartz certainly did.

He was a precocious kid living in New York who happened to worship Red Auerbach. "In Arnold," he says, "I saw a hero. I saw a short, loud, cunning, lying, cigar-smoking, Chinese food-eating — all of this I knew at a very young age, I don't know how — genius. And all of this was before he had won anything."

Young Schwartz's interest in the Celtics was originally an outgrowth of an abiding love for another Boston institution — the Boston Red Sox. Relocated to New York from Los Angeles in 1946, the only son of famed composer Arthur Schwartz (*Dancing In The Dark, That's Entertainment,* etc.), Schwartz had become infatuated with the regal Ted Williams, a verifiable loner with whom a boy in Schwartz's personal circumstance could identify. When Auerbach and Cousy arrived in Boston simultaneously in 1950, Schwartz plugged into the Celtics with the same fervor with which he had attached himself to the Red Sox.

To be interested in the NBA of the times, he explains, was to feel that you were a member of a small, select secret society. "It was the *enclosure* of it all," he explains. "Eight teams, people busing to small cities such as Syracuse, Rochester and Ft. Wayne. The enclosure of the arenas."

When the Celtics came to New York, whether it was to play in the first game of a doubleheader at the Garden or whether it was to play the Knicks at the 69th Regiment Armory at 25th and Lexington, he was there. "I was *absolutely* there," he says. "Twelve years old. By myself. Devouring it all. Rooting for the Celtics and hating the Knicks, who were always detestable to me. Those awful McGuire brothers (Dick and Al). Harry Gallatin. Vince Boryla. I hated them all."

He also hated Philadelphia owner-coach Eddie Gottlieb. "I threw myself into a detestation of Eddie Gottlieb, as well," Schwartz says. "I could not understand it when I learned that the owner of the Warriors made out the league schedule for everyone. How could this be? How could a league allow the owner of the Philadelphia Warriors to send *my* Celtics out on the road to play the wrong team at the wrong time?"

Jonathan Schwartz had three idols. "Red, Cousy and Lennie Koppett," he explains. Leonard Koppett was then a young sportswriter for the *New York Post*, and the young Schwartz was infatuated with both the knowledge Koppett dispensed and the richness of the language Koppett used to convey it. Schwartz was pretty much convinced that Leonard Koppett understood the mystery of life, at least the part pertaining to the National Basketball Association. "I haunted him," Schwartz says, "peppering him with questions. He once wrote a column about this 12-year-old kid who was bombarding him with questions about basketball."

This New York-based Celtics' fan was particularly enchanted with the annual home-and-home, Saturday night-Sunday afternoon brace of games his Celtics would play against the despicable Knicks. "They would be in January or February," he recalls. "They would play Saturday night in New York, and then both teams would get on the overnight train and play again in Boston the next afternoon. I vividly remember the sights: Red Auerbach challenging Harry Gallitin. (Knicks coach) Joe Lapchick, with his rolled-up scorecard. The frenzy of it all. And it seems to me that these games were seldom played in either Garden. The games in New York would be at the Regiment Armory and the games in Boston would be in the Boston Arena. To me, these games represented Auerbach, Cousy and Schwartz against the world."

This tradition of weekend home-and-home games continued into the '70s. By then the teams were no longer traveling back and forth by rail. But the intimacy of it remained. After the Saturday night game in New York, each team would head to LaGuardia Airport to catch the last available plane to Boston's Logan Airport. The players would mingle. They would then board the plane and the Knicks would take up all the available first-class seats while the Celtics, always in a penny-squeezing mode, would head to the rear. That's just the way it was.

The Celtics also maintained a similar Saturday night-Sunday afternoon scenario with Philadelphia. I even recall one or two with Buffalo.

The team young Schwartz had taken into his heart put a boa constrictor-like hold on the NBA. There were occasional moments of concern in the form of Seventh Games to win, but as long as Auerbach and Russell showed up, the basic task would be accomplished. In 1960 the Celtics defeated both Philadelphia (119-117) and St. Louis (122-103) in Seventh Games. Two years later it was again necessary to go to a pair of Seventh Games, and each was an epic. A Sam Jones jumper knocked off the Warriors, 109-107, while the subsequent 110-107 overtime triumph over Los Angeles in the Finals capped off what will always be remembered as the "Selvy Game."

That was the game in which the score was tied at 100-100 and the Lakers had the ball with five seconds left. In Elgin Baylor, who had established a new playoff one-game record with 61 points earlier in the series, and Jerry West, the Lakers had two superb offensive threats. The Celtics were definitely in trouble.

With Baylor covered by Satch Sanders, and with Cousy off double-teaming West, Rod Hundley hit an open Frank Selvy on the left baseline. He shot and missed. Russell grabbed one of his 40 rebounds and the Celtics were in overtime. Once there, they assumed command.

By this time, the Celtic images were fixed. Cousy, aging legs and all, was still the master of game tempo. Sam Jones was the man you wanted to take any big shot. Heinsohn was the swashbuckling forward who never saw a shot he didn't like and who had the uncanny knack of coming up with the sneaky offensive rebound. Sanders was the selfless defensive forward. K.C. Jones was the perfect Cousy backup with his flypaper defense and passing ability. Jungle Jim Loscutoff was the team policeman. Frank Ramsey was the game's reigning sixth man, a sound two-position player who, like a relief pitcher who could get completely loose with just 10 throws, was capable of entering a game and scoring a basket the first time he touched the ball.

And then there was the ultimate trump card — William F. Russell, the most dominant and intimidating player the game had ever known. There was only one Russell and the Celtics had him.

Auerbach was at his zenith, full of basketball knowledge, cockiness, bravado, moxie and maybe even a certain four-letter word, as well. "What would strike you about Red," says Marty Glickman, the Hall of Fame announcer and friend of Red's for almost six decades, "was that with Red there was only one thing, and that was the team.

Anything that helped the team was good. Anything that didn't help the team was bad. He was completely dedicated to the idea of the team."

Wilt Chamberlain had come into the league in 1959 amid speculation that he would put Russell, over whom he had a good four inches and, depending on Wilt's weight that given year, 30 to 70-some pounds, into his proper place. What Wilt did was spend the next 10 years proving just exactly how amazing Russell really was. Wilt did indeed become Russell's most challenging opponent. As good as Russell was before Wilt came along, he became even better afterward as he responded to the stimulus provided by this bigger, stronger opponent. Wilt vs. Russell remains the greatest individual duel in the history of the NBA, the competition extending right to the respective press tables, where the opposing stat crews spent a great deal of time accusing each other of doctoring the home guy's rebound totals (blocked shots were never an official NBA statistic during either of their careers).

The Wilt vs. Russell debate will never end. The sheer individual numbers favor Wilt in a big way. The two played against each other 142 times, with injury preventing one or the other to play in five other games. Wilt averaged 28.7 points and, unbelievably, 28.7 rebounds a game. Russell averaged 14.5 points and 23.7 rebounds a game. Boston was 87-60 in those 147 games.

Fortunately for Russell, basketball is not necessarily a game of stats. Chamberlain has never wanted to hear this, but Russell was the master of psychology, and the fact is there were many games when Russell, his team in full control of the game, eased up on Wilt at some point in the second half, allowing his foe to go on a minor rampage with meaningless points and rebounds so that Wilt would come away thinking he had had a good game and would therefore be feeling good about himself. The truth is sometimes very hard to digest.

Backers of both men devote much time and effort arguing the merits of each man's teammates. Well, let's get serious. Russell did have better teammates. But Wilt had some pretty good ones, starting with Paul Arizin, Guy Rodgers, Tom Gola, Tom Meschery and Al Attles; continuing on with Nate Thurmond, Billy Cunningham, Chet Walker and Hal Greer in the middle portion of the rivalry; and then concluding with Jerry West, Elgin Baylor and Gail Goodrich in Los Angeles.

Given Wilt's overwhelming size advantage, what Russell did to neutralize him over the years was downright miraculous. He played Wilt so well for so long that people began to ignore the fact that Wilt was so much bigger and powerful. Wilt had size, strength and a great degree of agility in certain movements. Russell was quicker laterally, quicker to the basketball (a vital, and thoroughly unteachable gift) possessed with a much better sense of anticipation and much sounder temperamentally. He knew exactly who he was — always. Wilt was forever trying to prove something. Russell was only thinking about winning the basketball game. He was Auerbach's dream, a player totally devoted to the team, and nothing else.

Oh, he had his pride, and it could manifest itself in mischievous ways. When Wilt became publicized as pro basketball's first $100,000 player, what did Russell do? He said all he wanted was $100,001. And Auerbach was very happy to give it to him.

The playoffs aside, Boston appeared to be willing to take or leave the Celtics. There was, of course, no such thing as "marketing" in those days. Auerbach gave his clinics, but that was that. Red was wearing every team hat imaginable, but he didn't have a ticket-selling bone in his body. His idea of "promotion" was to print up a few schedules and open the doors.

Now wouldn't you think that if a team coming off its fifth straight title were opening a new season at home, it would be difficult to find a ticket? I am here to say that was not the case because on the evening of Saturday, October 17, 1964, I walked up to the Boston Garden box office an hour and a half before the opener with Detroit and purchased a nice seat in the second row of the balcony. Section 99, row B, seat 8. It is one of two ticket stubs I still carry in my wallet. (The other is a seat in section 48, row L, seat 9, that being my location for Auerbach's last game on April 28, 1966). The Celtics defeated the Pistons, 112-81 for the first of their 62 victories before a crowd of 8,968. They would average 8,318 per game in a season that would culminate in a sixth consecutive championship.

Great players seemed to be leaving the Celtics on an annual basis, but it didn't seem to make any difference. Check it out: Bill Sharman (1961), Bob Cousy (1963), Frank Ramsey and Jim Loscutoff (1964). When Tom Heinsohn retired with shot knees at age 30 in 1965 it meant that Russell was the only player left from the 1957 championship team.

The Lachrymose Festival to end them all was Bob Cousy Day in 1963. The Cooz occupied a special place in the hearts of all Celtics fans, because there really hadn't been any real Celtics to speak of before he came along. The emotional Frenchman sobbed his way through a touching Thank You speech, the highlight of which came during one prolonged pause. A balcony dweller with a piercing voice boomed out "We Love Ya', Cooz!" And they surely did.

But in the end they were all replaceable, all except one. Sam Jones was Sharman and then some. K.C. Jones, patiently serving a five-year apprenticeship while waiting for Cousy to retire so he could take over the team, added a new dimension with his extraordinary individual defensive ability. By the time Ramsey retired he had trained John Havlicek as his replacement. Red didn't miss Heinsohn too much because he had in place both Havlicek and Don Nelson, the all-time bargain basement pickup.

Nelson joined the team just in time to see one of the great Celtic moments — Game 7 against Philadelphia in 1965. After six grueling games with the 76ers, it came down to Boston leading 110-109 with just a few seconds to play and the 76ers having the ball out of bounds under their own basket. A Russell inbounds pass had hit a guide wire which held up the basket, turning the ball back to Philadelphia with a chance to win the game.

But John Havlicek smelled out Hal Greer's inbounds pass and cut in front of Chet Walker, tipping the ball over to Sam Jones and thus preserving the game and the series. Up in his broadcast perch, Johnny Most lost it, launching into a memorable spiel, during which he kept screaming, "Havlicek stole the ball!" The account elevated Havlicek from good, reliable player to folk hero and *Havlicek Stole The Ball* became the title of a best-selling highlight album that is generally considered to be a pioneer of the genre.

By 1965 Auerbach was wearing down. He was only 47, but the 19 years of pounding around the country, attending to every team detail, was starting to get to him. The NBA was nothing like it is today. There were no assistant coaches. Red did everything himself, from making out the exhibition schedule to plotting the season's travel arrangements to scouting both college kids and pro opponents to making luncheon appearances on the road to acting as the team representative at league meetings and functions. All this was in addition to the thing he did best, and that was coach.

In classic Auerbach fashion, he announced to the basketball world that the 1965-66 season would be his last as coach. He did it before the season began in order that "everyone can take one more shot at me."

The 76ers ended Boston's run of nine straight regular-season crowns by a game, but when the playoffs came the Celtics were ready. Well, almost ready. Cincinnati, a smart, veteran team featuring such outstanding players as Oscar Robertson, Jerry Lucas, Happy Hairston, Wayne Embry and Adrian Smith, got up, 2-1, on the Celtics in a five-game series, before Boston came back to win. Sam Jones, who had scored 47 points in a 1963 Game 7 against Cincinnati, scored 34 clutch points in this hidden Game 7. That scare must have sobered up the Celtics, because they simply demolished Philadelphia in five games.

Then Lakers were the Western Conference foe in the Finals for the fourth time in five years, and the dynamics were the same as they had been since the first such confrontation in 1962. That is to say, the Celtics would know they were going to be dazzled by messrs. West and Baylor and the Lakers were going to be awed and intimidated by Russell.

L.A. battled its way to a Game 7, but the game was in Boston and at that point the Celtics — Russell, specifically — had never lost a seventh game, and were unlikely candidates to lose this one at home. By losing Game 6 in L.A., the Celtics certainly made my life better. That's because, as strange as it sounds to the modern ear, there were still seats available for a seventh game. The Celtics were announcing that they would put the seats on sale in the morning, four seats to a customer. We got together on our dorm floor at Boston College and dispatched one of our number to the Garden to get in line and stay overnight. He would, of course, get one of the four tickets. The other three lucky recipients were determined by lottery, and I was fortunate enough to be one of the winners. That is how I wound up watching Red Auerbach's last game from a nice seat in the stadium section from behind the basket.

The final score was 95-93, Boston, and it was and wasn't that close. The Celtics led by 13 with just four minutes left, and by 10 at the two-minute mark. Auerbach was even lighting up that final victory cigar. Then gangling Leroy Ellis threw in a couple from the parking lot, and with the crowd ringing the famed parquet in anticipation of the clinching, things began to get a little crazy down there on the floor. People were crowding around, even spilling liquids on the floor, and people were slipping and losing the basketball and it got down to two before the buzzer went off. The next thing you know, the BC Four was running around the floor along with all the other fools, just because.

There had been a lot of bravado attached to Auerbach's retirement announcement although there was a lot less involved as long as Russell was there to back him up. At the dawn of the 1965-66 season Bill Russell was 31 years old and the absolute master of all he surveyed. He had won two NCAA championships. He had won a gold medal in Melbourne at the 1956 Olympics. He had won five Most Valuable Player awards. He had won seven NBA championships in eight seasons, and it would undoubtedly have been eight in eight had he not sustained that ankle injury in 1958.

He was both Mr. Celtic and Mr. NBA. He was the individual who gave his team more of an inherent advantage just by showing up than any player on any team in any sport anywhere on the planet. He made Celtic fans feel invincible. In the entire world of sport, has there ever been a more rewarding experience than to be a Celtic fan in the mid-1960s?

"The degree of euphoria I felt after each important victory was so illuminating, so fulfilling, so gratifying and so nourishing," says Jonathan Schwartz, "that I could focus on it in subsequent months and years and there would dwell inside me the deepest kind of intimate pleasure. Those are the two words I want to hand over to you — intimate pleasure."

Schwartz has grown up to dispense his own brand of intimate pleasure as a one-of-a-kind radio personality. As listeners to New York's WQEW know, the depth and feeling of his appreciation for the American popular song has no equal anywhere in America. And that's without even mentioning the fact that he is the one Sinatra expert who knows more about Sinatra's career than Sinatra himself.

There was a temporary cessation of that intimate pleasure the following year when Chamberlain won his one and only clear-cut victory over Russell. The 1966-67 76ers were a team of great power and balance. They won a then NBA record 69 games, and they just weren't going to lose. The Celtics won a very impressive 60 games, but this one was in the zodiac. Philly blew out the Celtics in five games and the 76ers went on to win the championship.

Philadelphia appeared ready to replace Boston as the resident NBA predator. Wasn't Chamberlain at his peak? Weren't the Celtics getting too old? Was it conceivable the team missed Auerbach's aggressive and acerbic presence on the practice floor and on the bench?

If winning your first championship is supposed to be your number 1 thrill, then winning a later championship the world thinks is completely beyond your reach must surely be thrill number 1A. And if that is the case, what is there to say about winning one more beyond a championship believed to be unthinkable?

In other words, imagine the depth of Schwartzian euphoria which engulfed the Celtic faithful when the team won both the 1968 and 1969 championships.

Down three games to one and needing to win Games 5 and 7 on the road, the Celtics did what needed to be done in their 1968 Eastern Conference championship series with Philadelphia. Luck is always a welcome ally, and so it must be recorded that the 76ers played the entire series without superb sixth man Billy Cunningham, who had broken his wrist in the previous series against New York. But Cunningham's absence had nothing to do with Wilt Chamberlain's curious behavior in the second half of Game 7 in the newly-opened Spectrum. Wilt appears intent on going to his grave without ever having offered a satisfactory explanation why he attempted but two shots from the floor in the final 24 minutes of that game. Therein lies the essential difference between Chamberlain and Russell. Russell never, ever, left any loose ends. Either he did or he didn't, and he usually did. With Wilt there were always too many King of Siam puzzlements.

For further evidence of Russell's singular greatness, I submit the entirety of the 1969 playoffs when the 36-year-old center, after pacing himself during the regular season, was once again the consummate zenmaster in the playoffs. He dominated Philadelphia's Darrall Imhoff in the first round. He gave a pivot lesson to young Willis Reed in the second round. And he once again demonstrated to Chamberlain just what the game was really all about in the Finals.

The Celtics lost Games 1 and 2 in Los Angeles and needed a gift from a higher power in order to win Game 4 and avoid heading back to L.A. trailing three games to one.

Down by a point, but in possession of the basketball after Emmette Bryant had done everything to Johnny Egan but strip-search him, the Celtics needed a basket. Larry Siegfried, the team's *de facto* offensive coordinator, suggested an old Ohio State play nicknamed, cleverly enough, "Ohio." Sam Jones, who says he never really wanted to take the big shots, but who always seemed to make them, would be the shooter. Sam came off the pick and let it fly. The ball bounced around the rim and fell in as time expired. Sam said he just wanted to get it up there in order to give Russell a chance to get the offensive rebound, which would have been good thinking had Russell actually been in the game. The player-coach had removed himself in order to get another shooter out there.

Bryant had the most plausible explanation for the goings-on. "There were four-leaf clovers flying around all over the place," he said.

For the second consecutive year the Celtics found themselves playing a seventh game on the other guy's court. Lakers owner Jack Kent Cooke hired the University of Southern California marching band. He affixed balloons to the ceiling which would be released as soon as the Lakers won. The Celtics thought it was all pretty amusing.

Chamberlain was involved, so naturally Chamberlain became the postgame flash point. With 5:30 left, and the Celtics in command, he asked out of the game because he said his knee was hurting. Almost immediately the Lakers began a comeback, which happened to feature his replacement, 7-foot center (and ex-Celtic) Mel Counts. The lead fell to one at 103-102. Somewhere in here Wilt asked coach Butch van Breda Kolff if he could return. VBK refused the request, and not politely, either.

"We're doing well enough without you," Wilt was informed.

With a little over a minute remaining, and the Celtics ahead by a point, Keith Erickson poked the ball away from Havlicek. With any Laker luck, the ball would have gone to a Laker. It didn't. It went right to Don Nelson, who was standing at the foul line. Without a hint of hesitation, he rose up for a jump shot. The ball hit the back rim, rose several feet in the air and dropped cleanly through the hoop. That put the lead up to three, and the Celtics were able to live off that cushion and wrap up title number 11. More intimate pleasure.

That was the last official playing statement by Mr. Bill Russell, who closed out his career with 21 rebounds. The official announcement wouldn't come for two more months.

It was likewise the final game for the great Sam Jones, who had scored 24. Almost three decades later, the basketball world awaits a guard with a comparable first step.

It was a truly astonishing championship. The Celtics had finished fourth in the regular season. They did not have the home-court advantage in any series. They were positively Methuselean. And they were champions. Russell makes a statement in favor of this title every day of his life. The great man wears two championship rings. One is 1957, his first. The other is 1969, his last.

The Celtics had now won 11 championships in 13 years, and while they were loved, honored and adored elsewhere (either that or loathed, as all successful teams are by *someone*), at home they were still not the Bruins. They were still fully appreciated only by a cult following. A team of this magnitude would have owned New York. In Boston they were still the team that played on nights the Bruins didn't want.

That's the post-Russell climate I walked into as a 23-year-old beat man in October of 1969. The Celtics played on nights the Bruins didn't want. I was handed a beat no one with any stature in the sports department wanted. After 11 titles, the Celtics were still just an afterthought in the minds of more people than it is possible to imagine today.

I keep coming back to the word "innocent," but these really were sweetly innocent times. The Celtics still had to work very hard just to get their name in the paper on days when the team was not scheduled to play a game.

The publicity man was J. Howard (Howie) McHugh, and he was a certified American Original. All you need to know about the sheer physical toughness of this man is the following: he was a baseball catcher, hockey goalie and football center.

The one sport he knew far less than nothing about when the Celtics were formed in 1946 was basketball. But he was already on Walter Brown's payroll, and that little detail didn't stop him from appointing Howie as the team's PR man. He remained in the team's employ until his death in 1983.

Howie was known for his referee-baiting (he was once ejected from a playoff game), his essential good nature and his legendary press releases. I don't know what he was using for a mimeograph machine in those days, but his were the only releases I've ever encountered which ran diagonally on the page. But far more interesting than the angle of the copy was the nature of it. In Howie-speak, there were no such things as road games, or opposing courts. Uh-uh. If the Celtics were venturing out into the cold, cruel world, it was to play on such surfaces as "hostile hickory" or "enemy elm." God, I miss Howie McHugh.

Howie still had to prod people to write about the Celtics. They still had a weekly luncheon at which Auerbach and/or his coach, in this case Tom Heinsohn, had to start from A by going over the recent games and then discoursing on the upcoming opponents. The assumption was that if they didn't do this the press would have no idea what to write.

As the Celtics entered the '70s, Howie was only the second-greatest character in the entourage (the third, if you count Auerbach himself). The greatest was radio play-by-play announcer Johnny Most. Hired by Auerbach in 1953 on the recommendation of his good friend Marty Glickman, the Brooklyn-born and bred Most, a decorated World War II vet, composer of Japanese *haiku*, Big Band buff and relentless smoker of English Ovals (deadly cigarettes which made Camels taste like hard candy), Most had become the most passionate Celtics fan alive.

By his own admission, his voice sounded like the product of "a man gargling razor blades." As time went on he stopped broadcasting basketball games. What he was doing was narrating a nightly Passion Play in which the gentlemanly Celtics were forced, almost against their will, to defend the honor of the entire city of Boston against the endless succession of infidels in short pants who were trying to break into their homes, rape their women and steal their fine china.

But now everyone involved needed to adjust. Howie McHugh had to adjust. Johnny Most had to adjust. Red Auerbach had to adjust. The media had to adjust. The fans had to adjust. Russell was gone, Sam Jones was gone and now the Celtics were entering into a totally new phase of their existence.

The task was to rebuild without the greatest individual force the game had ever known, and the man in charge was Tom Heinsohn. He had no coaching experience, but he was smart and he was a quick learner. The cupboard wasn't entirely bare. He did have Nelson, Sanders and Siegfried, savvy veterans all. He did have talented kids in Jo Jo White and Don Chaney. And he did have John Havlicek, who was only the greatest all-around player in the game.

John Havlicek had spent his first seven years as a Celtic serving mainly as the consummate two-position sixth man. He would spend the remaining nine years of his career as the reigning two-position man, period. At 6-5 he was the ideal size for a big guard and he was plenty big enough to serve as a small forward. He was legendarily inexhaustible and he was emotionally unflappable.

The Celtics had exactly one down year. They went 34-48 in 1969-70 and then Red Auerbach drafted Dave Cowens and the Celtics were back on the right path. Honest to God. It really *was* that simple.

Whoever said it was better to be lucky than good had it right. Red had assumed Russell would be good, but no one on earth ever dreamed he'd be *that* good. He took Cowens thinking he'd be a real nice big forward and he lucked into a Hall of Fame center who would anchor two title teams. He hit the jackpot a third time with Larry Bird who was supposed to be very good but who instead turned out to be transcendent. I'm sure Red himself would prefer the Branch Rickey position that "Luck is the residue of design." As the kids say these days, "whatever."

Attendance fell back to 7,500 a night the year after Russell left, and it didn't pick up substantially the first two Cowens years. But there was clearly something in the air, even in the face of the phenomenal Bruins' surge of the early '70s. There was a buzz. People who came passed the word that something good was happening, that Cowens, White and Chaney were exciting young players and that Havlicek was better than ever. Heinsohn believed strongly in fast-break basketball, and even on nights when the Celtics were inefficient they were exciting.

They got themselves back into the playoffs in 1972, but when the Second Season began they were really no match for the smooth and polished Knicks. The prevailing theory was that the Celtics were one player away, that person being a power forward who could augment the dogged, but still undersized, Cowens in the trenches. Auerbach found his man. Red just happened to have the NBA draft rights to ABA guard Charlie Scott. When the skinny scoring machine wanted to jump to Phoenix in the NBA, Red bartered the rights to Scott for Paul Silas, a 29-year-old rebound monster.

With Silas added to the cast, the Celtics got off to a 10-0 start and never stopped running or winning. Cowens, now in his third year, had it all figured out. He was too quick for the tall guys to contend with and too strong for the ones his own size or smaller. His general *modus operandi* was to attempt to make every play, makeable or not. It was rather amazing to tally the successful unmakeable plays. He was the most aggressive and hustling center who has ever played in the NBA. I have absolutely no fear that anyone who ever played against him would contradict that supposition.

No man could be more eminently rootable. Unless, of course, he was on the other team. There was about him the look of a crazed individual. He had a linebacker mentality, and in the course of his nightly activities people occasionally got hurt. I rather doubt he was a comparable fan favorite on either hostile hickory or enemy elm. But he was an enormously popular player in Boston, and he probably did as much to put the game over in the town as anyone, Cousy and Russell included.

There was a new crowd coming into the Garden. Many of the new fans were the children of the befuddled hockey-lovers who had ignored the glorious teams of the '50s and '60s. They might have gone to an out-of-state college with a strong basketball orientation. There were also patrons who might have been transplants from a basketball-oriented school or locale. Boston was changing rapidly in the early '70s. It was becoming a happening place for young professionals, and a lot of them had been absentee fans of the Russell teams.

This Celtics team had great panache. It was a fearless, spunky team with great defensive flexibility. Heinsohn taught a tough, switching defense. Cowens was agile enough to handle most guards, while Chaney, a 6-5 guard with what was generally referred to as the wing span of a 747, was tall enough, strong enough and tough enough to take on big people. Havlicek was, well, Havlicek and Nuf Ced about that.

After encountering some stiff first-round opposition from a stubborn Atlanta team, the Celtics ran up against the seasoned Knicks. Since winning the 1970 title, the Knicks had lost a seven-gamer to the Baltimore Bullets in '71 and lost in the Finals to the great '71-72 L.A. team the following year. Late in the year, after the Celtics had beaten the Knicks in Madison Square Garden, Dave DeBusschere pulled me aside in the locker room. "Don't pay any attention to this," he said. "We're going to be a *great* playoff team."

Game 3 was in Boston on a Friday night. The series was tied at 1-1. Havlicek was trying to squeeze between DeBusschere and Bill Bradley and he got caught in a crunch. His right shoulder was partially dislocated.

The Celtics lost the game. The next game was on Sunday afternoon in New York and Havlicek wasn't going to play. But the kids played a magnificent game. Cowens, White, Chaney, Steve Kuberski, Nelson, Silas...they all rose to the challenge. The Celtics led by 16 after three periods.

They lost in double overtime. The Boston version is that referees Jack Madden and Jake O'Donnell were swept up in what I refer to as "unconscious crowd orchestration," making improbable calls in favor of the home-court Knicks. One neutral observation: Jack Kiser of the *Philadelphia Daily News*, a longtime NBA observer, labeled what he had just witnessed as "The Rape of Madison Square." At any rate, Boston lost control of the game. The Knicks' version is that the great veterans had pulled off a great comeback.

Havlicek returned for Game 5, and, playing mostly left-handed, scored 18 points as the Celtics remained alive. They were still breathing after winning an improbable Game 6 in New York.

The Knicks weren't taking any chances in Game 7. They had been too respectful of Havlicek in Games 5 and 6, backing off him and allowing him to make plays despite the fact that his right side was seriously impaired. When he came into the Game 7, they swarmed all over him, causing turnovers. The Knicks won easily, 94-78. It was the first time a Boston team had ever lost a Game 7, and the Celtics had lost it at the Boston Garden.

But the Celtics were back. They were among the league's elite, and the assumption was that the 12th title was imminent.

There was no more waiting. The Celtics did indeed win that 12th title in 1974. They beat Buffalo (not without controversy) in the first round. They eliminated an aging and battered New York in the second round. And they huffed and puffed a blew down a valiant, injury-wracked Milwaukee team in the Finals.

The 1974 championship series has stood the test of time. When we were all in the middle of it, we thought it was special, on and off the court. Now we *know* it was.

It was a seven-gamer in which there were only two home-game victories, Milwaukee in Game 2 (an overtime struggle) and Boston in Game 3. The Celtics won in seven but with a little bit o' luck they could have won in four. Kareem Abdul-Jabbar was relentlessly spectacular, save for one long dry spell in Game 7.

There was a crackle in the air right from the start. It was very much a coach's series, with Heinsohn and assistant John Killilea matching wits with Larry Costello and Hubie Brown. It was adjustment after adjustment after adjustment, with Heinsohn and Killilea having the final say. After allowing the 6-8½ Cowens to guard the 7-3 Abdul-Jabbar one-on-one for six games, the Celtics constantly double- and triple-teamed the big guy in Game 7, daring someone else to beat them.

The game most people remember was Game 6, the double-overtime thriller in which Kareem answered a John Havlicek basket with a 17-foot, game-winning corner hook. That set up a Game 7 I will never forget. Cowens was brooding after shooting 5-for-19 in Game 6. This was despite making a signature play, switching off on Oscar Robertson, knocking the ball away from the Hall of Fame guard and then belly-flopping on the ball to cause a key 24-second viola-tion. He believed that had he had a decent shooting night the Celtics would have won the championship in six games, and would have won it easily.

Milwaukee coach Larry Costello, somewhat frustrated after see-ing the younger Celtics press his team into all sorts of problems, said his major Game 7 concern was getting off to a good start. I wonder what he was thinking when the Celtics scored off the opening tap and then Chaney stole the inbounds and laid it in, making it 4-0, Boston, after 12 seconds?

Cowens had vowed to play better, and he kept that promise. He was 8-for-13 in the first half as the visiting Celtics moved to a 53-40 lead. Boston got up by as many as 17 before Milwaukee came roaring back, slicing the lead to three. Then second-year man Paul Westphal, whom everyone believed was a star in the making, broke the Bucks' momentum with a gorgeous baseline reverse drive. That righted the ship. The Celtics won it by a 102-87 score.

Auerbach had needed only five years in which to rebuild with-out Russell.

Red had also done it in true Auerbachian manner, manipulat-ing his roster while remaining completely loyal to worthy players. Red did not move people just to move them. From September 1, 1966, when he traded Mel Counts to Baltimore for Bailey Howell, until May 23, 1975, when he traded Paul Westphal and some future draft choices to Phoenix for Charlie Scott, he made no body-for-body exchanges. He sold and bought contracts, or he executed deals strictly involving draft picks, but he went nearly nine years without a strict player trade in a truly amazing display of loyalty and stability un-matched in American sports history.

The Celtics failed to defend in 1975, losing to the Washington Bullets in six games. But title number 14 materialized soon enough, as the Celtics regained the championship in 1976, taking care of Buffalo, Cleveland and Phoenix.

I recall saying in the early '70s that it would be a fine thing for the Celtics if they could ever average 11,000 a night. By the 1975-76 season they were up to 13,446, a very substantial average in what we had once presumed was too much of a pure hockey town for basket-ball ever to make a significant impact.

The Celtics were gaining parity. Cowens was a huge star and a compelling personality. He remains the most unaffected and natural professional athlete of stature I've ever met. Silas was a folk hero. White had established himself as a great player. And Havlicek was an icon. The great Russell teams had planted the seed and this group was now benefitting. It was now harvest time.

The Phoenix Suns weren't supposed to be hanging around in late May. The Suns were only a 42-40 team during the regular sea-son, but they discovered a new identity during the playoffs and ad-vanced to the Finals by defeating defending champion Golden State.

The pivotal game was the fifth. The Celtics played their best basketball of the entire playoffs, moving ahead by as many as 22 early in the second quarter. But the Suns wouldn't go away. They just wouldn't accept the idea of a KO punch.

They should have been finished after falling behind by nine with 3:49 left. They weren't. Led by Westphal, they forced an overtime.

There was all kind of weird stuff in the overtimes, the most bizarre occurrence taking place at the end of the second extra pe-riod. Trailing by a point with one second left after a Havlicek basket, and faced with having to put the ball in play at the far end of the court, the Suns appeared doomed. But Westphal had a good idea. By calling a timeout they didn't have, they would be assessed a technical foul, but they would then get the ball back at midcourt. Jo Jo White made the technical foul shot (good thing, too). Gar Heard then took the ensuing inbounds pass and fired in an arching jumper from the foul line extended to put the teams into a third OT.

Once there, with key players on both sides fouling out, the Celtics found themselves an improbable hero in seldom-used Glenn McDonald, who scored six vital points. The Celtics staggered home, 128-126.

The teams reconvened approximately 36 hours later in Phoenix, and even the Suns own crowd had nothing left. The Celtics won their 14th title by an 87-80 score.

It was the end of the second championship era. Silas couldn't get the money he wanted from Boston, forcing a three-way trade which sent him to Denver and brought Curtis Rowe from Detroit. Sidney Wicks was purchased from the Trail Blazers. Good times were not a' comin'.

The Celtics lost a seven-game series to Philadelphia in '77, a bizarre season which had begun with Cowens taking a two-month sabbatical after playing just eight games, and then dropped off the face of the earth the next two years. Heinsohn was fired near the halfway point of the '77-78 season, but his replacement, Satch Sanders, wasn't the answer. The Celtic won 32 in '77-78 and 29 the following year. Sanders was dumped 14 games into the '78-79 season and was replaced by, of all people, Cowens. It was becoming harder and harder to relate to Havlicek, let alone Cousy and Russell.

But something positive had already taken place. The Celtics had two first-round draft picks in 1978, and Auerbach took a chance. With the number six pick, he selected Larry Bird of Indiana State, a 6-9 forward who was the Player of the Year, but who had his doubters since he was alleged to be very slow and since he was quite obviously white. It was starting to become an article of faith in some NBA quarters that white men could no longer compete in what was becoming a black man's game.

Popular mythology holds that it was Larry Bird and Larry Bird alone who was responsible for the dramatic Celtic turnaround which transformed a lethargic 29-53 team into a dynamic 61-21 team the following season. I yield to no man in my admiration for my all-time favorite player, but there were a few more things going on that season. Such as:

■ A new coach. Bill Fitch brought an entirely new personality and direction to the team.

■ The off-season free agent signing of M.L.. Carr.

■ The almost complete rejuvenation of Tiny Archibald, an overweight malcontent in 1978-79.

■ The great personal comeback of Dave Cowens, who, freed from the coaching burden, got himself into the best possible shape and restored himself to an All-Star level.

But the number one reason was Bird, who was the Rookie of the Year and a first-team All-Star. As if that even begins to tell the Bird story.

Talking about numbers when discussing Bird is ultimately irrelevant. Larry Bird was not about statistics, although he had some juicy ones. The long and the short of it was that Bird was a basketball *objet d'art* who could be studied at different levels by fans of varying degree of sophistication.

The less sophisticated could appreciate the obvious, e.g., Bird shoots and the ball goes into the basket. No problem. But exactly how he got where he did in order to get that shot. Or what he did in close quarters in order to free himself for the shot. Or how he knew what opposing player X was going to do in order to get himself into the proper position, these were far more weightier matters of state, and were items understood only by aficionados.

Bird was something entirely new to the Boston eye. There were parts of many previous Celtic greats compressed in one package. At different times he passed like Cousy, shot like Havlicek or Sam Jones, rebounded like Russell or Cowens, and had an aggressiveness reminiscent of Heinsohn. He looked smooth doing some things (like shooting or passing) and awkward doing other things (running, for example), but he always played hard. And, according to his mentor, he took well to coaching.

He was a central energy force into which the team was smart enough to plug its outlets. Finally, he was a great *teammate*, showing deep respect for the feelings of everyone on the roster. Like Russell, his only concern was winning. He just happened to have the capacity to aid that process in a more diverse manner than any Celtic ever. Even the Celtic great to whom he bore the most general resemblance

Larry Bird gave the Boston basketball fan a combination of many previous Celtic greats compressed in one package. He passed like Cousy, shot like Havlicek or Sam Jones, rebounded like Russell or Cowens, and had an aggressiveness reminiscent of Heinsohn. (Photo©Tom Miller)

— Havlicek — said that the kid was better. John was right. In some ways Bird was a 6-9 Havlicek. High praise indeed.

The Celtics were back running, just like the old days. Bird and Cowens got the ball, and Archibald got it upcourt. Tiny was now into Phase 2 of his career. No more scoring titles. He was out there trying to be a consummate point guard, and he was succeeding.

The Celtics had a joyous season and a disappointing playoffs. They lost to hated Philadelphia in five games, and Fitch thought he knew the reason why. He wasn't telling the outside world, but what he was saying inside was that his team was too small. He didn't think he could get past Philly until he got bigger.

Auerbach and Fitch took care of that on draft day. The Celtics had the first pick in the draft via trade and people just naturally thought they would select 7-1 Purdue center Joe Barry Carroll, a smooth-functioning, low-energy player. The Boston brass had another idea. They packaged up the first pick and the 13th pick in the draft and they sent it to Golden State for the number three pick and four-year veteran center Robert Parish.

I found out about this deal an hour or so before the draft and I wasn't at all surprised. I used to enjoy sitting in airport or hotel coffee shops with Bill Fitch and talking basketball, and on more than one occasion he had expressed a desire to "get my hands on" Parish, whom he regarded as a vastly underused and unappreciated asset. I was skeptical, subscribing to the popular notion that Parish was a lazy, 7-foot slug. Fitch said no, no, no, the one thing I know Parish can do is run. He explained how impressive Parish had been at the 1975 Pan-Am Games practice sessions.

With the number three pick, the Celtics grabbed Kevin McHale, a center from Minnesota.

As for McHale, I was ecstatic, having seen him in person at the Coaches' All-Star Game the weekend of the 1980 Final Four at Indianapolis. I loved him. And I loathed Carroll. I was happy, even if no one else was.

Less than a year later, everyone in Boston was happy. Parish and McHale had fulfilled Fitch's vision perfectly. The Celtics were big and mean and once again champions. The last time it had taken five years to rebuild. This time it had only taken two.

The Celtics' draft-day genius played out when they took a chance on Larry Bird (33) in 1978 then in 1980 got Kevin McHale (32) from Minnesota with the third pick and traded for Robert Parish (00) from Golden State. (Photo©Tom Miller)

The pivotal series was the Eastern Conference Finals against Philadelphia. The Celtics trailed the series, 3-1, and the 76ers had a six-point lead in the Garden with 1:40 remaining in Game 5. They also had the basketball. But the Celtics pulled that game out, won Game 6 in Philadelphia (with Bird making a key basket reminiscent of the Nelson up-and-in job in 1969 and McHale making a monster block on Andrew Toney) and then won a relentlessly noisy and dramatic Game 7 in Boston. The Celtics had won those three games by margins of 2, 2 and 1.

And now every sports fan in Boston was paying attention. In December of 1980 the Celtics had begun a consecutive game sellout streak that would last until and beyond the closing of the Boston Garden in 1995. Celtic Chic was in vogue.

The Celtics polished off Houston in six, and they were champs once again. At a giant City Hall rally Bird, responding to a flippant Moses Malone remark that he and "four guys from Petersburg" could beat the Celtics, told the world that "Moses eats shit." Demosthenes, it wasn't, but from the heart it was. Bird's status as a Man of the People was secure forever.

There was a three-year wait for another title. The '82 season ended in stunning fashion when the 76ers, having blown Games 5 and 6 after again going up, 3-1, and having scored an embarrassing 75 points in Game 6, stunned everyone but themselves by rolling to a 120-106 victory in Game 7.

The next year was a step-back season. The Celtics essentially began divorce proceedings with the oft-abrasive Fitch during the second half of the 1982-83 season. I would go so far as to say that every prominent player with the predictable exception of Bird quit on the coach, and the team's ouster in four straight games by Milwaukee was not exactly a shock, especially since Bird was sick enough throughout to miss Game 2 entirely.

Fitch left at the conclusion of the season. K.C. Jones, the quintessential "Good Cop" to Fitch's archetypical "Bad Cop," replaced him. Bird, less responsible for the Milwaukee debacle than anyone, vowed to "take this personally," and to "go home and work on my game all summer."

Auerbach made a key move following the 1983-84 season. He took Rick Robey, a big man with a weirdly inscrutable overall game, and shipped him to Phoenix for volatile (or so everyone said) guard Dennis Johnson. DJ had been an All-Star for both Seattle and Phoenix. He had even been the MVP in the 1979 Finals. But he had a reputation as a malcontent and there were those who wondered how he would fit in at Boston.

The 1983-84 Celtics were an assembly line team. Bird averaged 24 a game. Parish had 19. McHale, who averaged 18 and was now being acclaimed as the game's resident sixth man (Cedric Maxwell, on board since '77, was still the starting forward alongside Bird), fit in perfectly. They won the division by 10 games over Philadelphia (62-52) and had the league's best record.

What everyone wanted was a championship series with Los Angeles. Bird and Magic Johnson had become linked in the public eye as far back as the 1979 NCAA Finals in Salt Lake City, and it was obvious that it was high time the two got it on in a seven-game series for the Champeenship of da Woild.

The Celtics took care of Washington in four games, but New York provided some unexpectedly strong opposition, in large measure due to the scoring genius of Bernard King, then as sure a two points as existed on this earth. It went down to a seventh game, and that turned into a classic Bird showcase. That nasty bit of business concluded, Milwaukee rolled over in five.

The Lakers had endured injury problems, but they had solved all their problems by the playoffs. They were ready for the Celtics.

The Celtics discovered this when L.A. won the first game by a 115-109 score, thus taking away Boston's home-court image. Nothing sets the tone for a great playoff series more than the road team winning the first game. The Celtics *had* to win the second game, and they did, thanks to a clutch steal and driving layup to get them into overtime and a game-winning basket by Scott Wedman in OT.

The Lakers demolished the Celtics in Game 3, 137-104. It was such a dismal Celtics display that Bird suggested that what the Celtics needed before Game 4 was "12 heart transplants." The word "sissies" also was emitted from his lips.

With Bird coming up with 29 points and 21 rebounds, and with Parish matching the mighty Kareem Abdul-Jabbar, the Celtics won another bone in overtime, 129-125, to tie the series.

Game 5 was won long before it started. This was the era of the 2-2-1-1-1 format, and so the teams flew back to Boston for Game 5. I was on the L.A. plane. When the Lakers landed at Logan Airport, they must have thought they were in Jakarta. It was 5:30 p.m. and it was in the mid-90s. And this was steamy, clinging East Coast heat. The airport was jammed. Babies were crying. I swear, all I could think of was *The Year Of Living Dangerously*. The state police would not allow the Laker bus to pull up to the curb, so the players poured themselves into taxis. I saw Kareem and Magic get into the same cab, and I remember thinking "I don't think this is what they had in mind."

The Boston Garden was not air-conditioned. The game-time temperature on Friday, June 4, 1984, was 97 degrees. The fans were determined to make this a certified happening. You have never seen an NBA crowd in such a state of undress or heard such noise. The fans made the conditions work for the Celtics.

The Lakers did not want to be there. Bird, of course, thought this was great. He shot 15-for-20 from the floor. He had 34 points and 17 rebounds. The Celtics won, 121-103. "I play in weather like this all summer back home in Indiana," shrugged Bird. The game remains one of my very special memories.

The Lakers went back home and took care of business, 119-108. Back we all went to Boston.

Game 7 was no classic. But it was a great night for Cedric Maxwell, a player who had worked hard to please Fitch by learning to play defense, who had been the Finals MVP against Houston in '81 and who had become less and less a part of the offense as Bird and McHale became the focal points. But Max was feeling it on this occasion. He made a little speech before the game. "Just jump on my back, boys," he said.

He backed it up, too, scoring 24 points while taking young James Worthy to school. Title number 15 was in the books.

The Lakers got their revenge in 1985, beating the Celtics in six games. But there was no reason to believe the matter between the two was settled.

The Celtics were at their peak of popularity. You could no longer get a ticket. Basketball was king of the Boston winter sports scene.

Some fans appreciated what was going on more than others. There were lots of bandwagon, nouveau rich sorts among the patrons, but there were others for whom Bird, Parish, McHale, D.J. & Co. were the culmination of a lifetime of sophisticated viewing. Such a fan was Peter Shankman.

He had grown up in Worcester and he was just old enough to know what Bill Russell represented. "I was 16 when Havlicek Stole The Ball in 1965," he says. "I was at Boston University in the late sixties, and I was at Game 4 against L.A. in sixty-nine, when Sam Jones hit the shot and Wilt slammed his fist against the support. I was a big Johnny Most listener, of course. I can still hear him making a call on Archie Clark sneaking away and Russell *"coming out of nowhere!"* to block the shot. I knew he embellished some of the things Russell did, but not a whole lot."

He relished the Cowens jousts with Abdul-Jabbar. He loved Havlicek. "I'll never forget game five in seventy-three, when he scored all those points with his left hand," Shankman says. "He didn't even have a left hand, but he *willed* himself a left hand for one night! I was always amazed how much Havlicek could accomplish just by running around."

He got tickets in the second balcony during the '70s, and when they did away with the second balcony in order to construct luxury boxes he was the lucky winner of a Displaced Persons lottery, if you will, which placed him in a far better seat, this time in the first row of the regular balcony, in what had once been the press box.

He was enough of a general basketball fan to have expected good things from Bird, but what he saw astounded him. Peter Shankman knew far more than good from bad. He knew good from great. That's why he represented the perfect audience for the greatest of all Celtics teams and the greatest of all Celtics seasons.

The 1985-86 Boston Celtics were made for all the Peter Shankmans out there. They would become the only team I have ever seen capable of rendering meaningless the concept of the "meaningless game."

5

The 1985-86 Boston Celtics

The 1985-86 Boston Celtics were not the same team that lost the 1985 Finals to the Lakers in six games.

Auerbach, general manager Jan Volk and assistant coach/player personnel director Jimmy Rodgers had done some serious work in the off-season to give their team more depth and balance. Coach K.C. Jones had lost faith in his bench during the playoffs. Changes would have to be made.

Rodgers had a good idea how to improve the backcourt, for example. He recommended the Celtics pry guard Jerry Sichting from the Indiana Pacers.

The Boston public didn't know much about the 6-1 Sichting, but basketball insiders prized him as a very reliable jump shooter who would also give you an honest day's work on defense. The Celtics were always concerned about having enough outside shooting.

But the real prize was hanging out in San Diego, waiting to see what his future might be. Bill Walton's time was running out. The team had never gotten enough bang for the many bucks invested in his fragile 7-foot body, and he was eager to move on.

Walton was emotionally ready to become a Celtic. His boyhood idol had been Bill Russell. He believed in the time-honored Celtics' virtues of fast-break basketball and selfless team play. He would also be a good fit because he had no illusions about being a starter in Boston. He had respect for Robert Parish. He just wanted to make a contribution.

There was a lot of hemming and hawing in the finest sports tradition before a deal with the Clippers could be consummated, but Auerbach was persistent, and it got done. On September 6, 1985, the Celtics traded Cedric Maxwell, a 1986 number one draft pick and cash to the Los Angeles Clippers in exchange for the services of William Theodore Walton.

NBA reaction was mixed. In theory, Bill Walton made the Celtics a much better team, but the sobering reality was that Bill Walton was the most physically unreliable great player in the history of the league. He had turned professional in 1974, and during the first 11 years of his career had only been able to participate in 51 percent of the 902 available regular-season games. He had missed the 1978-79, 1980-81 and 1981-82 seasons entirely. He even missed 24 games during his MVP season of 1977-78. He was a wonderful physical specimen from the shins up.

But the price was cheap. Maxwell had earned a spot in the back room of the Auerbach doghouse by his increasingly lethargic play. Red felt that Max had not worked hard enough to get himself back into the lineup after undergoing arthroscopic knee surgery midway through the '84-85 season. When the playoffs came, Maxwell was essentially useless.

No one was quite sure what was going on inside his head. Bird usually had a great handle on people, and Bird was president of the

The Celtics' gamble on Bill Walton paid off in a big way. Injury-prone for much of his NBA career, Walton played in 80 of Boston's 82 regular-season games and in all of the Celtics' playoff games. (Photo©Tom Miller)

119

Cedric Maxwell Fan Club. But one day in January of 1985 Bird said to me, "I don't know what's going on, but I can tell you that Max just doesn't want to play for us anymore."

The Celtics figured they could live without Max. Not having Max around meant more time for McHale, who had been improving on a yearly basis and was now one of the most feared and respected players in the league. The Celtics also felt adequately protected at forward because they already had a former All-Star in Scott Wedman in uniform. So losing Maxwell was never the issue. The only question was whether or not Walton would be able to participate often enough to make a difference.

Bill Walton is the Great Asterisk in any discussion of all-time great NBA players. When the roster of great centers is read, certain names are on every list: Bill Russell, Wilt Chamberlain, Kareem Abdul-Jabbar, Nate Thurmond, Hakeem Olajuwon, George Mikan, etc.

Bill Walton? In the eyes of most people, the body of professional work is just too thin. How can a man who takes part in half his team's games and who misses three years entirely be ranked with someone such as Kareem Abdul-Jabbar, who plays for 20 years and 1,560 regular-season and 237 playoff games? In terms of evaluating complete careers, you can't. But in terms of comparing skills and influence on any given game, you can. We saw enough of Bill Walton at his best to understand the unique nature of his game. Others had greater career statistics, but no one played the center position quite the same way Bill Walton did.

The Celtics were hoping to get lucky. They were hoping they could at least extract the 67 games the '84-85 Clippers had gotten from Walton. He had actually played pretty well that year for a 31-51 team. The Celtics began to fantasize about what Walton could accomplish in the company of great players such as Larry Bird, Kevin McHale and Dennis Johnson.

They were hoping, in short, for something more than they received on the night of October 25, 1985, when the Celtics inaugurated the new season with an aggravating 113-109 overtime loss to a team I always refer to as the "Exit 16 W Nets." (In Gertrude Stein terms, the New Jersey Nets play in a place where there truly is nothing there). The Celtics couldn't hold a 19-point third-quarter lead.

Dennis Johnson missed a pair of free throws which could have won the game in regulation. Bird, trying to work his way through a bad back, looked stiff and sore while shooting 5-for-15 from the floor. But no one felt more responsible for the loss than Bill Walton, who contributed little to the offense (no assists) while being charged with an appalling seven turnovers.

"I played a terrible game," he sighed. "It was a disgrace to my team and to the sport of basketball."

Walton had not played at this kind of tempo, with such a collection of skilled and intelligent players, since 1978. He needed a little time to get used to the idea. Within a week he was starting to feel somewhat comfortable in his new surroundings, and by Thanksgiving he was locked in. The Celtics were beginning to reap the benefits from employing the most creative all-around center who has ever played the game.

The Celtics did not stand around feeling sorry for themselves after the embarrassing loss in the Brendan Byrne Arena. They won their next eight games, grabbing an Atlantic Division lead they would never relinquish while establishing a feeling in the minds of the average opponent that there really would not be the proverbial snowball's chance in Hades of winning a game in the Boston Garden this season. On the road, under the proper circumstances and alignment of stars and planets? Perhaps, but only perhaps. In Boston. No way. As Ralph Kramden might have said, "Har-har-har-de-har-har!"

The team could play any way an opponent wished. If the foe liked the running game, the Celtics could run better. If the foe decided that walking the ball up the floor and playing a strict half-court game was the way to go, that was fine with the Celtics because they were the most overpowering and efficient half-court team in basketball. Depth was no longer an issue, not when you were bringing Walton, Sichting and Wedman off the bench.

There was really only one impediment to perfection in the first quarter of the season and that was the questionable physical condition of Bird, who had injured his back during the off-season and who was, by his exalted standards, struggling. In the first 14 games of the season he only exceeded 30 points once, and this was distinctly un-Bird-like. He carved out a sneaky 47-point game which included a 13-for-13 performance at the foul line against Detroit on November 28, but then he fell back into the realm of the mortal for the next month or so.

On the night of December 6, the young, aggressive and quite fearless Portland Trail Blazers came to the Garden. Portland was leading by a 53-35 score late in the second period when rookie Sam Vincent led a comeback which got the Celtics within four (56-52) at the half. At this point the nightly sellout gathering of 15,320 assumed it was going to be just another night at the office.

The Celtics kept the pressure on, and when they went ahead for the first time all evening at 75-74, everyone assumed the Trail Blazers would get the message and blink. They did not. Portland closed out the third period with an 11-2 run and the Celtics had no appropriate response. The final was Portland 121, Boston 103.

It was to be the only Celtic loss in the Garden all season.

"They just outplayed us in every department," said K.C. "They did a royal job on us."

This was just an annoying little bump in the road, at least until Christmas Day, when the Celtics found themselves some place they did not wish to be (Madison Square Garden), doing something they did not wish to do (playing basketball). One of the penalties the NBA exacts on teams who become good and who are desirable TV commodities is the requirement to provide entertainment for the masses on Christmas Day.

Leading by 25 points in the third quarter, the Celtics shut off the mental energy switch and began daydreaming about nicely wrapped presents, sugar plum fairies and a quick charter flight back home. The Knicks took advantage of some Boston largesse, seized control of the game and eventually walked off the court in possession of a 113-104 double-overtime triumph.

More disturbing than the loss was the sight of Bird struggling to get up and down the floor. He shot a shocking 8-for-27 and emerged from the game with a season's shooting percentage of 43 percent. It speaks volumes for the quality of his teammates that, despite his continuing inability to play like Larry Bird, the team was still among the league's elite.

What the world at large didn't know was that Bird was even then receiving daily treatment for his back from orthopedic physical therapist Dan Dyrek, and that things were imperceptibly making a turn for the better. As Bird later explained, "I was in pain all the time. It affected everything I did. I couldn't bend over or extend myself in any way. If a ball was on the floor, the only way I could reach it was to go all the way down. I couldn't bend from the waist. If I drove for a shot, I couldn't extend my arm and finish off. I couldn't take the bumping all the way to the basket."

Question: Given all this, how could a man *still* be averaging a shade under 20 points a night playing against the best basketball players in the world?

The Knick loss was sobering. The Celtics had just seen their record drop to 21-7, and, to be frank, they knew they were no ordinary, garden variety .750 team. They had been around the league once and what they had seen was that few teams honestly had the capability of beating them. It would be impossible not to have a game here or there reminiscent of the Portland affair, but, that aberration aside, there really was no reason to lose when just by being reasonably attentive to detail they could win just about every game, especially at the Garden.

Each season has flash-point games in which a team comes out of it with a new and vital sense of self. The Celtics had just such a game on the night of January 18, 1986, when they ventured into the Omni to play the Atlanta Hawks.

The Hawks were relatively young, and they were undeniably talented. They jumped to a 70-47 halftime lead before a sellout crowd of 16,522, and they had something to say about it as the teams walked off the court, too. Bad move. Bird fired in 17 during the third period and the lead went from 23 to 8. He kept pouring them in and the Celtics won by three in overtime. Larry had 41.

He was feeling better.

The matchups with the Lakers and Kareem Abdul-Jabbar were lumped in the Armageddon category. (Photo©Tom Miller)

It was the start of a great week. The following Wednesday Los Angeles came to town for the annual Armageddon. This was the night when Bill Walton officially and irrevocably became a Celtic. He blocked the first Kareem shot attempt, sending the maniacal Garden crowd into a frenzy. That was the beginning of an 11-point, 8-rebound, 7-block contribution, all of which was accomplished in 16 minutes of play! This was precisely the type of Walton performance about which the Celtics' brass had fantasized when he was imported from the Left Coast. The Celtics won it by an easy 15, 110-95. They were now 31-8.

Armageddon II took place on Super Sunday when the despised 76ers entered the Garden. Philly was no longer a team of championship caliber, but they were still a solid 50-win kind of club on a 17-2 roll and they were still an ancient rival. Bird never had any trouble getting himself up to play against the 76ers.

The Sixers were ready. They led by as many as 13 in the third before Bird began to heat up, capping a late run with a buzzer-beating 35-footer. Walton was immense again, this time with 19 points and 13 rebounds in 25 minutes of exceptionally valuable playing time. The Celtics prevailed, 105-103.

Boston was now playing without McHale who was idled with a sore achilles tendon. There was only one McHale, one absolutely unstoppable low post scoring forward, but the Celtics had a very suitable replacement in Wedman, a completely different type of player. Wedman was a perimeter shooter of the first degree.

McHale or no McHale, the Boston Celtics were now in total team synch. They had more diverse weapons than anyone, and they went into each game trying to make life easy for each other. They also were in the custody of the perfect coach — for them. K.C. Jones is a gentle, low-key individual who has never made the mistake of overcoaching. These great players loved his easygoing ways and they loved playing for him. In other circumstances, where an aggressive, technically oriented approach has been needed, K.C. has not thrived. But if you were going to select the one man best suited temperamentally to coach this veteran team of All-Stars, that man would have been K.C. Jones.

After losing a game in Detroit on January 7, the Celtics had casually run off 13 straight heading into the All-Star break. Bird was clearly mending. Walton was everything he could possibly be. Life was great.

And it would only get better.

The highlight of All-Star Weekend was the first Three-Point Shot contest. It was a given that Bird would enter, and it was even more of a given in his own mind that he would win it. As the contestants were getting themselves composed in the locker room prior to the contest, Bird took charge.

"Which one of you guys," he wanted to know, "is planning on coming in second?"

It wasn't just a gag line. Bird obliterated the competition, sinking 11 shots in a row during the deciding round. He had people babbling about the sight of two basketballs in the air simultaneously, one swishing and the other about to swish.

"I'm the Three-Point King!" Bird bellowed as he entered the interview room. Someone asked him what he was planning to do with the $10,000 check for first prize. "It's going to the Larry Bird Fund," he smiled.

With this jocular air setting the tone for his entire team, Bird led the Celtics out to the West Coast. The trip opener was a stunner. With Bird himself missing two big free throws in the final minute, the Celtics lost to the downtrodden Sacramento Kings, 105-100. But Bird responded with a triple-double in Seattle, and the Celtics were back on track.

When you are discussing a player like Bird, who is half-athlete, half-legend, the subject of truly memorable performances comes up. What he did in Portland on the night of February 14, 1986, is surely on his Top 10 List.

It wasn't just that he scored 47 points in a 120-119 overtime win. It wasn't just that he had a career double with 14 rebounds and 11 assists to augment those 47 points. It wasn't just that he scored the game-winning basket on a cramped fallaway (Jerome Kersey in his shirt and Sam Bowie and Steve Colter close by). The hook this time was that he had scored as many as 10 of his 21 baskets *with his left hand*.

Bird is overtly ambidextrous. He writes left-handed and he eats left-handed. He has always had a far better-than-average off-hand. But this was another realm entirely.

He had been working on his left hand since the summer of 1983. It was part of his "I'm-taking-this-personally" vow following the humiliating Milwaukee sweep. The following year he was conspicuously more capable with his left hand. Now the Portland players and fans learned just how proficient he had become.

"I feel better than I've felt all year," Bird said, adding that "I'm saving my right hand for the Lakers," who were the next opponents on the trip.

The Celtics could imagine few better satisfactions than winning in the Forum, and they insured this sweet brand of happiness with a

Larry Bird showed Celtic opponents he was just as capable of shooting with his left hand as his right. (Photo©Tom Miller)

truly magnificent all-around performance which even included significant bench performances from deep-on-the-bench kids David Thirdkill and Rick Carlisle.

The Celtics got excellent outings from the usual suspects, but what distinguished this one was the play of the bench. With the game still in doubt, K.C. had his subs on the floor during the third period. In one sequence Walton took a medium high post feed and, without looking right or left, dumped an overhead pass to a cutting David Thirdkill for a reverse layup.

What? David Thirdkill? Now if the cutter had been Bird, Johnson or Ainge there wouldn't have been any questions. You would simply say that Walton knew how any of these savvy veterans would react to any given situation. But *David Thirdkill*? How did Walton know that David Thirdkill would make the proper cut? What would prompt him to throw a blind pass to David Thirdkill? The answer was, of course, that if you're Bill Walton, this is what you do. It's who you are on the basketball floor.

As for Carlisle, ask any Celtic fan — Peter Shankman, for example — what he thinks about when the name Rick Carlisle is introduced into the conversation and he will say "Sunday afternoon in L.A." This was the defining moment of Rick Carlisle's Celtic career. He shot 5-for-7 from the floor, scoring 10 points, and one deep corner jumper late in the third quarter was a particular killer.

The Celtics were no longer just a good team, or even a great team. They were, in the minds of the grateful fans, an entertainment entity sent here by a loving deity to serve some higher purpose. They were playing a style of basketball truly unlike anything that had ever been seen before. This is not to say that it was worthier than the Best of Russell & Cousy or the Best of the Havlicek-Cowens teams, but that it was something new and different and unique.

Speak to me not of this team or that team if it is not, first and foremost, a superior passing team. This is something people seldom discuss in their foolish attempts to insert these Michael Jordan-led Bulls teams in discussions of the all-time great teams. Passing changes the game. Passing transforms basketball into an art form. And the 1985-86 Celtics were the greatest all-around passing team of the last quarter-century. I would say "of all-time" were I not so enamored of the great Knicks teams of the early '70s. They could move the rock a little, too.

Passing was this team's *raison d'etre*. Bird was, of course, 1A to Magic Johnson's 1 as the greatest passer of his time (or was it the other way around?). Johnson was a passer. Ainge was a passer. And good God almighty, was Bill Walton a passer!

There were two guaranteed nightly rituals. The first took place within a few possessions of Walton's initial entrance into the game. Bird would dump the ball into the post and make a cut to Walton's left, along the right baseline. If the game was taking place in Boston, everyone in the Garden knew what was coming. Bird was going to get a return pass from Walton and score an easy give-and-go layup right out of the 1921 Original Celtics playbook. It was all so simple and so obvious and so repetitive, and yet no one ever stopped it. Surely, I used to think, every team has watched the video tape 100 times. They *must* know what Walton and Bird are up to.

The second ritual could occur at any point in the ballgame. There would be a moment when Johnson would be a step or two on the offensive side of midcourt. Bird would be lurking along the baseline, ostensibly minding his own business. It didn't matter which side. With only eye contact and instinct as triggering mechanisms, Bird would make a quick cut and D.J. would fire a 40-foot bullet off the dribble for a backdoor layup. Many little hairs would snap to attention on many heads in the Garden.

Great passing is invariably contagious. Bird's effect on his Indiana State team was astonishing. Average players were moved to make creative passes when so inspired by something they had just seen Bird do. It was the same with the '85-86 Celtics, except that there were now *two* extraterrestrial passers to provide inspiration, and not just one. For Bill Walton was the finest pivot passer in the NBA in at least 20 years, or at least since Johnny Kerr had stopped throwing those backward between-the-legs to cutters for the Syracuse Nats and Philly 76ers.

Up in section 88, row AA, Peter Shankman and his friends were wondering what they had done to deserve such nightly treats. "I can't think of anything that was ever more enjoyable in a pure aesthetic sense," he says. "We were as lucky as we were ever going to be. It was the ultimate rush."

The W's rolled off the assembly line. February turned into March and the Celtics simply kept getting better and better. The Garden

Bill Walton became a favorite of the Boston fans during the Celtics' championship season. (Photo©Tom Miller)

crowd meant no disrespect to the great Robert Parish, the beloved "Chief," (so nicknamed by Cedric Maxwell because his stoic manner was so reminiscent of the Will Sampson character in *One Flew Over The Cuckoo's Nest*), but it was clear that one of the great anticipatory moments each evening was Walton's first appearance on the floor. He brought such creativity and such overt *joie de vivre* that he made everyone in the building feel he had been invited to a private birth-day party. And for Bill Walton, every night in the 1985-86 season was a cause to celebration. This man never complained about the schedule or the travel, or any other trivial matter.

This is what he had long waited for. He was on the best team and *he was playing every night*.

There was no accounting for the Celtics' good fortune. Bill Walton would play in 80 of 82 regular-season games and every one of their 18 playoff games. The man who had missed three entire seasons participated in every training camp two-a-day session. He missed one regular-season game when he broke his nose and another when he was sick, but he never missed a game or practice due to a complication of a lower extremity.

Walton even got to start two games when Parish went down. In the combined first two periods of those games he had 25 points and 12 rebounds. His full-game totals for a March 28 start against Washington were 20 points and 12 rebounds. "He is one of the greatest players ever when healthy," said Bullets coach Kevin Loughery, "and right now he's as healthy as he's been in a long time. He put on a show tonight, and it looks like he really enjoys playing again."

I had resumed covering this team for the third time in the wake of a *Globe* domino game which had begun with Peter Gammons leaving the paper to work for *Sports Illustrated* and resulted in Dan Shaughnessy leaving the Celtics' beat to take over Red Sox coverage. I got on board on a day-to-day basis in late February at a point when the nightly issues far transcended winning and losing. It was all about aesthetics and style points, and whether — I am not making this up — Bird could collect on a side bet with Knicks trainer Mike Saunders, the subject being whether or not Larry could *bank* in a three-pointer in the course of a game (he could).

One day I was standing around just before the start of practice chatting with someone when I saw a basketball in flight out of the corner of my eye. The ball swished through the cords and then I heard a great roar and I saw Bird dancing around.

It seems that K.C. Jones had said that if anyone on the team could make a shot from midcourt — one shot per customer — he would dispense with that day's practice. Bird, of course, had demanded the first shot. No additional shots were needed. The day had begun, like all Celtic days, with Bird ringing up Walton at his Cambridge home, reminding him to make sure he wasn't late for practice so that Bird could get on with the task of beating Walton's butt on the basketball floor.

The truth is there was fierce competition between the first string and the Walton-led second team, which K.C. had dubbed the "Green Team," that being the color of their practice jerseys (the first string wore white. The jerseys were, of course, reversible). Woofing was the order of the day, before, during and after practice. Such was life with the 1985-86 Boston Celtics.

The Celtics won their final 13 home games by an average margin of 16 points. Bird was his old self by that time. He had been the NBA Player of the Month for February. And March. After one of his unique displays, Detroit coach Chuck Daly attempted to put it all in perspective. "There has never been, and never will be, a player like Bird," he decided.

They weren't about to argue that point in San Antonio, where he had an 11-for-11 first half, or in Hartford, where he had helped himself to 34 by halftime of that home-away-from-home affair.

McHale's achilles problem cleared up and he resumed his low post dominance. One of the great stories in the stretch run was the amazing shooting of Sichting, who, according to *Globe* columnist Leigh Montville, "has never in his life been to the paint." The quintessential Indiana backyard jump shooter was a 63 percent marksman for the final 17 games.

They clinched the divisional title with 13 games left, the conference title with 11 games left and the best record overall with six games remaining. Their 67-15 record was the fourth-best of all time. Only two of their 15 losses were not connected with outright giveaways, ejections or missing personnel. If you were grading them for the season, your only conceivable mark would have been an A-plus.

6

The 1986
NBA Playoffs

The Celtics knew it before anyone else. Michael Jordan up and exploded in their face, and the Celtics knew right then and there the rest of the league was on borrowed time. They knew that some day Michael Jordan was going to be an NBA champion.

What was supposed to be a routine dispatch of a number 8 team by a number 1 team was anything but. The Celtics did sweep this first-round best-of-five series against the Chicago Bulls, but it happened to be a monumental ordeal.

Everyone recalls the 63-point Jordan statement in the epic that was Game 2 of this series, but Game 1 was a bucking bronco ride of its

Chicago's Michael Jordan was a handful for the Celtics but they held the player who was the become the league's next superstar enough in check to win the series with the Bulls. (Photo©Tom Miller)

own. Jordan scored 49 points in that one, and had Dennis Johnson not submitted a 7-for-7 second half (after an 0-for-7 first half) the Celtics might not have pulled away to a 123-104 victory. Jordan had 30 by halftime, and it's not telling any tales outside classroom to point out that the Celtics didn't appear to have anyone on the roster who could guard him.

The least that can be said about Game 2 is that it was one of the great Celtic playoff epics ever. For most of the 58 minutes it felt and looked like Michael vs. The World. "I didn't think anyone was capable of doing what Michael has done to us the past two games," said an exhausted Bird when the 135-131 double-overtime victory was safely recorded in the record books. "Michael is the most exciting, awesome player in the game today...I think it's God, disguised as Michael Jordan."

In Game 1 Jordan had scored a very forced 49, most of the points coming from isolations. It had very little to do with team basketball. But in Game 2 Jordan got 63 points out of the routine flow of the game, which is a lot more frightening to contemplate and a far better tribute to him as a basketball player.

About the only thing he did wrong during the course of a spectacular Sunday afternoon's work was miss an open jumper with two seconds left in the first overtime. The score was then tied at 123 apiece.

Otherwise, Michael Jordan kept his team in the game with an assortment of shots not routinely on display when the Minneapolis Lakers were in control of the NBA. He was scoring horizontally, vertically and diagonally, frustrating every chosen Celtic's attempt to guard him.

The Celtics didn't gain control of this game until Sichting, a Studebaker to Jordan's Porsche, took an inside-out feed from McHale and swished a foul-line jumper with 57 seconds left and Parish, who hadn't made a single outside shot all day, converted a pick-and-roll jumper on a feed from Bird with nine seconds left.

Bird shrugged off his apparent misplaced confidence in a man who was far off his normal game. "When he goes, you've got to give him the ball," Bird declared. "You don't worry about Robert Parish. I never do, because he's made a whole lot of big plays for this team."

Bird had an inconspicuous 36. Measured against the pyrotechnics of Jordan's record-breaking 63, anything else was a mute statement. Walton had made a major contribution, scoring 10 points and grabbing 15 rebounds in 25 minutes of work before fouling out. As proof of just how disruptive Jordan had been, Walton actually fouled him more than anyone else (four times).

Generally overlooked in analyses of Walton's game was his superb rebounding. He had unrivaled technique. His timing was absolutely impeccable. More than any player in history, Bill Walton had the knack of taking the ball away from the rim at the exact instant before it began to fall off the rim with a move which looked like someone sweeping crumbs off a table. In so doing, he was actually guilty of goaltending, but because he was so quick and the timing was so superb, his transgression would invariably go undetected by the officials.

One hidden story in Game 2 was the unofficial coming out party of Danny Ainge. Held to just two points midway through the third period, he began to assert himself to such an extent that he wound up with 25 very valuable points. He had once said that he knew his place as the fifth man on a star-laden starting five. "If they were to make it a 4-on-4 game," he said, "I wouldn't be playing." He seemed to discover exactly who he was and what he could accomplish after this game. The next year he was in the All-Star Game.

Game 3 was an anticlimax. The Celtics had made a reasonable policy decision: Michael Jordan was *not* going to beat them. Every time he touched the ball in the first quarter, a platoon of green-clad guys rushed to him, making him relinquish the basketball. He grew irritable, even picking up a technical. No one on his team stepped forward to relieve the pressure. The Celtics won easily, 122-104, to close out the series.

Consider it a Preview of Coming Attractions.

Atlanta was next on the menu, and the Celtics weren't concerned. The Hawks hadn't beaten the Celtics all year, and, what's more, the Celtics didn't particularly like them. Just what the Hawks needed to hear. Boston, needing no additional edge aside from their own brilliant basketball ability, was going to be motivated.

The Celtics breezed through Games 1 and 2 at home. It was strictly no muss, no fuss. They won a grinding Game 3 in Atlanta

(111-107) and then affixed a mental postage stamp to the right-hand corner of Game 4 and slipped it into the nearest corner mailbox. Their hearts just weren't in it.

And lucky for every Celtic fan on earth they weren't, because Game 5 was very well worth the wait. Specifically, the third quarter of Game 5 was worth the wait. The Celtics came out of the locker room leading by 11, 66-55. They went into the fourth period leading by 41. Do the math. That's 36-6.

It included a period-ending run of 24 unanswered points. The burst began inauspiciously enough with a technical foul shot. It peaked artistically with a trailing Walton stampeding down the lane for a thunderous dunk. It was a dazzling and enlightening demonstration of athletic prowess.

"It was the best quarter I've ever played in," said Dennis Johnson. "Probably the best I ever will play in."

"All you can do is wince and make substitutions and call timeouts," said Atlanta mentor Mike Fratello. "What else is there? The league doesn't let you make trades during games."

"If you want to see how the game of basketball is played," said Sichting, "put that third quarter on film. And show it to the kids."

Don Nelson was a pragmatic man. He knew exactly what his Milwaukee Bucks team would be up against in the Eastern Conference Finals.

"It's like, what is it? — *Man of La Mancha*," he joked.

It was a brilliant analogy, and it looked very prescient indeed when the Celtics took Game 1 by the comfortable margin of 128-96. Right away the winning or losing issue was settled, and therefore the Milwaukee role in this production became to give the Celtics just enough honest opposition to make the series entertaining for the fans.

They did just that in both Games 3 and 4. Milwaukee actually led by 13 in the third period of Game 3 before the Celtics decided to get serious. Bird made the game's most memorable play late in the third period when he went diving into a pile for a loose ball. Milwaukee's Paul Mokeski had actually gotten there first, but Bird ripped the ball away from the startled Buck, rolled over, sat up and fired a pass to McHale for a layup. "I'll never forget it as long as I live," gushed Nelson. "What a basketball player."

Bird finished the game with 19 points, 16 rebounds and 13 assists, one of which was an almost incomprehensible first period over-the-shoulder feed to Parish, who had gotten open barely a millisecond before.

That 111-107 victory in hand, the Celtics wanted an avenging sweep. They got it in Game 4. K.C. pulled this one out by hitting Milwaukee with a fourth-period lineup of McHale, Parish, Walton, Bird and Johnson. Larry drilled four consecutive fourth-quarter three-pointers to put an exclamation point on a spectacularly diverse two day's work in which he had done everything to torment the people of Milwaukee short of drinking up all their beer. The final was 111-98.

The Celtics would like to have played the Lakers in what would have been the Finals' rubber match, but, as the Rolling Stones long ago informed us, *You Can't Always Get What You Want.* The 1986 Western Conference champions happened to be the Houston Rockets.

But the Rockets did provide one intriguing subplot. The coach of the Rockets was none other than Bill Fitch.

The Rockets had gotten to the Finals by knocking off the Lakers in five games. Their biggest strength, aside from the shrewd coaching of Fitch, was the frontcourt of Akeem (the "H" came later) Olajuwon, Ralph Sampson and Rodney McCray. They were young, active on the backboards and relatively carefree. They were smart enough to know that the pressure was all on the Celtics.

The Celtics had gained control of the first three series by winning Games 1 and 2 at home. They made it 4-for-4 with routine dispatches of the Rockets by the scores of 112-100 and 117-95 this time.

Houston found out just how classically well-balanced in the opener. Parish led the team with 23. Bird and McHale each had 21. Johnson had 19. Ainge had 18. Walton came off the bench to shoot 5-for-5. How are you going to contest all that?

The Celtics were alert at both ends, taking pains to make their defense work to ignite their offense. "Every time we stole the ball (which the Celtics did 15 times), it seemed like there was a guy going in for a layup down at the other end."

Larry Bird dives for a loose ball against Houston. (Photo©Tom Miller)

Bird and McHale made sure the Celtics would get their customary 2-0 series edge in Game 2. Larry had 31, as he toyed with McCray. Kevin had one of his casual 25s. But the real story was the aggressive defense.

"You've got our little guys," analyzed Walton. "Dennis Johnson and Bird and Ainge, who really aren't so little. And they're constantly running in and out and darting here and there, chasing the ball every time you throw it. They're going to dive for loose balls; they're going to make you absolutely miserable."

Houston figured to play for God, mother and country down in the Summit, and so their 106-104 victory in Game 3 did not come as a great shock to anyone. The Celtics hung around and hung around, but Mitchell Wiggins had the last say with a game-winning tip-in.

The ever-blunt Parish was not impressed with his team's effort. "We haven't given away one like this since Christmas," he grumbled.

All season long, K.C. Jones was a benign, soothing presence. He seldom had to make a big decision. But in Game 4 he made a humongous one, and it won the game.

No matter how well Walton had played, or, correspondingly, no matter how poorly Parish had played, if the outcome of any game was still in doubt in the final few minutes, Parish was going to be in there. This policy held through 82 regular-season and 15 playoff games. But with about 3½ minutes left in a well-played, tense, taut Game 4, K.C. made his move. Out came Parish, in came Walton. And so the big redhead was in there to a) grab a missed shot and pitch it back out to Bird for a major three-pointer and then b) grab another offensive rebound and shove back in a huge reverse layup.

"Games like this are why I came to Boston," Walton said. "This is what I've been waiting nine years for."

From a Boston viewpoint, Game 5 was a bad movie. The focal point of the game was a weird second-period fist fight between 7-foot-4 Ralph Sampson and 6-foot-1 Jerry Sichting. The two were thrown out, and Houston seized the emotional edge, pounding the Celtics on the glass and walking off with a 111-96 decision.

It just wasn't Boston's night. "We were organized chaos," said K.C.

So it was back to Boston for Game 6 (and maybe 7), and back home there were a lot of Chicken Littles worried about the Boston sky. The younger Rockets had simply annihilated the Celtics on the offensive boards as the Houston portion of the series unfolded, pulling down 25 offensive rebounds in Game 4 and 23 more in Game 5.

Bird was more amused with the local panic than he was anything else.

"I don't guarantee victory," he said. "But I just know we'll play well. We've got two games here and we only need one...We just play better here. I'm not saying it's a great advantage, but I know I'd rather be up, 3-2, than down, 3-2."

The game was already over for Ralph Sampson, incidentally, and it wouldn't even start for another 20-some hours. The Boston crowd hated him, and he wasn't noted for his ability to handle these kinds of pressure situations.

As for himself, Bird was oozing with confidence. "I'm going to have a good game. I know that. Rebounding's a problem, so I'm gonna rebound. I don't have to score a bunch of points 'cause everyone's got to get involved."

Summing it all up, Bird said, "I think everything's going to be fine."

In those days, it was always wise to heed Larry Bird.

Bird watchers, Bird listeners and Bird historians love to rank the great performances, but they might as well know that the one nearest and dearest to his own heart is the one he submitted for our perusal on the afternoon of Sunday, June 8, 1986. On that day the Houston Rockets simply had no chance to beat any team fortunate enough to have Larry Bird in its starting lineup.

In 897 regular-season and 164 playoff games, he maintains he was never more ready to play than he was that day against the Rockets.

"That was the only game I thought I was *totally* prepared for," he insists. "As far as focus was concerned, none better. I should have quit right there."

He had many games with gaudier numbers (29 points, 11 rebounds, 12 assists). But he never had a game where he was as involved in every crucial aspect of the game at both ends of the floor. His hands and feet were in constant motion, particularly in the first half. Hubie Brown once described him as a "total menace," and that is exactly what he was in the eyes of the Rockets on this spring afternoon.

Is it shameless to quote from your own game story? Probably. But I'm going to do it in an attempt to convey the honest emotion and reaction of one observer after watching Bird play this magnificent game.

"The Houston Rockets were like an unwary couple pulled over on the highway for going 3 miles over the speed limit by a burly Georgia cop with the mirrored sunglasses.

"It wasn't their day. The cop's name was Bird. The bailiff's name was Bird. The court stenographer's name was Bird. And the executioner's name was — guess what? — Bird."

And that was before I found how much Bird himself loved his own performance in that game.

The final was 114-97. The Celtics never trailed. Bird had 16 points, 8 rebounds and 8 assists by halftime, at which point the Celtics led by 17 (55-38). He was so pumped he even won a jump ball from Olajuwon.

The Rockets only knew they had been undone by a superior being. "I just saw him take on five men by himself," marveled Houston's Jim Petersen. "At times, he doesn't even need teammates."

Just the opposite was true, of course. For Larry Bird was all about team and all about abetting teammates. Michael Jordan is the one who can beat teams by himself. Bird's great gift was an ability to utilize his physical and mental gifts to extract the utmost from his teammates. He could organize a basketball team into a frighteningly efficient unit. That was his goal. And this was his happiest hour in that quest. He was a champion for the third and final time in his career.

There have been many great Celtic teams, but this was the most diverse and entertaining. The '85-86 Celtics had an answer to every basketball question.

They beat people by running, by bombarding them with three-point shots, by making them submit to their will in a halfcourt game, by outdefending them and by, when all else failed, handing the basketball to Larry Bird and asking him to think of something.

The Celtics led every series 2-0. The only time they were in serious trouble during the entire postseason was that brief moment when Jordan was all alone with an open jumper at the end of the first overtime in Game 2 of the opening series. All other events were under their control.

The Celtics had gotten everything possible out of Walton. Walton had gotten everything possible out of the Celtics. "Walton was the trump card," says Peter Shankman. "He was the reason the '86 Celtics were what they were. We already had the smartest player in the world, Larry Bird, and now we had his cousin. No disrespect to Robert, but Walton was the one we couldn't wait to see get into the game."

Bird does not fancy himself as a hoop historian, but he certainly speaks with passion about the NBA *he* knew. "The best team I ever saw had to be the '85-86 team," he says. "I would honestly put that team up against any NBA team I ever played against. The fact is that Bill Walton made everyone on the second team twice as good as they really were."

Take my advice. Never argue with Larry Bird on a basketball matter.

Epilogue

The Celtics have never again hoisted a championship banner.

They got back to the Finals in 1987, but they did so with just about no bench and they did very well just to extend a great L.A. team to six games. Walton played in 10 regular-season games. He had injured his foot riding an exercise bike. He was riding the bike because he couldn't play. He couldn't play because he had already broken his hand. He was, in short, once again the Bill Walton they knew and didn't love in Los Angeles. He never officially retired, but he never played again after a token appearance in the '87 Finals.

The Celtics deteriorated, almost by the year. They reached the Eastern Conference Finals in 1988 when a storybook 20-point fourth quarter by Bird got them through a Game 7 against Atlanta. But Detroit's time was coming and Boston's was past.

Injury became the story of Bird's career. He had double heel surgery and he had back surgery. He had some wonderful moments, and against Indiana in 1991 he enhanced the legend when he came back into a deciding Game 5 after banging his head against the parquet floor.

He retired in 1992. McHale, himself bedeviled by injury from 1987 on, followed him a year later. They had always laughed that The Chief would outlast them all, and so he did, playing till age 43. Walton, Bird and McHale were all brought down by injury. Parish simply got old, but he did so with another championship ring, courtesy of Michael Jordan and the 1996-97 Chicago Bulls.

The 1985-86 Celtics represented the apex of the Boston Celtics rooting experience. Those old enough to have seen the Russells and the Cousys had been preparing for this quintessential fan joyride all their rooting lives. Those new to it, or only acutely aware of the sport's possibilities via the Cowens-Havlicek clubs, were somewhat spoiled. Teams don't go through a whole season losing just one game at home. Teams don't get better and better and better before your very eyes. Teams don't take a game and continually elevate it into an art form. The '85-86 Celtics did all these things.

Something like that can actually be harmful if you're planning on watching new teams and new players. Your rational self tells you it

Robert Parish outlasted everyone from the 1985-86 team, retiring in 1997 after winning another championship ring with the Chicago Bulls. (Photo©Tom Miller)

can *never* get this good again. So what do you have to look forward to? Another championship, sure, but the feeling will never be the same. It has been noted that the Boston fans have become passive over the past 10 years, that no matter what a specific Celtic team does, it is never enough to get anyone really excited.

But there is no doubt that the great Bird teams, climaxing in the best-of-all 1985-86 aggregation, made Boston a basketball-savvy town. Far more people do, in fact, know not only good from bad, but, more importantly, great from good. Because they understand the game's possibilities in a way others less fortunate than they do not, they have become very hard markers, as Rick Pitino and friends will now discover. Tradition is a healthy thing. Too much tradition can be a heavy burden.

One man's Intimate Pleasure is another man's Ultimate Rush. Bird may have been onto something. Maybe *everyone* should have quit and gone on to some other pursuit after the events of June 8, 1986, fans included.

The Patriots

The Patriots meet the Packers in Super Bowl XXXI. (Photo©Tom Miller)

7

Almost
Orphans

The very fact that this professional football team carries the appellation "New England," rather than "Boston," sets this franchise apart from the others.

The Patriots have been orphan-like since their inception. They have played their home games in Braves Field, Fenway Park, Harvard Stadium, Boston College and, since 1971, a stadium in Foxboro, Massachusetts, known successively as Schaefer Stadium, Sullivan Stadium and Foxboro Stadium. Because the city of Boston would not truly embrace them, schmooze them, stroke them and house them, the franchise had no choice but to relocate to a site 25 miles from downtown Boston. The team has been playing in a stadium located equidistant from Boston and Providence. The season ticket clientele is skewed south and west of Boston. A significant number of regular patrons hail from Rhode Island and even Connecticut. Unlike the perceived regionalization of the Red Sox, Bruins and Celtics, the Patriots' regionalization is concrete. They really *are* the New England Patriots. Unless they are planning on becoming an Arena Football franchise some time in the future, they are unlikely ever to play another game in the city of Boston.

The Patriots are the third major professional football franchise in Boston history. In order to find out what happened to the first, you need look no farther than the new Jack Kent Cooke Stadium in Landover, Md., wherein reside its direct descendants, the Washington Redskins.

The Redskins came into being in 1932 when Vincent Bendix, Jay O'Brien, M. Dorland Doyle and George Preston Marshall kicked in $7,500 apiece to secure a franchise in the National Football League. The other three were insistent that the flamboyant, bombastic, never-to-be-ignored Marshall be the team president and its public face.

Boston wasn't asking for a professional football team. The city was chosen, in large measure, because of O'Brien's friendship with Boston Braves owner Judge Emil J. Fuchs. The team set up shop in Braves Field, and was therefore christened the "Braves."

Hardly anyone cared. Most of the press ignored the team, as did the fans. College football was king.

Marshall switched his base of operations to Fenway Park in 1933, but fan support remained minimal. The team kept advancing its on-field stature, however, and by 1936 the Redskins, as they were now known, had earned a berth in the NFL championship game against the Green Bay Packers. The title game was scheduled for Fenway, but when advance sales lagged an enraged and exasperated Marshall made an amazing decision. He moved the game to New York and the Polo Grounds, and that is where Green Bay defeated the Redskins, 21-6, to secure the 1936 championship. Marshall was through with Boston. The Redskins moved to Washington in 1937.

A thought: The great Sammy Baugh came out of TCU in 1937 and joined the Redskins. He was the foundation of the franchise for the next 16 years. Would the presence of this dynamic player been enough to put pro football over in Boston? Just thinking out loud...

Six years later Boston found itself with a new professional football team, this one called the "Yanks." The owner was Ted Collins, who was known to the public as the manager of singing star Kate Smith. The team merged with the Brooklyn franchise in 1945 and then moved to the upstart All-America Football Conference in 1946. The Brooklyn part of the operation was killed off.

The team floundered for three forgettable years, winning 9 and losing 24 and creating very little interest in a city that was quite happy with its baseball and hockey franchises, and which was satisfied to spend its autumn weekends following the likes of Harvard, Boston College and Holy Cross.

Collins moved the franchise to New York in 1949. His games in the Big Apple were likewise distinguished by the huge numbers of patrons who arrived at the stadium cleverly disguised as empty seats.

Professional football went on its merry way throughout the '50s without Boston, Mass. The All-America Football Conference and the National Football League merged in 1950 without Boston. The great teams and stars of the '50s — the Cleveland Browns, the Detroit Lions, the New York Giants, the Baltimore Colts, the Otto Grahams, the Crazy Legs Hirsches, the Cloyce Boxes (I just wanted an excuse to get Cloyce Box into this book), the Charlie Conerlys — they all thrilled football-loving audiences from coast to coast, but not in Boston. Boston was a town of professional pigskin *voyeurs*.

New England was New York Giants territory. The football fans of Boston and the rest of the extreme Northeast corridor of America got their pro football thrills vicariously, much the way people in Los Angeles have done since 1995. Giants' games were televised into New England. To this day there remain staunch diehard fans of the New York (Football) Giants. They will remain loyal to the Giants, even should the Patriots reinvent themselves as the Vince Lombardi Packers.

The Boston Patriots came into being in the fall of 1959. William H. (Billy) Sullivan Jr., a well-known local figure, had first come under public scrutiny as the public relations spokesman for the athletic program at Boston College, his alma mater. He was at Frank Leahy's side when BC went undefeated in 1940 and then concluded its most successful season ever by defeating Tennessee in the 1941 Sugar Bowl. He later surfaced as the public relations director for the 1948 National League champion Boston Braves.

His baseball career was a diversion. The sport nearest and dearest to his heart was football, and he was one of a growing number of professional people in Boston feeling left out of the excitement being created by the National Football League. He and his friends were rebuffed when they tried to get a franchise in the NFL, and so when the American Football League came into being Sullivan thought he and Boston had found the right home.

Billy Sullivan was not a man of great means. The NFL was formed by a weird assortment of legitimately wealthy individuals (such as hotel magnate Baron Hilton) and wannabes. Sullivan was definitely one of the latter. In order to secure the eighth and final franchise in the AFL, he had to borrow money in order to come up with the $25,000 entry fee. The following April the Patriots became the first pro team to issue public stock.

Boston did not have, and still does not have, a modern football stadium. The Patriots were either going to play in a baseball park (Fenway) or a college stadium (Braves Field, then owned by Boston University, Harvard or Boston College). In time they would play in all of them. They would even play an official "home" game in Birmingham, Alabama.

Lou Saban, who in the course of a truly amazing four-decade career has seemingly coached every high school, college and professional football team in America, was the first coach. He went 5-9 in the first year and was 2-3 in 1961 when he was removed in favor of former Boston College hero Mike Holovak. The Patriots responded to his direction by going 7-1-1 the rest of the year.

People who followed the Patriots in the '60s sometimes attempt to convey the impression that the Patriots were a constant juggernaut. Well, they weren't. They had some good years, but they never won a title, and in their only appearance in an AFL championship game (1963) they were destroyed by the San Diego Chargers. That is, unless you consider a 51-10 score to be a squeaker.

They moved to Fenway Park in 1963, but during their entire AFL history they never had a decent practice facility. Tales of management penury persist. They had quality players such as wide receiver/kicker Gino Cappelletti, quarterback Vito (Babe) Parilli, fullback Jim Nance, defensive end Larry Eisenhauer and linebacker Nick Buoniconti, but there was always the aura of a glorified semipro franchise attached to the franchise.

Sullivan himself was capable of making himself a friend in the first of a sentence and making that same guy an enemy following the comma. Many members of the media considered him to be a faker, because he talked a much better financial game than he delivered. He always considered it to be a badge of honor that he was able to compete with multimillionaires such as Hilton and Lamar Hunt. What he never understood was that many people resented his Irish *chutzpah*, preferring to have as the primary owner of a major local sports franchise someone who actually had some money. Everything about the franchise was second-rate, the aforementioned players (and many others) excepted.

But say this for Billy Sullivan: he was able to keep the franchise afloat long enough to hit the jackpot. When the NFL and AFL announced their merger in 1966, the Boston Patriots assured membership in a very important club.

But nothing was ever easy for the Patriots. They schlepped around from inadequate stadium to inadequate stadium, playing the 1969 season at Boston College before begging their way into ancient Harvard Stadium in 1970, but not before being forced to listen to the sanctimonious wailing of various Cantabridgians bemoaning the campus invasion of these, these *professionals*!

They haggled for years with various municipal officials before arriving at the conclusion that they were never going to get a stadium in Boston, and so it was with great reluctance that Sullivan & Co. accepted an offer to get a stadium on land adjacent to a race track owned by E.M. Loew. Schaefer Stadium was constructed in nine months for less than $7 million.

Since the team would no longer be playing in Boston, it had to be renamed. Sullivan's first instinct was to call his team the Bay State Patriots. Then someone asked him to think about the ramifications of the "B" and the "S." For one of the few times in his life, Billy Sullivan paid attention to something someone else was saying. It was decided to call the team the 'New England' Patriots.

151

Their first taste of NFL success was due to one wise Sullivan decision. After failing in an attempt to woo Penn State coach Joe Paterno (Sullivan shadowed the Nittany Lion mentor at the 1973 Sugar Bowl), he turned to Oklahoma's wildly successful coach, Chuck Fairbanks. Sullivan's faith in his new coach/general manager was immediately rewarded when Fairbanks made some sensational selections in the 1973 draft. The Patriots were in possession of three first-round picks and Fairbanks used them to take guard John Hannah, wide receiver Darryl Stingley and fullback Sam (Bam) Cunningham, all three of whom would be key figures on one of the two best Patriots teams in the first 36 years of their existence — the 1976 club that came within one game of getting to the Super Bowl.

The Fairbanks regime would end in extreme acrimony, but not before he constructed a team that was clearly of Super Bowl caliber. That '76 team went 11-3 and was pushing the Oakland Raiders all over the Oakland Coliseum field (leading, 21-10) before Kenny Stabler led a comeback. The Raiders pulled it out, 24-21, but what Patriots' fans still talk about was a key roughing the passer call by referee Ben Dreith on Ray (Sugar Bear) Hamilton, who, alleged the official, hit Stabler after he released the football.

Sullivan fired Fairbanks on the eve of the 1978 playoffs, claiming that he had caught his coach negotiating with the University of Colorado while still under contract to the Patriots.

The Patriots finally got to the Super Bowl in 1986. It was the climax of a three-year building period under Raymond Berry, the once-great Baltimore Colts receiver who had something of a mystical approach to coaching. He often spoke in code, he frequently quoted scripture, and he had excellent rapport with most of the players because he was no screamer and yeller. His team was a wild card entry, and it became the first, and thus far the only, NFL squad to reach the Super Bowl by winning three road games.

The game itself was a colossal nightmare. The Patriots had the distinct misfortune of running into one of the great one-season teams of all time. That Chicago team has gone down in history as perhaps the pre-eminent defensive team of them all. The Jim McMahon-led offense wasn't bad that day, either. The Patriots lost, 46-10.

At this point in their history the Patriots were firmly established, but not what you would call beloved. Greater Boston was the only metropolitan area in the country in which the professional football team was an unquestioned fourth in the local pecking order. You would not know this had you been present during the month of January 1986, when the Patriots were making their thoroughly improbable march to New Orleans and the Super Bowl. There was enormous football euphoria. Entrepreneurs couldn't print up the "Squish The Fish" or "Berry The Bears" T-shirts fast enough before the Miami and Chicago games. The Patriots, for perhaps the first time in their existence, were the prime topic of conversation at every water cooler in every office in town.

But Boston was not New York, where Giants season tickets have been parcelled out in wills and divorce decrees. Boston was not Denver, where every John Elway sneeze and bowel movement was a stop-the-press bulletin. It was transitory. The Patriots were a phenomenon, not a way of life. Things gradually slid back to normal, in every way. The Patriots could not count on unconditional civic love. By 1992, the last year before Sheriff Bill Parcells was hired to clean up the mess, the Patriots had the lowest season ticket base in the league, a measly 17,000.

Billy Sullivan was once described by an enemy as a "smiling cobra," but he wasn't doing much smiling over the next few years. Finances were a constant problem. A scheme hatched by his son Chuck, a New York-based attorney, to back the Michael Jackson "Victory" Tour turned into a disaster of almost unimaginable proportions, as the gullible Number One Son was fleeced by both the Jackson Family and Don King. Sullivan needed money to pay disgruntled stockholders. The truth is he always needed money, period.

The Patriots were the product of Billy Sullivan's blood, sweat and tears. He had conceived them, wet-nursed them and loved them as only a parent could. Whatever his faults, no one could ever say he didn't always want the best for his team and its fans, even if he lacked the capacity to deliver what he promised.

So it was with enormous regret that he was forced to sell his beloved Pats to Victor Kiam in 1988. He was kept on the payroll as a $250,000 a year "president," and his youngest son Patrick was retained as the general manager, but Billy was no longer the man in charge, and it hurt.

Kiam was an abysmal owner. He, too, turned out to be a financial fraud. After four disastrous years, on and off the field, Kiam sold the team to St. Louis-bred Budweiser heir James Busch Orthwein. Every New Englander with any interest in the welfare of the Patriots worried every waking second of every day that Orthwein's only interest was to move the team to his native St. Louis. Orthwein insisted throughout that he regarded himself as a caretaker, that his goal was to safeguard his investment until he could find an appropriate local buyer. It was hard to take anything he said seriously. Standing there, resplendent in double-breasted blue blazer and grey slacks, fresh drink in hand, James Busch Orthwein looked for all the world like Mel Brooks' vision of an NFL owner.

But Orthwein turned out to be a man of his word. He signed Bill Parcells as head coach and general manager in January of 1993. He came across with the money to sign first draft pick Drew Bledsoe. And he found what everyone was hoping for — a local buyer.

On January 21, 1994, James Busch Orthwein reached an agreement with Robert Kraft to sell the Patriots. A month later the deal became official. The Patriots were back under local control, and this time the man in question was someone who had been in possession of six season tickets since the first game in Schaefer Stadium back in 1971 and who actually appeared to have some money.

But let it be recorded that if this is regarded as being a story with a happy ending, that the silent hero of the tale was James Busch Orthwein. He could have done anything with the team. In the end, he did the Right Thing.

8

In Search of Credibility

If you were the 1993 New England Patriots, and you were 9-39 in the three previous years, and your season ticket base had shrunk to 18,000 or so fans, and you were the only franchise in the National Football League fourth out of four teams in terms of local interest and prestige and you were in truly desperate need of a move that would give you instant credibility, you would probably do what Patriots owner James Busch Orthwein did on January 21, 1993.

You would zip open your checkbook and you would throw money at Duane Charles (Bill) Parcells. You would convince him that it was time to stop his two-year self-imposed (and, to a large degree, health-

New England owner James Busch Orthwein's decision to sign Bill Parcells as coach resulted in the Patriots' return to the Super Bowl. (Photo©Tom Miller)

related) exile from the coaching ranks. You would tell him that he wasn't fooling anybody, that his gigs on NBC and the Madison Square Garden networks were obvious busy-work. You would tell him it was time for him to do what he might do better than anyone in the world. You would tell him to get back in the football arena on a day-to-day basis. You would give him control of your football team.

Thus did James Busch Orthwein save the New England Patriots. Thus did James Busch Orthwein start the process that would result just four years later in the second Super Bowl appearance in team history. Had this man not signed Bill Parcells to coach the New

England Patriots in January of 1993, there might not even be a New England Patriots.

James Busch Orthwein was the perfect Parcells boss in that he allowed him to do whatever he felt prudent. When Bob Kraft purchased the team at the end of Parcells' first season, things were much different. Whereas Orthwein had been a benign, hands-off and largely unseen presence who had allowed Parcells complete autonomy, Kraft would prove to be more the scrutinizing sort. He would also prove to be much more the publicity-seeking sort. In time, the Kraft management style and personality would conflict with the Parcells ego and the Parcells self-image. In the end the two would wind up like litigants in a bitter mutual divorce. But before the partnership would dissolve in bitter and phenomenally public fashion in late January and early February of 1997, the two would preside over the happiest days in the history of a very beleaguered franchise. With Bob Kraft owning and prodding and probing and questioning and just plain nudging (also signing a few hefty checks); and with Bill Parcells utilizing coaching and organizational skills bequeathed to a very few, the Patriots would rise from a 2-14 launching pad in the final pre-Parcells year to an American Football Conference championship and a berth in Super Bowl XXXI, where they would engage the mighty Green Bay Packers in a legitimate battle of football equals.

Before leaving for his home state of New Jersey with a wallet newly stuffed with pictures of Alexander Hamilton, Bill Parcells had performed an almost immeasurable service for the New England Patriots. Bill Parcells had taken the New England Patriots from the middle pages of the sports sections and gotten them onto page 1. In the middle of a legitimate American League pennant race, he had created football conversation in Boston and throughout New England. And by virtue of just being himself, he had evolved into the single biggest sports personality in the six-state region, far bigger than any player.

He was a master media manipulator. He controlled the entire agenda, and he was able to get away with it because 10 minutes with him was meatier than two hours with most coaches. He could be informative, witty, caustic, charming and insulting in a five-minute span. He was completely autocratic. Alone among NFL coaches, he forbade his assistant coaches from speaking to the press. This happens to be a preposterous pretension, but he got away with it, and he continues to get away with it in his latest incarnation as coach of the New York Jets.

Charming or nasty, he was a writer's dream. During the 1996-97 Super Bowl run, he was the O.J. to many journalists' Geraldo. His daily chats, better known as Tuna Talks, were often virtuoso performances. Had they all been collected on tape, they would have provided a stunning football education.

He had a spin on everything, including his own universally employed nickname, The Tuna. One look at him would seem to explain everything. Let's just say he has to shop in the Big Man's department. The nickname would seem to be extremely apropos.

But that wasn't his version. *His* version is something very different.

According to Bill Parcells, he acquired the nickname in 1980, when the Starkist Tuna people had an ad campaign featuring a know-it-all tuna named Charlie. Parcells says it stemmed from a practice field situation in which he said to a player, "You think I'm Charlie the Tuna?" or some such thing. That's his story, and he's sticking to it.

What's undeniable and not subject to negotiation is the record. He made the Patriots respectable by the end of his first season, when, after a 1-11 start, they won their last four games. He steered them into the playoffs in Year 2. The third year was a step back (6-10), but the team never really recovered from a shoulder injury sustained by Drew Bledsoe in the fourth game of the season.

Parcells was very displeased with himself in the aftermath of the 1995 season. He thought he had not run a tough enough training camp and he also thought he could have coached better. He said that the 1996 camp would be "a camp like 1985 — a *Giants* camp." And everyone knew what had taken place at the end of the 1985 season. The Giants had gone to the 1986 Super Bowl. Final score: New York 39, Denver 20.

And by all accounts he had run just that kind of camp. The inside word was that the camp was a cross between basic training at Parris Island and a re-enactment of *Beau Geste*.

Away from the field, everything was said to be copasetic between the fidgety owner and the feisty coach, even though there was reason to believe the contrary. The storm clouds had already been brewing, dating back to Draft Day, when the owner had sided with player personnel director Bobby Grier against his coach on the subject of the first pick. Parcells wanted defensive help, but the owner reasoned that he had just invested some $42 million in a new contract for quarterback Drew Bledsoe, and the QB needed someone to throw to. No one on the outside world then knew the depth of the rift between the two. All the outside world then knew was that Bill Parcells had been signed by James Busch Orthwein with the understanding that he would have the final say on all personnel matters, that he no longer had that authority and that he was, at the very least, agitated.

Kraft went out of his way to play down The Troubles. "You can see how Bill and I interact on the field," said Kraft, referring to public chats back at the Rhode Island practice field. "Everything's fine. We're in this thing together. The goal of all of us is to make the team better. Bill and I are getting along fine."

The exhibition season was satisfactory. The first foe was, interestingly enough, Green Bay. Parcells liked the idea. "I very much like to play the Green Bay Packers. Lambeau Field's a wonderful place to play. The stadium's been redone, the game's a sellout, it's almost like a regular-season environment. And I think it's good for the team."

One of the beauties of NFL exhibition games is the fact that there are seldom any losers. Anybody can rationalize anything. In this case the Patriots were able to rationalize a 24-7 loss by noting that the game had been very competitive when both teams were employing their first offensive and defensive units. The Patriots could also reason that Drew Bledsoe had looked like someone heading to the Pro Bowl, connecting on 11 of 12 pass attempts for 140 yards, one touchdown and one interception.

After that game, the other coaches did all the rationalizing as the Patriots walked all over Dallas, Washington and Philadelphia.

There was one classic Parcells exhibition season flap. First draft pick Terry Glenn, the Grier-Kraft first-round pick, was not able to participate in practices or exhibition games because of a pulled hamstring. Asked one day in a quite innocent manner how the rookie was progressing with his injury, Parcells started out, "Well, *she's*," and he didn't have to go any farther. The press had its story for the day. And this baby had, as they say in show biz, "legs."

What Parcells was doing was reinforcing the ultramacho image of the football coach. Parcells is wary of rookies in the first place. Then consider that this kid was not merely a rookie, nor merely a number one pick. He was a symbol of a deteriorating relationship between the coach and the owner. The amused media was free to assume that the real object of the Parcells barb was not Glenn, but Kraft.

All his latent frustration with his changing situation leapt out with that line. Glenn himself was not flustered. He was a savvy kid. To him, it didn't mean a damn thing other than his new coach was irked because the prize prospect was unavailable for duty. Glenn was bright. He knew all about Tuna's reputation. Glenn couldn't help it if both the press and various women's organizations were going to make a big deal out of this.

Bill Parcells is always serious in the pursuit of football excellence, but this time the players knew he was not merely serious, but *serious*. He had negotiated himself out of the final year of the five-year contract he had signed with Orthwein, but no one was exactly certain what that meant in the long run. In the short run, he was as dedicated to the task as he had ever been. He was coaching them as if he were being paid by the minute. He felt he had never really been able to reach the 1995 team. He has often spoken of his annual postseason ritual, wherein he cross-examines himself to see what kind of a job he has done. He didn't like the answers he was giving himself about 1995. He was determined that in 1996 the world would see both the real New England Patriots and the real Bill Parcells.

Assessing the upcoming season in as objective a manner as possible, he believed that, given reasonable health, he had a team that could accomplish a great deal. The schedule was more than manageable. The opponents had a combined 1995 winning percentage of .495. The interconference opponents were coming from the NFC East, a conference which was deteriorating. And whereas in 1995 the Patriots had to play such playoff-bound teams as San Francisco, Kansas City, Pittsburgh and Atlanta — all on the road — this year they would be playing Jacksonville, Baltimore, Denver and San Diego. At the start of the season, the idea of either Denver or Jacksonville being considered among the league's elite was remote.

He did have one major concern — the first two games were in Miami and Buffalo. Both teams were division rivals, and both figured to be rugged opponents. The Miami game would be Jimmy Johnson's Dolphins debut, while Buffalo was, well, Buffalo. It would be very easy for the Patriots to get off to an 0-2 start. He had a young team, with an accompanying fragile psyche. A veteran team could handle an 0-2 start. He wasn't sure this team could.

Bill Parcells had ample reason to fear two people in Miami. The first was Jimmy Johnson and the second was Dan Marino.

For two years Jimmy Johnson had been South Florida's resident football government in exile. After parting company with Jerry Jones and the Dallas Cowboys he had contented himself with hanging around his houseboat and making breezy, flippant remarks on football gab shows. He had turned down the head coaching job in Tampa, partly because he had little faith in Buccaneers quarterback Trent Dilfer and partly because he was content to await the inevitable and then secure the actual job of his dreams.

He wanted to coach the Miami Dolphins.

He didn't want to appear *too* anxious for the job. After all, Dolphins coach Don Shula was pretty close to the most respected man in Florida. But he couldn't just couldn't restrain himself before the 1995 season. He picked the Dolphins to win the Super Bowl.

You can imagine how grateful coach Shula was for the endorsement.

Now the job was his. Shula had finally been forced out by Dolphins owner Wayne Huizenga. And if there was anything Jimmy Johnson wanted it was to make a good impression on both the fans of South Florida and the NFL in general.

The Patriots cooperated, playing as if they had been rounded up at random at Green Airport in Providence and given a few elementary instructions on how to behave on the flight to Florida. The final score was exceptionally kind to them. It was 24-10, but it felt more like 124-10.

"We got whipped very, very soundly," said Bill Parcells, "and I knew it wasn't our best. I told the players, if it was, we're in trouble. I know we can do better. We'll just have to see what happens next week."

Bledsoe actually threw for more yardage than the great Dan Marino, but that only served to illustrate just how deceptive sports numbers can be. Marino threw for a modest 176 yards (and, unbelievably, no touchdowns), simply because he didn't have to throw for any more. In a radical departure from modern Miami tradition, Marino was actually blessed with a running game in the person of Karim Abdul-Jabar, who picked up 115 yards in 26 carries.

The Dolphins controlled the line of scrimmage. There were seven runs of nine or more yards and five of 12 or longer. That's ugly. Johnson had decided earlier in the week that his team could simply line up behind left guard Keith Sims and left tackle Richmond Webb and run right over the Patriots. Come Sunday, that's exactly what they did.

"They pretty much manhandled us up front," admitted linebacker Chris Slade.

Bledsoe threw for a fraudulent 222 yards. He couldn't move the team inside the Red Zone (i.e., inside the 20-yard line). He threw a horrible interception to Louis Oliver. He would easily have been responsible for five interceptions had the Miami defensive backs been able to hold onto the ball.

Another Patriot who would have preferred to make the return trip to New England with a bag over his head was Shawn Jefferson, a veteran wide receiver the Patriots signed as a free agent during the off-season. On two separate occasions he made a reception and then fumbled the ball away when hit after turning back inside in a vain attempt to pick up additional yardage. His day ended in symbolic style when he sustained a concussion when hit by demonic Miami rookie linebacker Zach Thomas. Jefferson wound up spending the night in a Miami hospital, which, come to think of it, wasn't a bad thing. That way he didn't have to look at Parcells. Or Parcells at him.

The question one week later was whether or not Parcells and offensive coordinator Ray Perkins had outsmarted themselves with their play selection on the final play of the game. Parcells, you shouldn't be surprised to learn, said no. He said he'd authorize the same play call, in the same situation, again. But this time he'd prefer everyone to make his assigned block.

The situation: Buffalo leading the Patriots, 17-10. Patriots' ball on the Buffalo two-yard line. Just enough time left for one offensive play.

The decision was to give the ball to Dave Meggett on a draw play and allow him to skip into the end zone. It might have worked, too, if only Max Lane had made his block on Buffalo defensive end Phil Hansen. Max may have zigged when he was supposed to zag. Whatever happened, Hansen broke through and tackled Meggett.

But this game was lost long before. The Patriots could not take advantage of superb field position in the first half. Given the football in such locations as their own 41, the Buffalo 41 and the Buffalo 45, they had come away with three points. That was the first-half story. In the second half the Patriots took over on their own 40, the Buffalo 38 and the Buffalo 33. Total point potential: 42. Actual points: 10.

You screw up like that, you deserve to lose.

The defense was not exactly a bargain, either. Buffalo scored one touchdown when a blitz call on a Buffalo third-and-23 resulted in a blown coverage and a touchdown pass from Jim Kelly to Quinn Early.

It was an all-around Patriots' mess. A fake field goal at the Buffalo 11 turned into an incomplete pass. Rookie kicker Adam Vinatieri was 1-for-4. Two of his kicks hit the upright. Meggett, a veteran kick returner with great hands, fumbled away a kickoff at the 15, leading to the first Buffalo TD. Chris Slade intercepted a pass, stumbled around, hit the deck, and then, thinking the play was over, left the football on the ground. Sorry, Chris. No one had hit you. The ball was live. Hot. Free. Up for grabs.

Bledsoe? Don't ask. He was 21-for-46 for 210 yards and one touchdown. Ah, but the touchdown pass was caught by Terry Glenn. "I thought he did all right," grunted the Tuna. "Nobody's perfect."

The press corps braced itself for a classic Parcells postgame tirade. The Patriots had made a sickening number of mistakes.

Well, guess what? The Tuna was Mr. Optimist.

"That was a hard-fought game," he said. "I thought both teams fought real hard...I think there is something to build on here," he said. "I think if we continue to get that kind of effort, we'll win quite a few games."

He said it was "too early" to worry about the team's impotence inside the Red Zone. He stuck up for his field-goal kicker, saying "he will be all right." And he admitted that, as anyone could see, enough was enough. Losing at Miami in a Jimmy Johnson *jihad* wasn't totally unexpected and losing at Rich Stadium to the four-time AFC champion Bills wasn't a shock, but 0-2 was as far as it could go if the team was to get its way back into the playoffs. Suddenly the upcoming contest with the Arizona Cardinals wasn't merely a game. Now it was a crusade.

"This week's a critical week for us, without question," he said. "I think we need a win, or a couple of wins here. If we don't, we're gonna be in trouble. But I think we'll be all right. I know not a lot of people in here (i.e., the media) do, but I think we (are going to be all right). I saw some pretty good improvement. If we can smooth out a few things we'll do better."

One thing which did concern him was Drew Bledsoe. His quarterback had developed a phobia concerning the dump-off pass. It was a variation of "Steve Sax Disease," the allusion to the ex-Dodger second baseman who suddenly found himself unable to make the routine throw on a simple ground ball. Bledsoe had no technical problem with the medium or the long pass, but he was consistently bouncing screen passes or dump-off passes. Parcells had referred to the need for his receivers to make what he called the "American League Play of the Week" in order to catch Bledsoe's short passes.

"You could grab a guy off the street and he can throw it five yards and hit Dave Meggett and you take that for granted sometimes," Bledsoe acknowledged. "I try and make it easy for them to catch...if you throw it too hard, it's a tough play. But it's something I have to be more accurate with. To say it's frustrating to me is an understatement."

He had no need to apologize for anything after the Arizona game. Once again the final numbers were lying little bastards. So he finished with not especially dazzling totals of 21-for-35 and 221 yards.

The reality was that Drew Bledsoe had pistol-whipped the Cardinals and was one of the primary reasons the Patriots helped themselves to a comforting 31-0 victory.

Backed by Ray Perkins' superb, imaginative game plan, Bledsoe was 9-for-12 for 112 yards and a touchdown in the first period. He finished with three TD passes and he jacked up the crowd with a rare run for a first down and an even rarer spike of the football after securing a first down for his ballclub.

"My confidence has been there all along," he said. "I don't doubt myself. Ever. We have been saying all along we have the talent to play and be very competitive in this league. We know we have that talent, but when you're 0-2 you wonder what's going on. It was important for us to come out and demonstrate that the talent we have is not an illusion."

The defense matched the offense with a shutout. Meggett returned five punts for 87 yards. Offense. Defense. Special Teams. That should pretty much cover it.

"This," declared defensive end Willie McGinest, "is the *real* Patriots."

Parcells was subdued. He wasn't going to gush over this team simply doing what it was capable of doing, and doing it at home against a very sorry opponent. "We were pretty good in every phase of the game," he said. "If we play like this, we can be competitive with anybody. If we play the way we did the first week, we won't be competitive with anybody."

Just in case anyone forgot.

Kraft was a bit more ebullient. "Our fans deserve this," beamed the owner. "I think our season began today, and this is when you should start judging our team."

One more game, and then the players could enjoy their bye week. Second-year team Jacksonville was the next opponent. "They ought to be a good test for us," Parcells said. "They have a good, scrappy team and good talent, particularly offensively."

Most people laughed, but The Tuna knew whereof he spoke. After going ahead by a 22-0 score, the Patriots were fortunate to escape with a 25-22 victory in overtime.

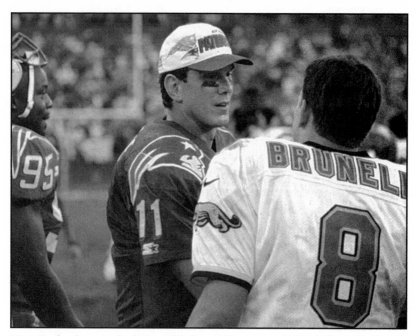

New England quarterback Drew Bledsoe (11) meets with Mark Brunell after the Patriots' 25-22 victory. A few months later they were facing each other again for the AFC championship. (Photo©Tom Miller)

The big problem was the New England inability to combat the well-known desperation play known as the "Hail Mary" pass. The Jaguars scored on one such pass late in the first half when a Mark Brunell heave into the Pats' end zone deflected off a falling Willie Clay's leg and was caught by Jimmy Smith for a touchdown. The play almost worked again in the final series of regulation. With eight seconds left Brunell flung another one in the direction of the end zone. Jacksonville's Willie Jackson caught the ball while falling backward. The officials ruled that he was a foot or so shy of the end zone. "When you're at home, you get that call," said an aggravated Jackson. "I reached up with one hand and when I twisted and landed, the ball was in my chest and my body was over the line." Fortunately for the Patriots, the officials did not agree. Vinatieri won the game in overtime with a 40-yard field goal for his first game-winning NFL kick.

The good points in the game included six Glenn receptions for 89 yards and the big kick by Vinatieri, who needed a boost after his tough afternoon in Buffalo.

166

Parcells on the "Hail Mary" epidemic: "We've been playing pretty much the same defense for 10 years on that thing, but that is the first time I can recall being victimized by it. I know they didn't do anything special. They just heaved it up there and you have to make the play. You see a game like that, and you know why the NFL is exciting. I am getting a little too old for those."

Thank God for the bye week.

More than one Patriots offensive coordinator, Ray Perkins among them, has been criticized over the years for lacking imagination. But there was no such complaint in the Baltimore game as Bledsoe passed on first down 14 times in 18 opportunities as the Patriots spanked the Ravens, 48-36.

The great revelation in this one was the improved work in the Red Zone. We all discovered how the team had been spending its practice time after watching Bledsoe and friends execute their offense inside the 20.

"With our bye week, we worked on some Red Zone passes," explained Bledsoe, who threw on 12 of 17 downs inside the Red Zone. "We were kind of excited about getting them into the game and seeing if our new toy worked."

Shawn Jefferson was officially welcomed to the fold with four passes, good for 88 yards. And second-year running back Curtis Martin perked up with some fancy running.

Bledsoe was wonderfully democratic in the dispersal of his passes, completing them to seven different receivers, including a career-first touchdown to tight end-long snapper Mike Bartrum.

The Tuna had plenty to worry about, however, as he watched his defense take a collective *siesta* after the Patriots had constructed a comfortable 38-14 fourth-quarter lead. He had seen the same thing in the Jacksonville game.

If Parcells thought a collapse was imminent, his fears were justified the following week when the Patriots were beaten at home by the Washington Redskins in what had been billed as a battle of young contenders. "We're having trouble," said Parcells. "We had problems in the secondary, but it was the whole defense...the discipline was lax. It's a discipline breakdown."

The offense also suffered a relapse. Potential in six trips to the Red Zone: 42 points. Actual tally: 22 points. Not good, when you wind up losing by five.

Meggett suggested the team had paid the price for a lazy work week. "It's like making deposits in the bank all week and then going to the bank on Saturday and Sunday and trying to make a withdrawal and you can't," he said.

People even had reason to question The Tuna's judgment after Martin, having gained 164 yards, was essentially told to go sit on the bench and don't bother anybody when the team fell behind by a 24-16 score.

"We couldn't go out there and just run the ball because he was going good," Parcells explained. "There were only 10 minutes left, and we were down by eight. That's two scores to me."

The next four games were against division opponents. They weren't necessarily glamour games, but in the Tuna's eyes they were vitally important games in which it was necessary to concentrate. If you're gonna win the division, he reasoned, then you'd damn well better win the division games, especially if you're already 0-2 in the division.

Good thing there are no such items as style points in the NFL. If there were, the score in the RCA Dome would have been New England 0, Indianapolis 0.

This was the heist of the year. The Patriots played a putrid first half and didn't ever do much of anything offensively. But they walked off with a 27-9 victory.

Indy could easily have led by a 28-0 score at the half. Instead they were down 10-6 after rookie defensive lineman Devin Wyman forced a Cliff Groce fumble and Bledsoe hit Glenn for an eight-yard TD pass and Vinatieri added a field goal on the heels of a 28-yard Meggett punt return.

The Colts penetrated to the New England 5, 4, 8 and 18, and from those four superb opportunities they generated a mere six points.

So credit the defense and credit the special teams. "We played real good on special teams," said Parcells. "Our punter (Tom Tupa) was magnificent. Our coverage was good. I feel real positive about

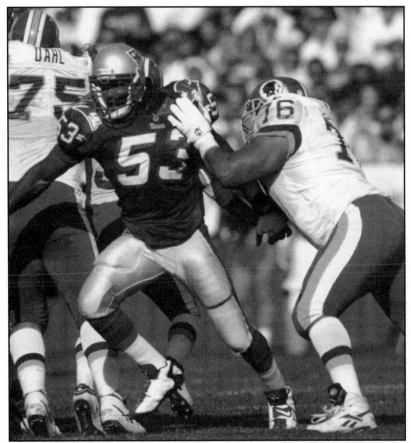

Chris Slade is pushed around by a Washington lineman in the Patriots' 27-22 loss.
(Photo©Tom Miller)

our punt return, our kickoff return and our kickoff coverage," he continued.

One more thing. "Turnovers," he said, "are the most significant statistic in football, and our game was a good case in point."

And let the record show that for the first time in the 1996 season the Tuna was heard to utter one very significant "P"-word.

"I'm proud of these guys," he said. "They came in here and did a good job."

Drew Bledsoe had thrown for a whole lotta yards during the first three years, plus seven games, of his NFL career, but he had yet to have that true defining moment.

It was Sunday night football, and so the entire NFL was watching as Drew Bledsoe led the Patriots on a clutch 84-yard drive to defeat the Buffalo Bills, 28-25. Taking over with the B team trailing, 18-15, and just 2:47 remaining, Drew Bledsoe did the first big John Elway imitation of his career.

It was a great win for the Patriots, and for Parcells, who has enormous respect for septuagenarian Buffalo mentor Marv Levy.

"Every year the media and the fans say, 'What's the matter with the Buffalo Bills?'" Parcells had said earlier in the week. "But they're always there. They're always in the picture."

Bledsoe took the team those 84 yard not once throwing in the direction of Ben Coates, Shawn Jefferson or Terry Glenn. But he did complete four passes on the Big Drive, throwing to whoever happened to be open. On two occasions that man happened to be Troy Brown, a versatile special teamer-returner-wide receiver.

"He may not have all the size or all the speed," lauded Bledsoe, "but I'll throw to him any time."

The game marked the Pats' debut of Keith Byars, a well-seasoned and well-rounded fullback who had been deemed expendable by Jimmy Johnson in Miami, and who had introduced himself to his mates by catching seven passes. "I know I have a lot to offer this team," he declared.

The ending was again scary. After Curtis Martin scored the go-ahead touchdown on a 10-yard run, Vinatieri missed the extra point. McGinest picked off a Jim Kelly pass and returned it for a TD, and it *still* wasn't over, because Kelly connected on a — are you ready? — Hail Mary pass to make it 28-25. One unsuccessful onside kick later (the ball recovered, fittingly, by Byars), and one Bledsoe kneel-down later, the game came to its conclusion.

Afterward, everyone wanted to talk about Bledsoe, who had gone 32-for-45, good for 372 yards. "If you continue to affect the outcome of games by big plays," said Parcells, "then you've become a dominant player."

The Parcells dream of sweeping those four division games came closer to becoming reality when the Patriots smacked around the Dolphins by a 42-23 score. Bledsoe sliced them up with 419 yards and three

Miami coach Jimmy Johnson(left) may have been smiling before the game, but Parcells was the one smiling after New England's 42-23 win. (Photo©Tom Miller)

touchdowns. Glenn had 10 catches for 112 yards. Bledsoe had become the master chef, and he knew he was fast becoming the envy of the AFC because he so many choice ingredients in the cupboard.

"We have as many weapons as probably anyone in the league right now," he declared. Living up to his image as an equal opportunity feeder, he completed passes to nine different receivers.

Keith Byars had a unique viewpoint of the New England-Miami series. "I'm the only man here who was on the winning side in *both*," he pointed out.

Bill Parcells absolutely dreaded Game 9, because Game 9 was against the New York Jets, whom everyone from Fairbanks to Ft. Lauderdale believed to be the worst football team in the league.

When The Tuna looked at the films, he didn't see a 1-8 football team. He saw a team with a terrific running back in Adrian Murrell, with some good pass receivers and with a game-breaker or two on defense. He also saw a team feeling better about itself following a victory over the Cardinals just one week before.

And when the score rose to New York 21, New England 0, The Tuna was ready with the "I-told-ya-sos."

Then reality set in, both ways. After a no-show first period, Bledsoe threw for 24 completions, 297 yards and three touchdowns in the final three periods.

The critical juncture in the game occurred in the fourth period. The Jets were ahead, 27-24 and the Patriots had a fourth-and-2 at their own 49 with just over six minutes to go. Parcells had only two weeks before publicly taken the pledge by saying he was through going for dangerous first downs on fourth down.

So naturally he went for it.

Bledsoe threw a pass to Coates in the flat. The big tight end was brought down close to the Jets' 49, and just about everyone in Giants Stadium assumed he was short of the first down. Well, there was this one dissenter, and he just happened to be referee Charles Stewart. He gave the Patriots a very generous spot for a first down. Five plays later Bledsoe hit Byars for the game-winning touchdown pass.

What bad first quarter? The Patriots had outscored the Jets, 31-6, when it really mattered.

So there it was. The Patriots had their four straight division wins. And curmudgeonly Bill Parcells was admitting in public what was becoming increasingly obvious to one and all. He was now in love with his football team.

"This *is* a team," he said. "No doubt about it. We may lose what's left on the schedule, but as long as they're out there trying their best not to lose, that's all a coach can ask."

He had perused the Jets' game and come away with a renewed adoration for both teams. "I admire what (Jets coach) Rich Kotite is doing," he said. "I really do. They don't have a whole lot to show for what they've been doing, but I have some compassion. He's done a pretty good job of holding them in there."

And as for his own team..."One more turnover, one blocked kick, one long pass and we lose the game. No doubt about it."

He elaborated on his team's psyche a little more. "From the beginning this team has done what I asked them to," he pointed out. "And once you get something invested, it's harder to surrender."

The Tuna was feeling philosophical, but not for long. There was too much work to do, because the next opponents on the schedule were the Denver Broncos.

The 9-1 Denver Broncos.

◆   ◆   ◆

The Broncos weren't supposed to be major AFC factors at the beginning of the season, but they had made some personnel changes and they were getting a John Elway performance out of John Elway, who, it was only pointed out 40 or 50,000 times, had never lost to the Patriots. Because the Patriots were on a roll, and because they were at home, they were even installed as slight favorites. Parcells thought that was ridiculous. He was afraid that the press was starting to get a bit carried away with his team, and he was even more afraid his team would start believing everything it was now reading about itself.

What The Tuna believed was quite simple and straightforward. He believed he had a good team that had a chance to become a very good team, the key words being "a chance."

"We're 7-3," he said, "and like I always say, you are what your record says you are. We still have some things to get resolved, and if we don't, we won't go very far. This isn't going to be smooth sailing. But we do have a chance to do something."

As usual, Tuna knew more than we knew. He wasn't at all sure the Patriots were ready for this challenge. He was right.

The Broncos scored first. The Broncos scored second. The Broncos scored third. So had the Jets, but these weren't the Jets. The final score was 34-8. Welcome to reality.

"We were completely outclassed," said Parcells. "We had no chance to win this game. This is very disappointing. I can't put my finger on why we responded the way we did. Maybe it was the pressure of the big game. Maybe we're just not ready for that. I don't know. A lot of it was poor tackling. If that's the team that shows up to play, we won't win another game. I don't know who was wearing those jerseys today. That's what I told them after the game."

Parcells may have himself set the negative tone with either a (pick one) bold, creative, curious or lunkhead decision on the Patriots' first possession of the game. It was fourth-and-one at their own 32 on the game's first series. Parcells sent out the punt team.

But Tupa, a quarterback by trade who had once thrown for 312 yards and three touchdowns against the Patriots while wearing an Arizona uniform, took the snap and began to search for a receiver.

173

Fake punt! He threw to linebacker Tedy Bruschi, who was open at the 45. He dropped the ball. After all, his name was Bruschi, not Glenn. Five plays later Terrell Davis was taking it in from the 15-yard line. Forget the team. The entire stadium audience was deflated.

"I wanted some momentum," said Parcells. "It was a perfectly executed play. We just didn't make the play and dropped the ball."

"I dropped it," said Bruschi, a definite stand-up guy..."I (censored) up. It would have been a big play for us."

Tedy Bruschi's oopsie didn't lose the game. The Patriots never generated any serious offense. Bledsoe had a brutal day. The Broncos toyed with the home team, and then exercised their woof privileges.

"It was supposed to be tougher than that," said tight end Shannon Sharpe. "They were supposed to be Goliath. We came in as nobodies and we looked at the Patriots and said, 'Let's kick some butt.' We did that Now we're the best team in the AFC."

It was Game 11. Life would go on.

After going through what Parcells would call "the worst week of practice for me all season," the Patriots rebounded with a convincing 27-13 triumph over Indianapolis. Right from the start, the offensive game plan was evident.

Here is how it went on the Patriots' first possession: Martin, Martin, Martin, Martin, Martin, Martin, Martin, pass, Martin, Martin, Martin, field goal.

And here is how it went on the second New England possession: Martin, Martin, Martin, pass, Martin, Martin, Martin, Martin, Martin, pass, Martin touchdown pass.

Having ridden Curtis Martin to victory, Parcells said he hoped not to do anything like that in the future. "He'll always do what you ask," Parcells said. "But he's gonna have a short career if we continue to give him the ball 35 times."

The big question after the Denver debacle was just how brutal the practices were going to be, and just how cantankerous The Tuna himself would be. But he demonstrated why he is such a great leader by fooling everyone. For the most part, the bombastic Tuna was Mr. Silent. He wanted to see if he had internal leadership, without which there can never be a championship team at this level.

"The players got themselves together," Parcells was happy to report. "I really didn't have much to do with this one."

It wasn't quite that simple. Parcells altered the routine, and when someone like The Tuna alters the routine, players get the message that they are now engaged in very serious business. Corwin Brown summed up the reaction of all the players when they arrived at practice on Friday, normally a light, walk-through kind of day. On this particular Friday the players were told to strap on the pads. "We knew this was an important week when he did that," Brown explained. "Nine in the morning? We hadn't even watched films yet, and we were practicing. When he did that, we all thought '*Whoa*.' I got a sense then that he really, *really* wanted to win the game. We left here last week with our tail between our legs."

The Indy momentum carried over. San Diego was next and the Chargers were embarrassed in front of their own fans. The Patriots beat them 45-7, and now the air was filled with playoff talk.

With this powerful display the Patriots were tied with Buffalo for first place in the AFC East and in possession of the necessary tie-breakers. They could actually start talking about and planning on the playoffs, and not just sneaking into the playoffs, either. They could fantasize about the entire package — the division title, the first-round bye and the home field.

'I'm so excited," said Kraft. "It's a wonderful thing, and this is why you get into the business. I've always said there are easier ways to make money, but it doesn't get any better than this. Now we just have to keep it going."

As so often happens in sport, one play affected the course of the entire game. The second-quarter sequence began with the Patriots leading by a 14-7 score and Tupa punting the ball out of bounds on the Charger 2. Quarterback Stan Humphries, who would take a frightful beating before the night was over, then hit receiver Charlie Jones at about the San Diego 40. Jones appeared to have made a sensational diving catch to get his team out of trouble, but the official on the spot ruled that he had caught the ball on the bounce, video tape evidence to the contrary.

On the next play, Ferric Colons deflected a Humphries pass and linebacker Ted Johnson picked it off. Bledsoe hooked up with fullback Sam Gash for a 7-yard touchdown pass, and the Chargers were never in the game again.

The players were, of course, quite taken with themselves. "None of us could have imagined this," said Willie McGinest. "To travel this far and beat a good team like this handily..."

Enter The Tuna with a more sobering analysis. "I wouldn't make too much of this if I were you," he groused. "But if we play like we did tonight, we're gonna be effective."

As the Patriots were readying themselves for a perfunctory 34-10 dispatch of the Jets, Professor Parcells was broadening the parameters of Football 101, the ongoing course he was conducting for the benefit of the players, media and, by extension, the fans.

For some time he had been discoursing on the difference between a "club fighter" and a champion, about how a club fighter is content to remain at a certain level of competence and how a champion aspires to something greater.

Now the part-owner of two thoroughbreds was about to change sporting analogies. "The third month is over," he told them. "We're starting the fourth quarter. For you racing guys, we're at the top of the stretch. We've got to go three wide and go to the whip now. We're in the hunt at the end of the season. No doubt about that. But we've got to win a couple more to get into the tournament."

Only one bad thing came out of this game. Valued fullback Sam Gash, little appreciated by the public but almost revered by his teammates, injured his knee and would be lost for the season. What made this even more disturbing was the fact that he had been done in by the wretched Foxboro Stadium grass field and not the New York Jets. Trying to make a cut on a bad field made worse by overnight rains, he tried to go one way while his knee tried to go a way nature never intended.

Gash would be missed, both for his superb blocking and for his pass catching ability. He was one of those receivers who *always* got you additional yardage after the catch.

There had been some interesting off-the-field news during the week. It had been everyone's understanding that when Parcells had met with Kraft the previous January in order to negotiate his way out of the fifth year of the contract he had signed with Orthwein it meant this would be his final year of coaching, period. But now Parcells' agent, Robert Fraley, was saying this was not necessarily the case. Fraley reported that Parcells wished to remain in coaching "in the right situation."

The public was confused. What exactly, they wanted to know, was wrong with the current situation? Why would he be interested in walking away from such a young, talented team? The only conceivable answer: he no longer wished to work for Bob Kraft. From this point on, the issue of Parcells' future was Topic A, more often than not overshadowing whatever good things the team was accomplishing on the field.

Oh, one more thing. With this victory, the Patriots were in the playoffs. "It's the first time in 37 years we made the playoffs with two weeks to go," Kraft gushed. "Did you know that?"

Things were really looking up. They were in the playoffs, but it did not have to end there. They were in sole possession of first place in the division. There was now a very real chance of getting a first-round bye because the Patriots had the tiebreaking edge should they wind up tied with Pittsburgh.

◆ ◆ ◆

The penultimate game of the season was intriguing: New England at Dallas.

No one had been fooled by an easy exhibition victory over Dallas. Many of the Cowboys' stars had been out of the lineup. Beating the 'Boys in exhibition play didn't mean squat.

It had not been a smooth season for the Cowboys, who were beset with injuries and problems in what we shall refer to as the extra-curriculars. The tangible manifestation of the injuries was a low-octane offense. They had been surviving on defense and on the right foot of kicker Chris Boniol, who had kicked seven field goals in a victory over Green Bay.

But the defense was in good shape. They were still the Cowboys and they were playing at home. The Patriots had no illusions.

177

There wouldn't be much scoring. Everyone new that. The most points Dallas had scored all year was 32. Dallas had only scored five touchdowns in its four most recent games. And despite the fact that the Patriots were flying to Dallas with 79 points on the board in their last two games, nobody believed the Patriots would score a whole lot on the 'Boys, at least not in Texas Stadium.

This turned out to be a classic shoulda-coulda-woulda game from the Patriots' viewpoint. It was right *there*. The Patriots had their chances. It was an all-field goal game, and they came away 12-6 losers.

"I'm disappointed," announced The Tuna. "That game was winnable."

On the very first New England possession, Bledsoe drove the team to the Dallas 4, whereupon the Patriots discovered that being at the Dallas 4 was not the same as being at the Jets' 4 or the Colts' 4. Bledsoe threw three incompletions and Vinatieri was brought on to kick a 21-yard field goal.

They also got as far as the Dallas 13 and Dallas 16 without getting the ball into the end zone. Dallas was only marginally better on offense. The Boniol field goals were from distances of 23, 36, 35 and 29 yards.

There was a lot of nice defensive play on both sides, but the single most dramatic physical act of the day was not turned in by either an offensive or defensive player.

After the second Patriots field goal, Vintieri kicked off to Herschel Walker. The veteran burst through the usually reliable Patriots coverage and suddenly it was open spaces, extra bases. He appeared headed to the end zone when, out of the corner of your picture a Patriot player materialized. He was gaining on Walker with every step, finally hauling him down at the 25-yard line, saving, as it turned out, a touchdown. The Cowboys were forced to settle for a field goal.

So who was this masked man? Who had saved these four precious points? Special teams mainstay Larry Whigham? Corwin Brown? Marrio Greer? Which fleet young defensive back or wide receiver had run down Herschel Walker, who, at age 34, could still run, and was actually having a great year as a return man?

Turns out it wasn't any of the DBs or WRs. It was Adam Vinatieri. The *kicker*?

"I didn't know I could run that fast," admitted Vinatieri. "Herschel is older now, but he can still run. I guess the adrenaline was flowing at the time."

With this spectacular tackle Adam Vinatieri elevated himself in the eyes of his teammates. He wasn't just some geeky kicker, standing around the sidelines at practice while they were out there banging each other and taking years off their lives. No, sir. This Vinatieri kid isn't just a kicker. He's a *football player*.

Tuna has had better days than this. He admitted the play calling might have been better, and he was willing to accept the responsibility. Sort of.

"I'll take the credit," he said, meaning, of course, the blame (psychologists are hereby invited to explain the mind-set of someone who, even while admitting it, can't bring himself to a direct association with the word "blame"). Maybe we weren't quite patient enough with the running game."

But the one thing which really concerned him was the fact that the entire Dallas experience seemed to be a bit too overwhelming for a few of his players. "I think 95 percent of our guys were OK," he said. "They weren't distracted by everything that was going around. But there might have been two or three young guys...this thing might have been a little bit too much for them."

The Patriots felt a lot better about the defeat when they learned that conference rivals Buffalo, Kansas City and Pittsburgh had all lost. With one game remaining, the Patriots were in the blissful position of being able to control their own destiny. Denver would have the best record in the AFC, and would thus be at home for any and all conference playoff games. But the Patriots could become number 2. Beat the New York Giants in the Meadowlands, and they would secure a first-round bye and get a home game.

No one knew quite what to make of the Giants, a team good enough to have beaten Dallas, Minnesota and Miami (at Miami), and bad enough to have lost to the pathetic New Orleans Saints at home.

It was 22-0 at the half, the Patriots having the doughnut.

Things were so bad that when Bruce Armstrong, the great left tackle, came out of the locker room he looked up at the scoreboard and made an interesting discovery. The board read *23*-0.

Armstrong pointed this out to The Tuna and the necessary correction was made.

"Well, yeah simple mathematics," Parcells confirmed. "A safety, two field goals, two touchdowns and two extra points. That's 22."

The Patriots were worse than bad in the first half, gaining all of 21 yards in eight plays from scrimmage on their first two possessions. On the third possession Bledsoe was assessed a safety when he was called for intentional grounding in the end zone.

With 30 minutes of football left, the Patriots decided to be professionals in the second half. A Vinatieri field goal got them on the board just before the end of the third period. An 88-yard drive, finished off with a 26-yard TD pass to Glenn, made it more interesting.

Things got a *lot* more interesting when Dave Meggett took a Mike Horan line drive punt and returned it 60 yards for a touchdown to make it 22-17. It was his 31st game as a Patriot, and people had pretty much given up hope that he would ever run anything back. His timing was impeccable.

The winning drive was every bit as dramatic as the 84-yarder against Buffalo. The key play was a miraculous catch by Troy Brown at the Giants' 16 on a third-and-13 situation. Brown reached up and snatched the ball out of the air while half-sitting, half-lying.

"I've caught a couple on my back before," Brown said, "but this was the biggest one I've ever caught."

The Patriots still weren't in the end zone. On a fourth-and-7 play at the New York 13, Perkins and Parcells put Bledsoe and his skill players into a formation in which Ben Coates normally plays no part. But this time Bledsoe threw him the ball. He caught it around the two and was trying to lug a pair of Giant defenders over the goal line when suddenly he got an extra boost.

It was Meggett, shoving him from the rear. That's illegal, of course, but only if you get caught. "You saw that, huh?" winked Meggett. "It was a team type thing. The play wasn't over. I just gave him a little nudge."

Parcells on the key pass to Coates: "We didn't improvise the play. We improvised the people."

Dave Meggett's 60-yard punt return for a touchdown sparked the comeback against the Giants. (Photo©Tom Miller)

Parcells on the new AFC East titlists: "They've got champions' hearts. We may not be the best team, but this is as happy as we've been in a long time."

Parcells on what he was going to do by way of celebration after the game: "We've been at this for 23 weeks without a break. I've got my daughters with me, and we're going out for dinner and a few beers. It's Miller Time."

◆　◆　◆

Parcells had used his Giants team as a frame of reference, and why not? They had won two championships for him. And now he was willing to discuss his Patriots team in the same breath, at least on occasion.

For one thing, he was willing to say that, yes, he had started to develop as much confidence in the Patriots' offense as he once had in the vaunted Giants' defense. Secondly, he was seeing the same type of dedication and heart in this team as in the great New York teams.

"They've paid the same price," he said. "Same sweat. Same blood. Same turned ankles. Same IVs on the plane coming home. It's all the same."

With a week off the Patriots had a chance to polish things. The defense was the number one Tuna concern, because the defense is always what separates the pretenders from the true contenders. The Denver game had terrified everyone. If the Patriots weren't any better than that, they really weren't going anywhere. But they had started to play better defense, although they weren't quite up to a proper Parcells standard.

Said The Tuna, "Let me generally say, no matter what sport you coach — I don't care, any sport — until you play better defense than we are playing, you are not going to win. You *have* to play better defense. Anyone who disputes that knows nothing about sports. I don't think anyone would dispute that we have to play better defense."

Pittsburgh took out the Colts, 41-14 in the wild card round. The Steelers fit the description of the kind of team Parcells wanted. They were a defensive-oriented team which had not allowed any quarterback a 300-yard game, and which had only permitted one running back, Baltimore's Bam Morris, to gain 100 yards. The Steelers had represented the AFC in the 1996 Super Bowl and they naturally assumed they would be doing it again.

"We're not done yet," crowed linebacker Levin Kirkland after that destruction of the Colts. "We still have a lot we can accomplish. I think the national audience saw we were still (AFC) champions, and that we will be the champions until somebody beats us."

On the morning of Sunday, January 5, fog rolled into Foxboro, Massachusetts. NBC was planning on using 12 cameras, but guess

Curtis Martin rushed for 166 yards and three touchdowns in the 28-3 win over defending AFC champion Pittsburgh. (Photo©Tom Miller)

how many director Andy Rosenberg got to use? Four. Rosenberg would later say, "The pictures were as good as we could get them. It was a constant balancing act between clarity and depth of view. The fog changed the entire game."

Well, yes, the fog changed things for everybody, but nothing transpired during the course of the game to suggest the outcome would have been any different if the game had been played in clear blue skies and 78-degree weather. It was New England's day.

After his defense stopped the initial Steeler drive, Bledsoe went to work. On the first play from scrimmage, Bledsoe went deep, hitting Terry Glenn on the right sideline. Glenn, who had established a new NFL rookie record with 90 receptions, had simply gone beep-beep past Rod Woodson. The play was good for 53 yards. Martin, en route to gaining 166 yards, scored the first of his three touchdowns. The Patriots were in control, and we still had 59 minutes and 9 seconds left to play.

"Ray Perkins said we are not going to come out and be conservative," explained Glenn.

"Terry Glenn has speed," pointed out Dave Meggett, "but I know Woodson didn't know from watching film how fast Terry really is. You can't judge Terry's speed from game film...he's really *fast.*"

It quickly escalated to 14-0 and then 21-0 on a 78-yard Martin TD gallop. "That was probably my longest run ever," Martin said. "College, Pop Warner, *anything.*"

The Patriots settled for 346 yards only because Perkins, Parcells and Bledsoe went conservative in the second half, the only score being a highlight film 23-yard TD run by Martin, whose body did things on that run which were clearly anatomically impossible.

The Steelers were so badly beaten they probably still can't believe they had only lost by a 28-3 score. The Patriots never allowed them to think they were actually in the game. The most useful Steeler was punter Josh Miller, who was able to demonstrate his expertise nine times, including each of the first seven Pittsburgh possessions.

Now the working assumption all season long was that the road to the AFC title would eventually go through Denver. The Broncos had been the class of the conference all season long. The Broncos are generally tough at Mile High Stadium, if only because of the altitude problem visitors face, and they are just about unbeatable there if their team is any good at all. There couldn't have been three people in America who didn't think the Broncos, with the home-field advantage, would win the AFC title.

But that's why they play the game on the field and not on paper or a computer screen. On any given day...well, I think you know the rest. Everyone knew Denver would defeat Jacksonville at home, except they didn't. The Jaguars beat them, 30-27. The Patriots were going to be hosts of the AFC championship game.

Andy Rosenberg had nothing to worry about this time, fog-wise. Everything was great until 4:53 p.m., EST. That's when the lights went out.

Given the amount of stadium talk floating about at the time, the immediate speculation was that Bob Kraft had brazenly picked this dramatic forum to demonstrate just how badly, and how quickly, he needed a new venue for his team. But the actual source of the blackout had nothing whatsoever to do with Foxboro Stadium or the New England Patriots. The story was that a quarter-inch piece of steel twine some 12-15 inches long had burned out. The whole area had been plunged into darkness. Three repairmen from Massachusetts Electric replaced the fuse. The delay was a manageable 11 minutes.

The Patriots got an early break when rookie Jacksonville punter Bryan Barker reacted to a snap that was high, but not *too* high and decided not to punt from deep in his own territory. A veteran such as Tom Tupa would have gotten the kick off, but Barker allowed himself to be tackled at the one by special teams player *extraordianaire* Larry Wigham. Bledsoe sent Martin into the end zone. The Patriots would never trail. They would never dominate, but they would never trail.

Jaguar quarterback Mark Brunell discovered that the Patriots were not the same porous defensive unit he had shredded for 422 yards earlier in the season. This time he was held to 190.

The Patriots' special teams were magnificent. There was the aforementioned Whigham play and there was a blocked punt by Marty Moore, who created a Chris Hudson fumble which led to a Vinatieri field goal.

But the story of the game was defense, defense, defense. Willie Clay had an interception runback. Chris Slade separated James Stewart from the ball, allowing Otis Smith to pick it up and run it back 47 yards for another score.

The Patriots hardly needed an offense to ring up a 20-6 victory. And when it was over, the defenders all cited the same inspiration for their improved play — Denver 34, New England 8.

Willie McGinest shows off the AFC championship trophy after the win over Jacksonville. (Photo©Tom Miller)

"Denver?" said rookie safety Lawyer Milloy. "Embarrassing. I'm not saying everybody expected us to *beat* Denver that day, but we just didn't show up. We all knew how bad we had been."

Said The Tuna: "They can't call us club fighters anymore."

9

A Real
Football Town

Boston had officially become a football town. The town and region motto had become "In Tuna We Trust."

Patriots fever had engulfed everyone, and why not? The Celtics and Bruins had both become embarrassments and eyesores. It was too early to become fixated on the Red Sox. Anyone interested in sports who happened to live in Greater Boston had little recourse but to follow the New England Patriots who were now on their way to a Super Bowl date with the Green Bay Packers.

Here's how crazy things had gotten. On the evening of January 12, the same day on which the Patriots had defeated the Jaguars to become champions of the AFC, a 7-pound, 6-ounce baby boy was born to Tina and Donald Linscott in Anna Jacques Hospital in Newburyport, Massachusetts, a coastal town located about 35 miles northeast of Boston.

And what did they name this child? How about Curtis Martin Linscott?

"She is not a football fan," said the proud papa, "but I'm working on it. We were trying for months to come up with a name and we couldn't. One day, two months ago, I was watching a game and she heard the name Curtis Martin. She said, 'Hmmm, I like that name.' Of course, I didn't fight her."

This Patriots' euphoria had been building for four years, or ever since the day James Busch Orthwein signed Bill Parcells to put a little hair on the chest of the Patriots' franchise. That very day the Patriots sold 5,000 season tickets.

For years the Patriots had been the number four team in local esteem and Boston, though in possession of a franchise, had been left out of the national hubbub. There was the glorious month of January 1986, but when the Patriots were blown out of the Super Bowl so badly, and when within days of that humiliation it was revealed that several of the players were guilty of drug-taking, the team image did a 180. All the old Patriots' jokes — and there were plenty of them — were revived.

Now Kraft was ecstatic. Owning the Patriots was a true fantasy for a man who had long held title to tickets in section 217, row 23, seats 1 through 6. "I remember him coming home with those tickets," said son Jonathan, now a team vice president. "He was so excited, and so were we." The year was 1971. Kraft still regarded himself as a fan, and claimed to understand all the concerns of the working man. He was talking and talking and talking, probably too much. People thought he needed to get a grip when he began referring to the fans as "shareholders" in this enterprise.

Fan feeling was high because it was impossible not to have faith in Bill Parcells, who had turned out to be every bit as dynamic a coach as he was supposed to be. Life is, for most people, an endless string of disappointments and broken promises. Here was a man you could believe in. It's not as if people expected to beat the Packers, who had dominated the NFL to the rare extent of having led the league in both most points scored and fewest points allowed. But people expected the Patriots to give them a good fight. It wasn't going to be a repeat of the 1986 46-10 fiasco in which the Pats had gained seven yards on the ground.

It didn't take long for fireworks to go off once everyone settled into the Crescent City. On the morning of January 20, the *Globe* had a Will McDonough story with the headline: *Parcells Won't Return*. A prophetic subhead said, simply: *Controversy Looms*.

This wasn't news as much as it was a quasi-confirmation of an assumption. The key here was that McDonough was a close friend of Parcells. The story had to come from agent Robert Fraley and it had to have been authorized by one Duane Charles (Bill) Parcells.

Included in the story was the following paragraph: "However, Fraley maintained that there is no provision in the contract that would call for any type of compensation and that his client is free to do whatever he wants in '97."

That was most definitely not what Kraft was saying. The battle lines were now drawn. Other teams go to the Super Bowl and the talk is about football. Only the Patriots would go to the Super Bowl and make some 3,000 international journalists witness to a family spat.

Now it was charge-countercharge time, and it was ugly. The low point came on Wednesday, January 22, when both Parcells and Kraft took apparent leave of their senses. They participated in a witless Vaudeville-type exchange that was supposed to defuse everything and put a smile on everyone's face. These proud men would be well advised to buy up all available video tapes and toss them into the nearest furnace.

It was so bad that one neutral observer inquired, "Which one is the dog and which one was the pony?"

The football issue was straightforward. Green Bay had everything. The Las Vegas wise guys had them favored by 14. The Wise Guys were about to take a bow. Green Bay won Super Bowl XXXI by a 38-24 score.

In years to come, few outside of Green Bay will recall the jolting 81-yard touchdown pass Favre threw to Antonio Freeman. Few out-

189

side of New England will recall the 18-yard burst Martin made for the touchdown which reduced the Green Bay lead to 27-21. They will only remember one thing, and one man.

Desmond Howard.

Martin's score had the Super Dome fans thinking that maybe, just maybe, the Patriots could pull this thing out. And then...

And then Vinatieri kicked to Howard, who gathered the ball in at the one-yard line. Boom. 99-yard return for a touchdown.

"That kick return provided tremendous impetus for their team," Parcells said. "I thought we might have had them rocking a little bit at 27-21. We had momentum on our drive, and our defense was playing better, but he made the big play."

There was one interesting "What If." Troy Brown was a valuable member of the kickoff unit, but he had been battling valiantly with what was eventually diagnosed as a hernia — and by "eventually" I mean two months later — and had to be scratched just before the game. Howard ran right by the spot where Brown would have been.

Vinatieri had an interesting slant on the Howard return. "Write this down," he said. "I was coming up to get him, but I was held. Go back and check the film and tell me if I was wrong. Because if I didn't get held, I'll give you all the money I own."

And this was no ordinary wimpy kicker, as Herschel Walker would be the first to admit.

Favre, a two-time MVP, was himself. Bledsoe was not. He was 25-for-46 for 256 yards, two touchdowns and — this was the killer — four interceptions.

The Bledsoe postgame analysis could have come directly from the mouth of Bill Parcells. Bledsoe said the story of the game was big plays and turnovers. "Big plays, that's the bottom line in this game. You watch, year in and year out. Super Bowls are won on big plays. The Packers made more big plays than we did. They didn't turn the ball over and they basically played mistake-free football."

Events unfolded quickly after Super Bowl XXXI.

It was all My Lawyer vs. Your Lawyer. Parcells & Co. said The Tuna was contractually free to do anything he wished, whether it was to manage the Yankees or coach the Jets. Kraft & Co. said Parcells might manage the Yankees, replace Seiji Ozawa at the Boston Symphony or join the Peace Corps, but he could not coach the New York Jets, or any other NFL team, without the express written permission of Robert Kraft.

The matter was referred to commissioner Paul Tagliabue, who ran it by his own well-paid legal beagles. The decision was swift.

The headline of the January 30 *Boston Globe*:

Kraft Wins Sticking Point

That was on Thursday, four days after Super Bowl XXXI. The next day Kraft and Parcells held back-to-back press conferences. The Tuna said his differences with Bob Kraft were "not about power." He spoke of "philosophical differences."

The closest he came to identifying what was really bugging him was when he alluded to the draft day problems. "If they want you to cook the dinner," he said, "they ought to let you shop for some of the groceries."

Ha-ha. The fact is he had always been able to shop for *some* of the groceries. He just wasn't being allowed to shop for *all* of the groceries.

Kraft wanted there to be a division of power because he didn't want the organization to be dependent on the whims of one individual. He had always known that Parcells would not be a long-term coach. He wanted to have a stable organization that would be operating wisely even after Parcells left.

Kraft promptly hired San Francisco assistant Pete Carroll as his new head coach. That was simple enough.

Parcells provided everyone with some entertainment. He went to New York and signed an agreement that would make him a "consultant" for one year while longtime aide Bill Belichick would be an interim head coach. This, of course, was unacceptable to Kraft. In ruling in favor of Kraft and against Parcells, commissioner Tagliabue had specifically said that Parcells could neither hold the job of head coach, general manager or any "comparable position." The consultancy was, Kraft said, a "transparent farce."

The dispute was eventually tossed into Tagliabue's lap. His ruling: The Jets could have Parcells as a head coach. In exchange, the

Patriots would get the Jets' fourth-round pick in 1997, their second- and third-round picks in 1998 and their first-round pick in 1999. In addition, the Jets would contribute $300,000 to the Patriots' Charities.

The Parcells Era was now officially over. The ending was messy and even degrading, but none of it could change the fact that he had fulfilled his part of the bargain. Said The Tuna, "I said when I came to New England that I would not rest until this team could compete for the championship — and I've done that."

Parcells and Kraft each had reason to feel proud. As much as Parcells groused about the hands-on proclivity of his owner, The Tuna couldn't deny that Kraft had been ready with the checkbook whenever the necessity arose, and that the owner had been supportive in every way. And Kraft had to admit that even if he were to remain in football for three more decades, he was unlikely to find another coach anywhere near as good as Bill Parcells, who had left behind a sound young team which, thanks to him, had a very clear understanding of what it takes to win in the NFL.

The ultimate winners were the fans, For the first time in their tortured history, the Patriots were a solid team geared for long-term success. They were in the mainstream of the National Football League.

The Red Sox

Jim Lonborg in the season-ending pivotal series against Minnesota. (Photo©Dick Raphael)

10

A Legacy
of Frustration

There is a simple reason why Boston baseball fans feel so tremendously aggravated over their favorite team's inability to win a World Series since Woodrow Wilson was president.

They feel *entitled*.

They believe that Boston is the source of all baseball intelligence, insight and feeling, and so it would only be appropriate if the Red Sox could win one lousy title before the century expires. The typical Boston fan is unlike any other baseball follower in America, in that he regards the team's ongoing failure as a personal insult, and not merely a human failing.

When a Red Sox batter strikes out with the bases loaded, he doesn't understand that what he has just done is tell a guy sitting in section 12 along the first-base line to go bleep himself. When a Red Sox reliever throws a ninth-inning two-out game-losing home run ball, he doesn't know that he has just told some other guy sitting in the bleachers that he can just go kiss his butt. A baseball game in Boston isn't just a baseball game, the way it is in, say, San Diego, way out there in California where people just don't have, according to a classic Boston perspective, the proper appreciation for the finer things in life.

"You throw a home run ball in San Diego," Red Sox pitcher Mike Maddux once observed, "and some guy in the bleachers says, 'Man, that home run sure went faaarrr.' You thrown one in Fenway, and they want to kill you."

There is no other way to put it other than to say that the Boston baseball fan is frighteningly narcissistic. He thinks *he* is the only one who has ever suffered. This self-centered approached has not gone unnoticed in the outside world. Consider the following letter to the editor of the *Washington Post* dated Oct. 5, 1997:

> *...Red Sox fans wallow in failure, inviting all around them to witness their wailing. They're especially loud in Washington where rooting for the Red Sox is a way of saying you went to Harvard.*

Boston fans figure that they have unmatched credentials. Each was taught baseball from his father, who learned it from his father, and in many cases this lineage goes back far beyond Woodrow Wilson. The truth is that when Boston's first professional baseball team came into being, Ulysses S. Grant was living at 1600 Pennsylvania Avenue.

That was in 1871, when Harry Wright organized a team to play in the National Association of Professional Baseball Players. The league lasted five seasons, and the Boston Red Stockings won four of the championships. Harry Wright had been the prime force behind the celebrated Cincinnati Red Stockings, the first openly professional baseball team, and by the time he had shifted his operation to Boston he was justifiably known as the "Father of Professional Baseball."

The NAPBBP was not run in any manner you or I would recognize, but, hey, you've got to start somewhere. Each team was required to play all rivals five times, the time and place of said games to be determined by correspondence. Some teams played the required number of games, and some did not. The one absolute was that the best-run, most imaginative and most professional franchise was the one run by Harry Wright in Boston.

The team played in a park alternatively known as the "South End Grounds," the "Grand Pavilion," the "Walpole Street Grounds" and the "Boston Baseball Grounds." This site housed baseball teams in Boston until 1915, when the Boston Braves moved to Braves Field in the Back Bay section of Boston.

The new parks's rather bizarre dimensions bring to mind a venue somewhat similar to that of the famed Polo Grounds. It was 250 feet to left, 445 feet to left-center, 440 feet to center, 445 feet to right-center and 255 to right.

It was certainly hospitable to the home team. The 1875 club went undefeated at home and hardly defeated at all, finishing with a 71-8 record. Pitcher Al Spalding had a 57-5 record. (No one worried about how many of these appearances were "quality starts"). The Red Stockings were actually *too* good. There was no viable competition, and the league disbanded at the conclusion of the 1875 campaign.

The Red Stockings had left a powerful legacy in Boston. They had drawn 75,000 fans during that final season, and that was, by the standards of the day, a handsome figure. Wright had done much to promote the game, even going so far as to take the team on a trip to his native England. Just about everything Harry Wright did during those eventful five years reflected well on the game of baseball in the city of Boston.

When the National League was formed in 1876, Boston was, of course, a charter member. Chicago was the first winner, but the next year Boston was right back in the spot where its fans had come to expect it — first place. The Red Stockings won again in 1878. Thus were created the first generation of spoiled Boston fans. Six championships in eight years of existence clearly bred spectating arrogance.

For the remainder of the 19th century, Boston was in the forefront of baseball development. As Harold Kaese pointed out in a 1955 essay written for *Sport* magazine's *Book Of Major League Baseball Clubs*, "The Braves gave baseball the first outfielder to trap a fly ball for a double play, Tom McCarthy in 1894; the first first baseman to make the 3-6-3 double play, Fred Tenney in 1897; the first hitter to grab a rival catcher so he could not chase a foul fly, Johnny Burdock in 1883; and the first player to hit four consecutive home runs in a game, Bobby Lowe in 1894."

Boston did not develop, but gave great homage to, one of the great characters of early baseball history, Mike "King" Kelly, a flamboyant, albeit self-destructive, player who inspired a song entitled *Slide, Kelly, Slide*, written by the unrelated John W. Kelly in 1889. Kelly also loaned his name to the first "autobiography," ghost-written or otherwise, ever done by a baseball player. It was published by the Boston firm of Emery and Hughes in 1888.

Boston had more than its share of stars in the '80s. Among the contemporary greats who wore Boston uniforms were Dan Brouthers, John Clarkson and Charles "Ol' Hoss" Radbourne.

By that time the team was playing in the most magnificent baseball venue in America. In 1883 the original grandstand at the South End Grounds had been torn down and replaced by a graceful double-decked affair with six spires on the roof. The park even had special VIP seats which could be considered ancestors of the luxury box. This state of affairs came to an end when fire destroyed the grandstand in 1894. The replacement structure was far less grandiose. Boston has never again had a double-decked ballpark.

Boston baseball really took off in the 1890s. Though the rollicking Baltimore Orioles have lived on in folklore, the fact is that the dominant baseball team in the last decade of the 19th century was the team in Boston.

The Orioles won consecutive titles in 1894, '95 and '96. Boston won in 1891, '92, '93, '97 and '98. They were managed by Frank Selee, and their stars include such players as Lowe; outfielder Hugh Duffy, who set an all-time record by batting .438 in 1894; and third baseman Jimmy Collins, still regarded as among the handful of greatest players who have ever played the position.

The Red Sox came into being in 1901 as a member of the rival American League, having absconded with the great Collins, as well as center fielder Chick Stahl and right fielder/first baseman Buck Freeman.

The competition between the established Beaneaters and the upstart Pilgrims (or Puritans, as the terms were often used interchangeably) was fierce. The American League club even built a ballpark in close geographic proximity to the South End Grounds occupied by the haughty National Leaguers. This one was called the Huntington Avenue Grounds, and it served as the home of the AL team until 1912, when the Taylor family constructed a park in the Fenway section of Boston which took the name of the region.

Right from the start, the advent of the American League team wounded the National League entry. The Pilgrims outdrew the Beaneaters, 289,448 to 146,502, and in a very real sense that was the beginning of a slow death for the National League franchise. The process took 52 years, but there was never any doubt that the favored team in town was the one in the American League.

From 1901 through 1952, the last year of National League baseball in Boston, the National Leagues Braves outdrew the American Leaguers seven times, all in a stretch between 1921 through 1933, when the Red Sox finished eighth and last nine times and never finished higher than fifth. The Braves won two National League pennants, in 1914 and 1948, and in neither of those years could they outdraw the Red Sox.

The Beaneaters lost an important battle even before the first games were played in 1901. Boston was in possession of the most famous fans in the game, the celebrated "Royal Rooters," organized and ruled by saloon keeper Michael "Nuf Ced" McGreevey, so called because the argument was officially over when Mr. McGreevey declared "Nuf Said." The group was headquartered at McGreevey's Third Base Saloon at 940 Columbus Avenue in Boston's South End. The bar's slogan was "The last stop before you steal home."

The Beaneaters made the foolish mistake of raising ticket prices prior to the 1901 season, and Nuf Ced & Co. took exception. They immediately transferred their official allegiance to the Pilgrims. Gaining the official sanction of the Royal Rooters gave the Pilgrims impressive local credibility.

The shortsightedness of the Beaneaters' management was a perfect illustration of how the American League had come into being in the first place. The National League was notoriously penurious. There was a $2,400 salary ceiling. The ballpark itself was getting run-down, but the Beaneaters, coming off championships in 1897 and '98 refused to do anything to assuage either the players or the fans. When the new league came along, waving many dollar bills in the faces of the ballplayers, it was a very easy matter to induce some changes of allegiance.

The Pilgrims drew 11,025 for their first game. Cy Young went the distance in a 12-4 victory over Connie Mack's Philadelphia Athletics. The Beaneaters drew 2,000 for their opener against Brooklyn, the defending National League champions. It was a clear triumph for the Pilgrims, and it was the beginning of a love affair between town and team which has lasted for the duration of the century.

By the third year of their existence, the Red Sox were the best team in baseball. They won the American League pennant by 14½ games over Philadelphia, and they won the first modern World Series by defeating Pittsburgh, 5 games to 3, in a best-of-nine series.

Young, who had come to the Red Sox two years earlier after being inspired by the oratory of Jimmy Collins, was the team's marquee pitcher, but he wasn't the star of the first World Series. That was Bill Dineen, who won three games.

The fans had already made themselves a factor, if the accounts of a prominent Pittsburgh Pirate player can be believed. Tommy Leach told Lawrence Ritter in his classic *The Glory of Their Times* that the Royal Rooters had raised such a racket with their singing, starting in Game 5, that the Pirates could hardly concentrate on their playing. The song they were singing was *Tessie*, a ditty which had been adopted as the Pilgrims' theme song despite the fact that it had absolutely nothing to do with baseball. In other words, it was kind of the *Na, Na, Hey, Hey, Kiss Him Goodbye* of its day.

The Red Sox were denied an opportunity to defend their title after winning the American League championship the following year because cantankerous New York Giants skipper John McGraw, who had an irrational hatred of the new league, simply refused to participate in a postseason series against the winners of a league he thought was lower than pond scum.

The great, glorious Golden Era of Boston baseball in this century, at least insofar as playing field success is concerned, came between the years of 1912 and 1918, when the Red Sox won four American League pennants and four World Series while the Braves were making a name for themselves in 1914 (conveniently, a non-title year for the Red Sox) by coming from last place on July 19 to win the pennant. But that wasn't all. They put a giant exclamation point on the season by taking out Connie Mack's imperious Philadelphia A's in four straight games to win the one and only Boston Braves title.

The Braves finished second in 1915, third in 1916 and then were not genuinely competitive for the next 31 years.

The great Red Sox hero in 1912 was a 23-year-old right-handed pitcher from Missouri by the name of Joe Wood, nicknamed "Smoky Joe" because, as legend had it, his fastball was so good it was accompanied by a trail of smoke.

Coming into that season, he was 47-38 lifetime, but he was coming off a 23-17 season the year before, and there was a feeling he was ready to break through. So how does a 34-5 record, with a 1.91 earned run average and 10 shutouts sound? Toss in a .290 batting average and 13 runs batted in, and he had himself a pretty good year.

Wood received a great compliment that year from the highest possible source. Asked if he threw harder than Joe Wood, Walter Johnson looked at his inquisitor as if he had just arrived from Uranus and said, "Do I throw harder than Joe Wood? There isn't a man alive who can throw harder than Smokey Joe Wood!"

On Friday, Sptember 6, 1912, the two great fireballers hooked up in an epic duel. It was very much a staged confrontation, with managers Jake Stahl of Boston and Clark Griffith of Washington arranging their rotations so that the baseball world could enjoy this battle of mound titans who would combine for a 64-17 record that season.

Wood went into the game at 30-4. Johnson was 28-11. Wood, who had won 13 consecutive games, had to be at his best that day. Back-to-back sixth-inning doubles by Tris Speaker and Duffy Lewis produced the game's only run as Wood defeated his great rival.

What a day it was, wrote renowned sportswriter Melville E. Webb Jr. "It (the crowd) packed the stands and the bleachers and trooped all over the outfield inside the stand and bleacher boundaries. In the grandstand the broad promenade was packed solid 10 rows deep with fans on tip-toes to see what was going on. The playing field was surrounded completely by a triple, even quadruple, rank of humanity, at least 3,000 assembling in the banking in left field and the mass of enthusiasts extending around in front of the huge concrete stand."

I've often imagined that if I could have been any athlete in the 20th century at any given point in time, I'd choose to be Smokey Joe Wood in 1912. You're 23, you're very good looking, you've got a fastball, you can hit and you're playing baseball at a time when it is unchallenged as the true National Pastime in a city that is a wondrous combination of cultural sophistication and childlike enthusiasm for your chosen specialty.

That year would represent the peak of Smokey Joe's career. He came up with an arm injury the following season, and, though he recovered sufficiently to go 15-5 in the championship season of 1915, he did so without the fastball that had so awed Walter Johnson. But he did resurrect his career to a degree by abandoning pitching in favor of becoming an outfielder. He spent six years with the Cleveland Indians, helping them to a World Series title in 1920, batting .366 in 197 at bats in 1921 and finishing his career by batting .297 in 505 at bats the following year.

He would spend 20 distinguished years as head baseball coach at Yale. He died in 1985 at age 96. A noted gentleman, he was never heard to curse the fates or bemoan the cruelty of coming up with a deadened arm at age 24. After all, he always had 1912, when there was no finer thing in the world than to have been Smokey Joe Wood. If Walter Johnson was correct, then he, Joe Wood, and not Amos Rusie, Rube Waddell, Walter Johnson, Dazzy Vance, Van Lingle Mungo, Bob Feller, Rex Barney, Herb Score, Sandy Koufax, Sam McDowell, Nolan Ryan, Roger Clemens, Randy Johnson or even Steve Dalkowski, was the hardest thrower of all time.

The 1912 World Series was, in the opinion of some people with very weighty diamond scholar credentials, one of the great sporting events in American sports history. It had superb drama, both on and off the field, and it even needed eight games to resolve itself due to an 11-inning, darkness-induced, 6-6 tie in Game 2.

Game 7 was an epic almost beyond belief. An obscure pinch hitter named Olaf Henriksen had tied the game at 1-1 for the Red Sox off the great Christy Mathewson in the seventh with a pinch double off the third-base bag. The Giants scored a run in the top of the 10th off Wood, who had come on in relief of 20-game winner Hugh Bedient, and Mathewson was thus three outs away from victory.

The Boston 10th included two of the more celebrated *gaffes* in World Series history, sandwiched around one of the great plays. The inning opened with center fielder Fred Snodgrass dropping a routine fly ball off the bat of Clyde Engle. Snodgrass immediately atoned for the miscue with a spectacular grab of a blow struck by Harry Hooper.

Mathewson walked Steve Yerkes. That brought up Tris Speaker, and he appeared to be out number two when he hit a harmless pop foul along the first-base line. But neither first baseman Fred Merkle nor catcher Chief Meyers could decide who should take it, and the ball dropped in. A grateful Speaker singled home Engle with the tying run as Yerkes moved to third. Larry Gardner brought home Yerkes with a fly ball to right. It was the first World Series decided in extra innings in a no-tomorrow game.

Crowd decorum was a bit different in those days. Major problems arose when the Royal Rooters arrived *en masse* at Fenway Park only to discover that their normal seats had been given away to others, presumably higher rollers than they.

Nuf Ced and the boys were not the type to skulk away meekly. They took their banners and their attitude right onto the playing field. It was quite common practice in those days for management to accommodate overflow crowds at ballparks all across America by simply placing fans on the field in front of the outfield fence, throwing up a rope, declaring new ground rules and instructing the plate umpire to start the game. But this time management was not in control of the proceedings. It was necessary to summon police, and it took a good 25 minutes before the Rooters were assuaged. They took their new place in front of the left-field fence and then watched the Giants score six runs on the supposedly invincible Smokey Joe in the first inning to force a deciding eighth game.

The Red Sox won it again in 1915, defeating the Philadelphia Phillies, and in 1916, knocking off the Dodgers. The Chicago White

Sox prevailed in 1917, but the Red Sox came roaring back in 1918, a year shortened by World War I. The Red Sox nosed out Cleveland by 2½ games to win the American League pennant and then defeated the Chicago Cubs in six games.

The 1906 White Sox were forever branded the "Hitless Wonders," but in terms of actual World Series competition, what team ever accomplished more with less offense than the 1918 Red Sox, who hit .186 as a team while being outscored, 10-9, in a six-game series?

The Cubs even had the lower ERA, 1.04 to 1.70, but the Red Sox emerged as champs, anyway. That's just the way life was, in the opinion of Red Sox fans. We can outhit you, we can outpitch you or we can outthink you. Our team just has whatever it takes to win.

The fans didn't know it, of course, but the Red Sox problems had already begun. The chain of events which would lead to a championship drought which is now closing in on 80 years had begun back in 1916, when Red Sox owner Joseph Lannin sold the team to a consortium consisting of Hugh Ward, G.M. Anderson and Harry Frazee for the sum of $675,000, half of which was paid in cash and half of which was nothing more than promissory notes signed by the loquacious Frazee, a theatrical promoter of note. It is conceivable that Boston, and indeed American sports history might have been different had this Lannin fellow been a little bit more of a hard-nosed businessman.

Harry Frazee goes down in Boston sports history as the poster boy for dunce cap owners. On December 19, 1919, Harry Frazee sold Babe Ruth to the New York Yankees.

What else do you need to know?

At the time, Harry Frazee was a desperate man. He had been a dangerous owner to begin with, because being a theater producer in the teens is not exactly the same as being Bill Gates in the late '90s. You win some (*No, No Nanette*, for example) and you lose some, and when things get sticky you ask Peter to pay Paul. When things started to go sour on Broadway, Harry found it necessary to plunder his other assets, those being able-bodied baseball players. And the most valuable asset of all was a 24-year-old American original named George Herman (Babe) Ruth.

Ruth had joined the ballclub in late 1914. He was then a left-handed pitcher. It wasn't until 1918 that general manager Ed Barrow made the decision to make Ruth into more of an outfielder-slugger than a pitcher. This was a very controversial move, because Ruth was not just an ordinary southpaw. He had gone 65-33 in the years 1915-17, and in the 1916 World Series had begun a scoreless inning streak that would reach 29²/₃ innings and would remain the record until Whitey Ford broke it more than 40 years later.

By 1918 Ruth was a hybrid. He pitched often enough to go 13-7 with a 2.22 ERA. He played outfield and first base often enough to hit 11 home runs (tying Philadelphia's Tilly Walker for the league lead). He threw a six-hit shutout in Game 1 of the 1918 World Series. He began the sixth game as the starting pitcher and the number six man in the batting order, and he finished it in left field after giving up just two runs in eight innings, plus two batters in the ninth.

The basic transition took place in 1919. Ruth got 432 at bats, and he made good use of them, setting a new major-league record with 29 home runs while driving in 114 runs. It was rather obvious that he was a new kind of offensive force. Oh, and in his spare time he moonlighted enough to go 9-5 as a pitcher.

Frazee started out as a spender. He brought in quality players such as first baseman Stuffy McInnis, outfielder Amos Strunk, catcher Wally Schang and pitcher "Bullet" Joe Bush, and without these acquisitions there would have been no 1918 World Champion Red Sox.

No one has ever suggested that he was a nefarious man whose mission on earth was to destroy the Boston Red Sox and inflict misery on millions of New Englanders in perpetuity. He was just a businessman who did what he felt he had to do. For the last eight decades Red Sox fans have wished he had considered cyanide rather than selling Babe Ruth, and then compounding the felony by selling Babe Ruth to the *Yankees*.

Not that there was any great Red Sox-Yankees rivalry in 1919. How could there be? The New York franchise (originally known as the Highlanders) had been relentlessly irrelevant since its inception. After losing a very good chance to win a pennant in 1904 when 41-game winner Jack Chesboro threw a celebrated wild pitch in the ninth inning of the first game of a showdown doubleheader with the Pilgrims themselves on the last day of the season, the Yankees went back to their apartments and didn't bother anybody for the next 15 or so years. From 1911 through 1918 the best they could do was fourth. They were the "other" team in New York, because those were truly The Days of Mr. McGraw. John McGraw and his regal Giants owned New York. The Yankee games, were, as quintessential New Yorker Jimmy Bresin might have written, had he been born a bit earlier, "back by the girdle ads and overseas flight announcements."

By selling Babe Ruth to the Yankees, Harry Frazee *made* the Yankees. End of story. But it wasn't just Babe Ruth, I might add. Before he sold the team to J.A. Robert Quinn in 1923, Harry Frazee also sent New York Herb Pennock, a Hall of Fame pitcher; Carl Mays, a pitcher who probably *ought* to be in the Hall of Fame; Sad Sam Jones, a 229-game lifetime winner who was coming off a 23-victory year when Frazee dispatched him to the Bronx; Jumpin' Joe Dugan, a quality third baseman; Everett Scott, a reliable shortstop whose record of 1,307 consecutive games would be broken by Lou Gehrig, and a few others who could play the game.

By the time Frazee had finished his strip-mining of a baseball team, there were no players remaining from the team that had brought Boston a fourth World Championship in seven years back in 1918.

So suppose you're a Boston baseball fan in the early '20s. You had yourself a perfectly enjoyable teens. Your American League team won in 1912, 1915, 1916 and 1918. You saw Cy Young end his career. You saw Smokey Joe Wood light up the sky. You saw Tris Speaker, Duffy Lewis and Harry Hooper play the outfield as you had never seen it played. You saw two new ballparks open, each a state-of-the-art stadium. You also saw the Braves make history in 1914. (Proving himself and his followers to be front runners in the finest American tradition, Nuf Ced and his Royal Rooters re-embraced the Braves just in time for a grand round of World Series picture taking).

And you saw Babe Ruth.

Nuf Ced.

And now the owner of the Red Sox was systematically disman-tling a great team and selling the parts to New York. You saw The Babe go to New York in 1920 and put together the greatest offensive season the game had ever seen. Taking full advantage of a tighter-stitched baseball geared to stimulate offense, Ruth batted a healthy .376 and he hit an astronomical 54 home runs, increasing his one-year-old record by an outrageous 46 percent. He scored 158 runs and he drove in 137. He slugged a stratospheric .847. Then you watched him have an even better year in 1921. It may have been the single most productive year any batter has ever had:

Batting Average: 378
Home Runs: 59
Doubles: 44
Triples: 16
Runs Batted In: 171
Runs Scored: 177
Walks: 144
Slugging Percentage: 846

Worse yet, this was a pennant-winning year for the Yankees. It was the real beginning of the New York dynasty which would result in 27 American League pennants by the 1964 season.

True, the Polo Grounds, where the Yankees were still a tenant of the Giants, was a much different home run proposition than Fenway Park, but even if the actual numbers were scaled down a bit, Babe Ruth was now doing for New York what, in the eyes and hearts of the Boston baseball fans, he should have been doing for Boston, the town which had nurtured this refugee from a Baltimore home for boys and which had taken him to its heart. Babe Ruth was never once heard to say he hadn't been happy with Boston, or that he didn't wish to remain there. Babe Ruth had been happy in Boston. Oh, there were the usual disciplinary problems you'd expect from an essentially overgrown kid who felt he owned the world, but it was nothing the Red Sox couldn't have lived with.

The Yankees won the pennant in 1921, 1922 and 1923. The Red Sox, stripped down and bereft of hope, finished fifth in 1921 and eighth and last in 1922. The Yankees would win World Series championships in 1923, 1926, 1927 and 1928. The Red Sox would finish out the decade as follows: 8th, 7th, 8th, 8th, 8th, 8th, 8th and, yes, 8th.

Hey, Harry, thanks a lot.

The Braves? Get this decade for them: 4th, 8th, 7th, 8th, 5th, 7th, 7th, 7th and 8th.

Now you know why Boston grandpas feel sorry for themselves.

The Braves did not help themselves by marrying themselves to a ballpark which was easily confused with the Grand Canyon. The original dimensions were, and I swear I am not making this up, 402 to left, 550 to center and 402 to right.

402? 550? What were they *thinking* of?

Even Comiskey Park in Chicago, constructed in 1910 with pitchers' welfare in mind (Hall of Famer hurler Big Ed Walsh was actually employed as a consultant), was not this diabolically insane a ballpark. With the advent of the lively ball in 1920 and the official emphasis on offense, Braves Field was an instant dinosaur. The Boston fan could pick up his morning paper and read about The Babe hitting another one out down there in New York. Then he was expected to hop onto the trolley and go to Braves Field, where Walter Hagen couldn't hit one out with a driver?

Small wonder the longest game in major-league baseball history was played at Braves Field on May 1, 1920, when the Braves and Dodgers slogged through 26 innings without being able to break a 1-1 tie before darkness set in. Nobody was going to end it with one swing, that's for sure.

According to Michael Benson's *Ballparks of North America*, — and why should anyone have any trouble believing this? — it was 10 years before someone hit the ball over the left-field fence. Frank "Pancho" Snyder, a catcher who had a career total of 47 homers during a 16-year major-league career, became the first man to trot around the bases after hitting a baseball to left field at Braves Stadium when he connected off Larry Benton on May 28, 1925. Let's hope some enterprising scribe inquired as to what Pancho had for breakfast. Guess it was too early for drug testing.

That doesn't mean home runs weren't hit in Braves Field. From 1915 through 1925, there were 209 touch-'em-all homers hit in Braves Field, including four in one game with the Giants on April 29, 1922.

A semblance of sanity began to prevail in 1928, when the dimensions were reduced dramatically (340 to left, 390 to center and 340 to right). From 1915 through 1927, with the original dimensions, the only Boston Braves players to reach double figures in home runs were Ray Powell (12 in 1921), Tony Boeckel (10 in 1921) and

Jake Fournier (10 in 1927). When the park was scaled down to something resembling human proportions the following year, Rogers Hornsby came in and hit .387 with 21 homers.

The noted Braves of the era were usually men known for their personality. Rabbit Maranville spent the first nine and the final six of his meandering 23-year career with the Braves. Casey Stengel passed through. The Braves even had a lovable fool of an owner, Judge Emil J. Fuchs, who installed himself as manager for a spell during the 1929 season.

With a combined 11 eighth- and nine seventh-place finishes between 1921 and 1933, the Red Sox and Braves weren't exactly providing the people of Boston and New England with baseball they could sink their teeth into. And while there was always residual loyalty to the sport itself, the fans could not arouse themselves to patronize either team in any great numbers, the top attendance racked up by either squad during those many lost years being the 448,556 who came out to see the seventh-place 1924 Red Sox. Perhaps they were coming to see if Bill Wambsganss had another unassisted triple play up his sleeve. Let the record show that the veteran second baseman did lead the league in putouts, assists and errors.

The Red Sox entered a new and interesting phase at the conclusion of 1933 when the well-meaning, but financially overmatched Quinn found a buyer. The new owner was a 30-year-old heir to a tin and lumber fortune. In addition to a dazzling bank account, Thomas Austin Yawkey had one other thing to recommend him: he was as much in love with the game of baseball as a fashion model is with a mirror.

He would own the team for the next 43 years, and in his case it was until death do us part — and then some. He would renovate the ballpark into the basic edifice you see today. He would treat the franchise like a beloved toy. He would see his team win three American League pennants. And he would die unfulfilled, because each of those teams lost the World Series in a seventh game, two of them in positively excruciating seventh games. For better or worse, he would put as much of a personal stamp on his baseball organization as any man has on any team in the history of baseball, the only possible exception of Connie Mack, who was an owner-manager for an almost unimaginable 50 years. But whereas Mack's influence ceased the moment his crumbling team was sold and moved to Kansas City for the 1954 season, Yawkey's remains strong, more than 20 years after his death.

It is as if the old man never left us. The team is run by John Harrington, but is owned by the Yawkey Trust. Fenway Park is more Tom Yawkey's monument than the folks who originally had it constructed in 1912. Doing things in the "Yawkey Tradition"is very much an issue in Boston. Most of all, Tom Yawkey's pain is every Boston fan's pain. He died without seeing the Red Sox win a sixth World's Championship — or, at least, a World Series that could actually be broadcast on radio — and so has everyone else who has passed away in New England since 1918.

Just like Harry Frazee, Tom Yawkey started out as a big spender. Unlike Harry Frazee, he never stopped. He told his general manager Eddie Collins (a boyhood idol) to make offers for players any time he saw fit. The townspeople couldn't believe it. During the latter part of the destructive Frazee era and for the entirety of the Quinn regime, all the Red Sox ever seemed to do was liquidate assets. Now there was an owner whose only credo was "buy, buy, buy!"

He never, ever stopped. Rick Ferrell, George Pipgras, Billy Werber, Lefty Grove, Rube Walberg, Max Bishop, Wes Ferrell, Lyn Lary, Fritz Ostermueller, Joe Cronin (a record $250,000), Doc Cramer, Eric McNair... For three years, it never ended. He even bought the great Jimmie Foxx, and it wasn't as if the great slugger didn't have anything left. Double XX's 50 home runs and 175 RBIs in 1938 remain Red Sox standards.

He drew a deep breath after the 1936 season and scratched his head. The spending had gotten his team out of the American League basement, but his team's placements were 4th, 4th and 6th. Then he was persuaded that buying past-their-prime stars wasn't necessarily the way to go. OK, then, Yawkey said, let's do what Branch Rickey has done in St. Louis and build ourselves a farm system. We'll develop our *own* stars.

And he did. When the Red Sox finally won a pennant in 1946, it was done with such home-bred talent as Johnny Pesky, Dom DiMaggio, Bobby Doerr, Boo Ferris, Tex Hughson, Mickey Harris, and, of course, the inimitable Theodore Samuel Williams, to go with such veteran imports as Rudy York, Pinky Higgins and Wally Moses.

The Yawkey spending tradition continued unabated throughout the '50s, '60s and '70s. Yawkey made a splash in the winter of '57-58 when he offered the Cleveland Indians $1 million for the services of young pitching sensation Herb Score. The Indians politely refused. His final grand gesture in the spending department was to give Oakland A's owner Charles O. Finley $1 million apiece for outfielder Joe Rudi and premier reliever Rollie Fingers on June 15, 1976. Had this deal gone through, the balance of power in the American League might have been tipped in Boston's favor for years to come. But commissioner Bowie Kuhn, locked in an endless feud with Finley, voided the deal, saying it was not in "the best interests of baseball." Given that Yawkey had voted for countless proposals over the years which benefitted baseball's interests at the expense of his own, it would have been nice for the commissioner to realize that baseball owed Yawkey one. But it was not to be, and Yawkey would die before the year was out, frustrated in his 43-year quest to bring Boston and New England a baseball championship.

◆　　◆　　◆

In addition to spending money for ballplayers, Yawkey put his stamp on the ballclub during his first year as owner by spending at least a million dollars to renovate Fenway Park. He wasn't doing it because he wanted to impress people. He did it because it needed it.

The '20s had not been kind to Fenway. A 1926 fire burned down the bleachers along the left-field foul line, and owner Bob Quinn didn't have the money to make the necessary replacements. The park was in general disrepair, and then there was the matter of "Duffy's Cliff."

Having an incline of some sort leading up to a fence or wall was not an uncommon occurrence in those days. No one had yet thought of a warning track. But the left-field incline in Boston was exceedingly steep, and it was a real problem for most left fielders. Not so for Red Sox left fielder Duffy Lewis, who was so adept maneuvering up and down the incline that the sportswriters nicknamed the little hill in his honor. But Yawkey recognized the incline for what it was, and ordered it removed. He also changed the left-field fence into a 37-

211

The addition of Ted Williams to the Red Sox roster in 1939 may have been Tom Yawkey's most important move up to that point. (Photo©Fred Kaplan, courtesy Lee Kaplan)

foot left-field wall. He replaced the wooden center-field bleachers with concrete ones.

He continued to tinker with the park. A 23-foot screen was placed atop The Wall in 1936 so that fewer baseballs would threaten businesses on Landsdowne Street, the thoroughfare which ran behind it. Bullpens were added in right-center field four years later. Skyview boxes were built in 1946. The next year lights were added and advertising removed from the left-field wall. The last Yawkey touch was the construction of a $1.3 million electronic scoreboard in 1976, although there still remained, and remains, a manually operated scoreboard in the left-field wall itself.

But the most important Yawkey addition, if you want to look at it that way, was the advent of a brash young left fielder named Ted Williams, who joined the team in 1939 with the stated objective of being recognized as the greatest hitter who ever lived. When he retired, 21 years, 2,654 hits, 521 home runs, three Most Valuable Player Awards and six batting (but no World Series) titles later, he was, if not necessarily the greatest hitter, certainly included significantly in the discussion.

At the very least, Williams became the flash-point player in the Yawkey era. The old man loved Williams, and Williams loved him. Their bond transcended baseball, for each was an avid fisherman and outdoorsman. Critics snickered that Williams was the perfect Yawkey player, because he was, they believed, all about statistics. Ted's rigid approach to hitting, they said, precluded team play. It was more important for him to take a walk, and thus verify his strike zone judgment, than to swing at a pitch a couple of inches outside the strike zone if presented with an important RBI opportunity. Again according to the critics, Williams was essentially indifferent to anything but his own plate appearances.

Yawkey spoiled his babies, the critics said, and no one was spoiled more than Williams. Ted ran the locker room. Because Ted disliked photographers and harbored deep distrust of most (but not all) members of the printed press, the Red Sox had the most carefully guarded photography and media entree policy in all of baseball. Yawkey indulged Ted's every whim, and because of this, the critics claim, the Red Sox were never really a team, at least not in the sense that the damned Yankees were.

Well, maybe all of this was true, but whether or not it had anything to do with the difference between the Yankees and the Red Sox from 1939 through Williams' retirement in 1960 is highly arguable. The Yankees almost always had more consistent pitching and a deeper bench. Williams himself said that the difference between the Yankees and Red Sox during the '40s was that New York had Phil Rizzuto at shortstop and the Red Sox didn't.

Williams had to live with the fact that in his only World Series he was 5-for-20, all singles with one run batted in. That was in 1946, when the Red Sox were a resounding 61-16 in Fenway Park, winning the American League pennant by 12 games. Williams entered the Series with a bad elbow, but the critics didn't want to hear that.

The Red Sox as a group will always have to live with the fact that from 1946 through 1950 they won more games than any other team in baseball (764) with just one pennant and no world's championships to show for it. (Now you understand why all those Daddys and Uncle Eds in Greater Boston are so touchy about the Red Sox.)

They won the pennant in 1946, finished a distant third in 1947, lost in a one-game playoff to Cleveland in 1948, lost to the Yankees on the final day in 1949 and finished a strong third, four games out, in 1950. They were never serious contenders for the remainder of Williams' career.

Had they won in '48, Boston would have been the baseball capital of the known world. That's because the champion of the National League was none other than those out-of-sight, out-of-mind, Boston Braves.

The Braves had shown signs of life for the first time since the teens by finishing third in 1947. It was their highest finish since 1916. Honest to God.

People were actually coming to see the Braves play. Attendances were up everywhere right after the war, and the Braves were not left out of the frenzy. They drew a team-record 969,000 in 1946, increased that to 1,277,000 in 1947 and then set an all-time Boston Braves attendance record of 1,455,439 in the pennant-winning year of 1948. The Red Sox outdrew them by 103,000, but the Braves were thrilled, nevertheless.

Dreams of an all-Boston World Series were shattered when the Red Sox lost a one-game playoff to the Indians, 8-3. Red Sox manager Joe McCarthy created a furor which lasts to this day by passing over such candidates as Joe Dobson and Mel Parnell to entrust the important pitching assignment to journeyman Denny Galehouse. No one knew what Ol' Marse Joe (no stranger to John Barleycorn, by the way) was thinking then, and no one knows what he was thinking now. What we do know is that Cleveland player-manager Lou Boudreau banged out two home runs and two doubles in four at bats. We know that the Braves lost the World Series to the Indians in six. And we know that within four years attendance at Braves Field had dropped to 281,000 (less than a good Red Sox home stand now) and the team would move, lock, stock and Warren Spahn, to Milwaukee.

The presence of Williams kept people coming out to Fenway Park during the '50s, but when he retired following the 1960 season, a certain reality set in. The Red Sox were simply not very interesting, and people were contenting themselves with following the team on radio, where they had the great Curt Gowdy to entertain them, television and by reading the newspapers.

The Red Sox were still the Red Sox, an important part of the fabric of life in Boston and New England, but they were more and more becoming background music to people's lives. Yawkey was now being openly derided for running what the press was calling a "country club." His underachieving players were better paid than comparable, and in many cases, superior, players on other teams, most notably the Yankees, whose tight-fisted general manager George Weiss threw nickels around as if they were stone tablets on loan from Stonehenge.

Williams had once said, "All the American League has is me and the Yankees, and when I go, this league is going to be pretty damn dull." He was right about that, and he was righter than he wanted to be about the predictable Red Sox, who could usually hit home runs but do little else.

The Boston Red Sox finished ninth in a 10-team league in 1965 as a paltry 652,201 came to see them play. This represented a drop-off of nearly a million fans since the glory days of the late '40s, and a slide of more than 400,000 since Williams' farewell season of 1960. They finished ninth again in 1966, and, while attendance did pick up some (rising to a modest 811,172), it was nothing like the old days.

I came to Boston in 1964 as a college student from New Jersey. There was nothing more important to me than baseball. My primary team was the San Francisco Giants. I had been a staunch New York Giants/Willie Mays fan since 1954, and when the Giants moved to the Coast my heart went with them. I suffered from afar during the tense 1959 three-way race with Los Angeles and Milwaukee. I reveled in the spectacular comeback of 1962, when the Giants made up a four-game deficit with one week to play and then defeated the Dodgers in a three-game playoff, scoring four times in the ninth inning of Game 3. I wept when Willie McCovey's line drive didn't have quite enough oomph to get over Bobby Richardson's head in the ninth inning of Game 7 in the 1962 World Series (Recall the famous Peanuts cartoon, and Charlie Brown screaming out, "Why couldn't McCovey's hit have been three feet higher?").

My secondary team was Philadelphia. I lived through the exciting summer of 1964 and was crushed when the Phils lost 10 straight in September to take themselves out of the race. I still maintain that the 1964 Phillies actually won the pennant, only the season was too long.

I was the kind of kid who had read everything about baseball he could get his hands on. I read and reread the available biographies of great players (a particular favorite book was a paperback by Tom Meany entitled, simply enough, *Baseball's Greatest Players*). I was a certified Babe Ruth freak, and I must have read Meany's *Babe Ruth Story* a dozen times. I regarded the All-Star Games of the '50s and early '60s as High Holy Days.

My father had been associated with the Trenton Giants of the Class B Interstate League in the late '40s, and, as a result, he knew people in the game. Part of the family folklore was that future New York Giants catcher Ray Katt and pitcher Al Corwin had actually babysat me. Marv Blaylock of the Phillies once gave me a batting lesson in my backyard (I'm sure he doesn't remember). My mother and father both knew Willie Mays. We had connections in both New York and Philly, and it was a routine thing for me to wake up on a summer Sunday morning and be informed that we were going to either the Polo Grounds or Shibe Park/Connie Mack Stadium for that afternoon's doubleheader. I remember being on the set during Frankie Frisch's studio show while Sid Gordon was swinging a bat which came within two inches of rearranging my nose. Talk about memories...

This is the attitude and background I brought to Boston, Massachusetts, and Boston College in the autumn of 1964. Baseball was very central to my existence. At that point I had been to just two games in Fenway, a night game in September of '63 when I was in Boston investigating college choices, and a Sunday game in July of '64 which was decided by a tape-measure Tony Conigliaro home run.

Fenway was an interesting curiosity, no doubt, but in those days there was nothing electrifying about baseball in Boston. The Red Sox were just, well *there*. They were like an old, familiar sofa. They were a familiar part of the Boston landscape, but not the object of much fuss. They were the Red Sox. They would undoubtedly hit a few home runs, but no one was talking about the ballpark itself in any hallowed terms, either. This was four years after its sanctification in John Updike's famous *New Yorker* essay, "Hub Fans Bid Kid Adieu," written to commemorate Ted Williams' final game on September 28, 1960.

It was in this piece that Updike anointed Fenway in the very first sentence as "a lyric little bandbox of a ballpark." Continuing on, he declared that "Everything is painted green and seems in curiously sharp focus, like the inside of an old-fashioned peeping-type Easter egg. It was built in 1912 and rebuilt in 1934 and offers, as do most Boston artifacts, a compromise between man's Euclidean determinations and nature's beguiling irregularities."

Well. Until Updike came along, most people simply said that Fenway was just shaped kinda funny.

Three decades after its reconstruction, Fenway Park was simply being taken for granted by most everyone associated with it. People were used to the 302-foot distance down the right-field line, the short fence which ran complete from the seats running down the right-field foul line all the way out to the Red Sox bullpen in deep right-center and the astonishingly abrupt angling out of said fence just a few degrees past the right-field foul pole.

Now, 302 isn't much. It was the second-shortest right-field distance in the American League at the time (prerenovation Yankee Stadium's 296 being the shortest). But whereas the fence in New York sloped and logically, the one in Boston veered out dramatically.

If you didn't pull the ball right down the line in Fenway you needed to put a pretty good charge in it if you wanted to reach the seats. At the same spot in right field where Yankee Stadium was sporting a 344-foot sign, Fenway had one reading 380. And that was only because Yawkey had ordered the construction of the bullpens after seeing what Ted Williams had done in his rookie season of 1939. The Thumper had banged out 31 homers while taking aim at a so-called power alley that was more than 400 feet away. Yawkey wanted his new left-handed slugging sensation to have a better chance to deliver the long ball, so he built the new pens. They were immediately christened by the local scribes as constituting the new municipality of "Williamsburg."

The deepest part of the park was not straightaway center, but right-center, just to the left of the Red Sox bullpen in deep right-center. There the sign read 420. A high wall ran from the edge of the bullpen to the center-field flag pole, right at the intersection of the famed left-field wall.

The Wall. The Green Monster. How many words have been written about The Wall? There was, and is, nothing in baseball like it. The essential truth is that The Wall giveth and The Wall taketh away. It has never taken much to hit a home run to left in Fenway. For years the sign read 315 at the left-field foul pole. But over the years many people pooh-poohed that figure, saying it was very generous. More than one person (including, I am told, manager Joe Morgan) hauled out a tape measure in order to do his own survey.

The *Boston Globe* once conducted aerial surveillance and determined, with the help of some MIT sort, that the actual distance was closer to 300 feet. Estimates ranged as low as 291.

The Red Sox themselves 'fessed up in the early '90s. Without much fanfare, they painted a new figure: 310. Whatever. It's not much.

One problem: the ball must have loft. The Wall is 37 feet high, and that's pretty steep. Therein lies the ultimate charm of The Wall. Crappy little fly balls which would be routine outs in every other park in baseball can become three-run homers in Fenway. (Think Bucky Dent in 1978. Every Red Sox fan has.) But vicious line-drive shots ticketed for arrival in neighboring states smash off The Wall and become angry singles. The Wall rewards certain types of hitters more than others. One of the most fearsome men ever to swing a bat in Fenway Park was Harmon Killebrew, who had a great fly ball stroke. But Frank Howard, another slugger, was more the line drive sort. Fenway caged him. There are many other examples.

Fenway offered other peculiarities. Mounted on the left side of the manually operated scoreboard in left field is a ladder. It is used by members of the ground crew, one of whom mounts it at the conclusion of each day's batting practice in order to retrieve the many baseballs which have landed in the net atop the wall. A baseball occasionally strikes the ladder on the fly and bounds away.

There is also a corrugated door down the left-field line. It sits a few feet short of the wall, and when a hooking baseball enters the doorway it has been known to ricochet back and forth, eluding the grasp of a frustrated fielder, while men round the bases.

Then there is the wind. In the months of April, May and September, there is more of a chill in the air and the ball won't carry very well. But a ball which might go no farther than the warning track in those months might carry into the screen or even over the works in June, July and August. The wind direction is, of course, a known variable. When the wind is blowing in, at any time of the year, Fenway and Yellowstone might as well be twin brothers.

All these things were known, but in the mid-60s they were not dwelt upon. The great ballpark building boom was just starting to take place. Old, charming parks in such cities as St. Louis, Philadelphia, Pittsburgh and Cincinnati, to name four (all privately financed under an entirely different economic climate), were in the process of being razed in favor of multipurpose stadiums that were now being underwritten by the public. Ebbets Field in Brooklyn ceased having a function when the Dodgers left for Los Angeles at the conclusion of the 1957 season, while the Polo Grounds in New York would, after serving for two years as the home of the expansion New York Mets, meet its rendezvous with the wrecking ball, as well.

People just naturally assumed that newer, bigger and perhaps even cleaner would inherently be better, but it did not take long for people to discover that the reality was something far different. The old parks, cramped, and strewn with bothersome poles, and perhaps lacking in decent parking, had a certain *Je ne sais quoi* the newer parks would not have if they should last as long as the Pyramids. People were learning that the old, idiosyncratic parks actually contributed to the product. People were learning that there was actually something to be said for asymmetry (with the notable exception of the two warhorse ballparks in Chicago, most of the lovable old parks were outrageously misshapen).

Baseball is, as much as anything else, a game of *conversation*. There is a lot of down time in between pitches and innings and pitching changes, and there is always something to talk about. One of the endless topics of conversation among those people, like myself, who are fortunate enough to have the necessary frame of reference, is how the ball we have just seen hit would have had a different consequence somewhere else. You cannot do this in football, hockey or basketball. A touchdown is a goal is a basket, period.

219

Not so in baseball. A ballpark is not unlike a golf course, in that, while it may indeed be an inanimate object, it is, nevertheless, a significant contributor to the outcome of a game. That 317½-foot fly ball right down the line in Boston would be an out in Cleveland. But that vicious line drive home run in Baltimore is just a shrill single in Boston.

The old ballparks were all built with *landmarks*. The concrete ovals of the '60s had none. They were all symmetrical and dull, and they provided no frames of reference. Home runs were just home runs. You didn't threaten the windows of the laundry located across York Street in the new park in Cincinnati as you had when the Reds played their games in cozy Crosley Field. There was only one concave wall, and that was the right-field wall in Brooklyn. You could only take aim at the Goldenberg's Peanut Chew sign in Philadelphia. If you wanted the opportunity to see an outfielder frantically searching for a baseball enmeshed in ivy, your only option was to go to Wrigley Field.

No one planned it that way. No one sat down in 1909, when Forbes Field in Pittsburgh and Shibe Park in Philadelphia were constructed; or in 1912 when Navin Field (later Briggs Stadium and now Tiger Stadium) and Fenway Park were constructed; or even in 1924-25 when Sportsmans Park in St. Louis and Crosley Field in Cincinnati were renovated into their final configurations, and said, "We're going to jazz up the game by doing this or that." The ballparks of the day were all located in urban locales. The architect was told, "Here is your plot of land; build me a ballpark." They worked with whatever shaped piece of acreage they were presented with. They just happened, but the result was baseball magic.

People understand all this now. Since the construction of Baltimore's Oriole Park at Camden Yards in 1992, the new mantra of American baseball park construction is, "Everything old is new again." Retro is in. The new parks are simply the old parks with modern amenities. Everyone stuck in one of those multipurpose stadia wants his own new park. Even the football people are unhappy. It turns out the concrete ovals weren't much better for football. They were misnamed from the start. "Multipurpose?"

Uh-uh. "No purpose" better describes them.

But this was not readily apparent in the mid-60s. Updike's lofty tribute aside, the people of Boston did not regard Fenway as anything more than a distant cousin you might visit once a year, just to be sociable.

The Red Sox had last truly contended in 1950. There were a couple of feeble half-season runs thrown in there, but nothing more than that. The fans of the '50s had Williams, Jackie Jensen (the 1958 MVP) and wacky Jimmy Piersall to focus on, but not a whole lot more. The major preoccupation from 1962 through 1964 was hoping that hulking right-handed reliever Dick Radatz, nicknamed "The Monster," would get into the game. He was a 6-6, 225-pound terror who had a fastball which exploded out of an almost effeminate, soft 'n easy motion. They also had Carl Yastrzemski, who had succeeded Ted Williams in left field and who had even won the batting title in 1963. But he was generally regarded as a sulking underachiever who couldn't get along with his superiors. Some even said that his petulance had even cost the popular Johnny Pesky his managing job.

The one thing that could be said was that the ninth-place finish in 1966 was a better showing than the ninth-place finish in 1965. Instead of 60 victories and a 40-game deficit, the Red Sox had advanced to 72 victories and a 28-game deficit. They had come up with a slugging rookie first baseman, George Scott. Jim Lonborg was a pitcher of some promise. Yastrzemski was only 27, and — who knows? — he might get better. And there was a new manager. Well, sure, if you follow the Red Sox you understood that there was almost *always* a new manager, but people were saying there might be something different about this one.

11

The

Impossible Dream

Richard Hirschfeld Williams might have been a great ballplayer. He mighta been a contenduh.

Then he hurt his arm trying to make a play. He caught one coming in, but his momentum sent him tumbling forward. He felt something pop in his arm. The year was 1951. The trainer probably rubbed some alcohol into it. The manager (and since the manager was Charlie Dressen this is probably what he really *did* say) probably told him to rub some dirt in it. The year was 1951. He was 23. It's a terrible thing to be 23, and smart enough to know that you have just been removed from the ranks of the Indispensable and placed into the ranks of the Expendable, and that this would remain the case for the remainder of your career.

What Dick Williams turned out to be, through 13 years and 1,023 major-league games, was a roster-filler, a guy useful enough to be sought after, but not valuable enough to be protected for very long. He was an outfielder, third baseman and first baseman who played for the Dodgers, Orioles, Indians and A's, before closing out his career by playing 140 games over the 1963 and 1964 season for the Red Sox. The most memorable thing he did while wearing a Red Sox uniform was hit a ball in the direction of the Red Sox bullpen which was 99.999 percent certain of being a home run. But Cleveland center fielder Al Luplow made an airborne catch, plummeting into the enclosure while holding onto the baseball. This was pre-*Sports Center*, and even pre-local TV sports. There are sequence newspaper photos, but no video account. People who were there, including some veteran scribes who could answer in the affirmative if asked if they had ever seen the Speaker-Lewis-Hooper outfield play in person, swore on the spot it was the greatest catch in the history of the ballpark. It may very well be, but we'll never know.

What we *do* know is that for the 36-year-old Dick Williams it was just another "8" in the scorebook. It was, in fact, the story of his baseball life.

Dick Williams was one of those players who was destined to be a manager. Everybody knew it. He was a "student-of-the-game" type, if ever there was one, and so it came as no surprise when he was given a quite prestigious Triple A managing job as soon as he retired. What was surprising was that the team entrusting him with its top farm club was the Boston Red Sox. He did not seem to be the Tom Yawkey type.

Yawkey had always been partial to schmoozers and drinkers. With Williams, it was 1-for-2. He'd take a drink with you, but he was sure as hell no back-slapper. He was caustic, outspoken and very sure of himself. If the Red Sox really were interested in erasing the Country Club image, they had picked the right guy.

But what was he getting himself into? This was a ninth-place team two years running. Yes, the Red Sox had actually played some solid baseball in the second half of the 1966 season, but they certainly didn't have the aura of a contender.

Dick Williams was the type of player who was destined to become a manager. (Photo©Dick Raphael)

Williams ran a tough training camp and he did a lot of talking. One statement above all jumped out. "We'll win more than we lose," he vowed. The fans and the media were more amused than energized by the bold proclamation. The Red Sox had last won more games than they had lost in 1958, when they had finished a Gentleman's Third behind New York and Chicago by winning 79 and losing 75.

The favorites were Chicago and Minnesota. The Red Sox were picked by one and all to be a second-division team. But everyone knew that it would be an interesting season, for Dick Williams was an "in-your-face" manager before anyone had even conceived of the phrase.

By Red Sox standards, April was a very good month. The Red Sox emerged from the month with an 8-6 record, which was good for third place behind Detroit and New York. But the entire league was bunched. Minnesota was last with a 5-10 record, but the Twins were only 4½ games out of first. Ten teams were thinking, "Geez, ya think?..."

The highlight of the month came on Friday, April 14, when rookie left-hander Bill Rohr nearly became the second man in major-league history to pitch a no-hitter in his major-league debut. You can't come much closer, since he took his no-no against the Yankees right down to two outs in the ninth before cagey veteran Elston Howard lined a single to right-center.

I was no Red Sox fan then, but I was a baseball fan, and I recall listening to the end of the game on the radio. The seminal moment had come at the outset of the Yankee ninth when Tom Tresh stepped up and smashed one in the direction of deep left-center, a vast expanse which in Yankee Stadium was, and is, known as "Death Valley."

Carl Yastrzemski, even then a two-time Gold Glove winner in left, reacted perfectly. From the first stride, he ran after an uncatchable baseball as if he was going to catch it, no questions asked. As the ball was making its descent, he willed his body diagonally to a full extension and caught the ball just before he landed on the Yankee Stadium turf with tremendous force. I can still hear the voice of Red Sox announcer Ken Coleman saying, "And Yastrzemski makes a tremenjus catch!" I am certain of that, and I have heard that description replayed many more times over the years. Coleman has a wonderful voice and superb diction, but at that moment, in the heat of battle, he was so excited the word "tremendous" came out as "tremenjus." And it sure as hell was. That one, unlike the Luplow catch on Dick Williams, lives on in video.

But after retiring Joe Pepitone on a routine fly ball for out number two, Rohr was done in by Howard. He finished up with a one-hit shutout. Baseball being baseball, and arms, in particular, being arms, Bill Rohr won exactly two more Big League games, one more for the Red Sox that season and one for Cleveland the following year. No matter. When people begin rhapsodizing about the 1967 season, one of the first questions invariably asked is, "So, do you remember what *you* were doing when you heard Ken Coleman describe Yaz's catch in the Billy Rohr game?"

The other on-field April highlight came two days later, when the Yanks and Red Sox needed 18 innings to resolve matters. New York won it, 7-6, as the Red Sox stranded 13 men in scoring position.

The *real* story in April was that no longer was it business as usual at Fenway. There was a Captain Bligh in charge. He just wanted to win ballgames, not secure a nomination for Diplomat of the Year. George Scott found this out when he picked up the morning paper one day to read the following: "I'll have (Tony) Horton at first base. Scott has been awful hitting, and his fielding hasn't been so fabulous that Horton will hurt us out there...The last three times up, he struck out with men on base. Trying to talk to him is like talking to cement." And after the 18-inning, five-hour ordeal in Yankee Stadium, after which the team had flown directly to Chicago, he had ordered 17 members of the team out of bed for an early morning workout at Comiskey Park. Yastrzemski was not one of the conscripts, but he was so taken by the forceful personality of the new skipper he went to the ballpark, anyway.

May was a tread water month. The most important thing that happened was that no team in the league had established itself as the one to beat. All the contenders had flaws. The Red Sox came out of the month with a 22-20 record. Despite losing nine of 15 in one stretch they were still only 4½ games behind first place Detroit.

There was bad and there was good. One of the good days was Sunday, May 21. I remember it as the day I said to my girlfriend, Elaine Murray, "The Sox are playing two today. Wanna go?" And so we did. I bought two bleacher tickets and we sat in brilliant sunshine to see the Red Sox beat the Indians, 4-3 and 6-2. George Scott won Game 1 with a homer into the Red Sox bullpen. I can still see that ball coming toward us in the bleachers, Honest to God. And I've still got a ticket stub from that game. I had such a good feeling coming

By 1967 Carl Yastrzemski was a two-time Gold Glove winner, and by the end of May that season he already had 10 home runs. (Photo©Dick Raphael)

out of those games that I made a point to save the stub and write the scores, plus a "Scott HR wins 1st G" on the back. They were Games 1 and 2 of what would turn out to be the greatest pure fan experience of my life.

The Red Sox must have sensed something, too. Word is they had a pretty boisterous clubhouse celebration following the second game.

At the end of May one statistic was very interesting. Carl Yastrzemski already had 10 home runs. He had never been a big-time, flex-those-biceps, home run hitter, and why should he have been? He was 5-11 and about 175 to 180 pounds and he was a left-handed hitter in Fenway Park. Rather than aggravate himself and his manager(s) by swinging mightily and hitting 380-foot outs, he had taught himself to become a reliable opposite-field hitter. His offensive forte during the first six years of his career had been spraying singles and doubles off The Wall. Going into the 1967 season he had career totals of 227 doubles and 95 home runs. He had twice led the American League in doubles. He had hit 20 homers once. When a guy is 27 with those credentials, you can safely say he is what he is, and move on.

But now Yaz clearly wasn't the same guy who had hit 16 home runs in 1966. The story was that he had taken a good look at himself following that season and decided he wasn't getting enough out of his ability. It wasn't that he was out of shape, it was just that he wasn't in the *best possible shape*. The truth is that few baseball players were.

Oh, were these different times. Baseball players spent the off-season in a sedentary manner. Spring training was spent knocking off the extra 12 or 15 pounds the wintertime easy livin' had brought on. About the only ones who got any exercise were the rural guys who were into hunting ("Helps keep the ol' legs in shape"). Weight lifting? No way. The wisdom of the day said that weightlifting was foolish because all it did was make you tight and "muscle-bound," whatever that was.

Carl Yastrzemski was going very much against the grain of the times when he presented himself to a physical fitness expert named Gene Berde at the Colonial Golf Club in Lynnfield, Mass., in the winter of 1966-67 and said, "Get me in shape." The dour Hungarian was skeptical, because he regarded these American team sport athletes the way a French gourmet chef regards a hot dog. He thought they were indolent, spoiled, lazy and completely unworthy of his attention. He barely regarded them as athletes.

But Gene Berde soon learned that Carl Yastrzemski was different.

He was the son of a hard-nosed Eastern Long Island potato farmer, and he was not afraid of work. He had come to Boston under extraordinarily difficult circumstances, as would anyone whose task it

229

was to succeed Ted Williams as left fielder for the Boston Red Sox. He wasn't Ted, of course. He was Carl Yastrzemski, a completely different kind of hitter. He was also not geared to be a public person. He did not take well to the give-and-take process of the media, and Boston was then a very competitive newspaper town. He was shy, introverted and he had little to say. He just wanted to show up, do his job and go home without being forced to offer any explanations.

He was hard on himself. As he would point out in his dotage, the game never really came easy to him. He wasn't big. He wasn't fast. He was just a plugger. He saw others more naturally gifted who had no idea how to apply their gifts, and it really frosted him. In his mind he was the kid who stayed up all night, night after night, in order to get a B. He walked into the Hall of Fame never thinking of himself as an A student.

The workouts with Gene Berde, he figured, might be his edge. If nothing else, he would at least be giving baseball his very best shot. He would hate to be taking the gold watch some day in the future knowing that he could have squeezed more out of his career. Here he was, 27 years of age, with six unfulfilled years already in the books. Enough was enough.

The town was stirring. Years of baseball ranging from the mediocre to the downright insulting had created a town of diamond cynics. The '64 team had hung around the race until June. Then there was a weekend series in New York, and that was that. I happened to be at the Sunday game in Yankee Stadium with my good friend Tom Haney, a really serious Red Sox fan, despite the fact that he had been raised in Pennsylvania and now lived in Delaware (those who don't follow sports could never possibly understand). The big play in that game was a ball which went right through first baseman Dick Stuart's legs with the bases loaded. If I'm not mistaken Yogi Berra scored the third run all the way from first base with a head first slide (Don't hold me to that one). The 1964 Red Sox were never heard from again.

The idea of actually being involved in a pennant race had certainly not occurred to the fans of Boston before the season started. If the team could actually fulfill the manager's "win-more-than-we-lose" prediction, that would be great. They might actually draw a million into Fenway for the first time since 1960 (Williams' last year, if you're into cause-and-effect theories), and that might make the old man smile a bit. That would mean he'd actually lose a little *less* money, not that it really mattered.

But let the record show that on Memorial Day, 1967, a crowd of 32,012 came to Fenway to see a doubleheader with the California Angels. This was the largest Fenway gathering in five years. The fans were rewarded with a pair of victories. Tony Horton's pinch-hit double made a winner out of Dan Osinski in the first game, while shortstop Rico Petrocelli brought the crowd to its feet in Game 2 with a successful suicide squeeze bunt in the midst of a 6-1 triumph. It may have been a lot longer than five years since anyone had witnessed anything like *that* in Fenway Park, at least not on behalf of the home team. People left the ballyard that day skipping and humming and perhaps even dreaming. This Williams guy actually had the Boston Red Sox playing *baseball*. It was no longer just Home Run Derby.

The Red Sox were obviously better than they had been in years, and better than anyone (except, possibly, Williams) had expected, but were they good enough to win? Did they have enough? Dick O'Connell apparently didn't think so, and he was the general manager.

A Red Sox employee since 1946, Dick O'Connell was definitely from the old school. A Bostonian through and through, he was part of the cadre which kept Tom Yawkey company when he hit town each June. He had been appointed general manager on September 16, 1965, a five-star news day in Boston since it was also the day that Dave Morehead had picked to throw an afternoon no-hitter against the Indians.

He was the one who hired Dick Williams to manage the Red Sox after his two successful seasons in Toronto. He was a character in his own right. He quite literally talked out of the side of his mouth, and his thought process was anything but linear. An O'Connell conversation seldom went from A to B to C, and so on. He was Felliniesque, dealing in verbal flashbacks. But he always knew where he was going, even if you didn't.

He was a busy man during the first week in June. On June 3 he traded aging reliever Don McMahon and minor-league pitcher Rob Snow to the White Sox for veteran infielder Jerry Adair. The latter was a close-mouthed, Gary Cooper-type, "I-seen-my-duty-and-I-done-it" sort, so introverted that announcer Ned Martin quickly dubbed him "Casper, the Friendly Ghost." He was a second baseman by trade, but he could also play shortstop and third, and he could handle the bat.

The next day O'Connell made a move to strengthen a pitching staff which was a bit thin in starters. He shipped long-disappointing infielder Tony Horton and journeyman outfielder Don Demeter to Cleveland for right handed-pitcher Gary Bell, a solid starter with such a well-developed taste for night life that he was unashamed to tell the world that his pet dog's name was "Cutty Sark."

To this point the pitching load was being carried pretty much by one man, Jim Lonborg. He was a cerebral Californian — a Stanford biology major, in fact — who had joined the team in 1965 and who had shown some potential while going 9-17 and 10-10 for those ninth-place teams. He had gone to pitch in Venezuela after the 1966 season, and while there he underwent something of an epiphany when he was shown the value of pitching inside. Waaay inside.

He always had stuff. He had a good sinking fastball and a sharp overhand curve. What he needed was what the professionals call *command*, or what boxing people might call ring generalship. In his case the missing ingredient was attitude. Not for nothing was the 6-foot-4 inch Californian known as "Gentleman Jim." Off the field, he was scholarly and polite, courtly, even. At least one hard-bitten member of the Boston press corps would never cease referring to Lonborg as "Alice."

But the transformation from the 1966 Lonborg into the 1967 Lonborg was every bit as dramatic as Yastrzemski's. By the end of May Jim Lonborg had a 6-1 record and was leading the American League in strikeouts. He was also establishing a reputation as a tough guy. He was throwing inside on a regular basis, and if he was hitting a guy here or there, *c'est la guerre*. People were even going so far as to label him a "headhunter." For that, Dick Williams might have been willing to kiss him flush on the lips.

In the South and West, there is spring and then there is summer. In Boston, spring is a rumor. Here is the Boston/Upper New England weather calendar: summer, a little less summer, pretty much winter, winter, a little less winter, summer. Summer officially begins around June 21, but we all know that if you live in Tucson, or even

Charlotte, summer goes from May 1 or so till the end of September, and perhaps even beyond. In Boston summer goes from Memorial Day, if you're lucky, through Labor Day.

Many people in Boston pay only peripheral attention to the Red Sox in April and May because in their minds it really isn't baseball season yet. Too damn cold, windy and raw. Period. I am talking about the generic sports fan, the one who puts TV ratings over the top and who needs a *reason* to get interested in the team. I'm not talking about season ticket holders or fourth-generation fans or what we call in the late '90s, the get-a-lifers.

This was also a point in time, remember, when the ballpark had not yet become the superstar it is today. Fenway Park had not yet been discovered. Fenway Chic would come later.

So what had been happening in the post-Williams (Ted, that is) era is that the generic fans had never been able to get into the baseball season because, with the exception of 1964, for them it had never really gotten started. By the time they had checked on the Red Sox, they were 15 out and the only remaining issue was just exactly when the manager would get fired.

Things were different in 1967. Here it was, June 1, and the Red Sox were not only above .500 but *still technically in the race*. And the generics were hearing from the diehards that there was something very odd about this season. There were a lot of OK teams, but no team the Red Sox actually had to fear. I can just hear the water cooler conversations.

"Don't think I'm crazy, but I swear the Red Sox might be just as good as anyone else this year."

"Shoo-ah, and I'm the friggin' Queen of England."

"No, I swe-ah."

Lonborg cranked it up, but good, on June 2, taking a no-hitter one out in the eighth against Cleveland. He came away with a three-hit, 2-1 victory. He was now 7-1. Maybe it was too early to call it a pennant race, but one sure sign that the Red Sox were being taken seriously was that opponents were mouthing off. There was no one more strident in the American League than Chicago White Sox skipper Eddie Stanky, who early in his playing career which had begun in

1943 had been nicknamed "The Brat." No Yastrzemski fan, he was widely quoted as saying that Yaz was "an All-Star from the neck down." The Yastrzemski response was to bang out four hits and make three sparkling catches in a 7-3 victory on June 8.

Speak to any manager or player who has ever been part of a pennant winner, and he will tell you that during the course of the six-month marathon there are *always* a handful of defining moments, plays or games from which a team is able to draw energy and emotional sustenance as the season goes on. I know it is foolish in the minds of some to suggest that an April or May game can have season-long ramifications, but it can.

June counts, too, and on the night of June 15 the Red Sox got a huge lift from Tony Conigliaro.

Each sport has a unique brand of tension. One of baseball's contributions to the sports treasure chest is the true pitchers' duel. The unlikely mound combatants on this June evening were Bruce Howard for the White Sox and rookie right-hander Gary Waslewski for the Red Sox. Together they were 37-47 lifetime, but on this night they might as well have been Christy Mathewson and Grover Cleveland Alexander, for at the end of 10 innings the score was 0-0.

The White Sox pushed across a run off Boston reliever John Wyatt in the top of the 11th. After effervescent Walt (No Neck) Williams led off with a double, Don Buford came up to bunt. After squaring off, he tried to cross up the Red Sox by swinging away. The result was a vicious line drive down the first base line. Somehow, some way, George Scott, the best fielding first baseman in Red Sox history, contorted his body to make the catch. One away.

Wyatt struck out Tommy Agee. Two out. But Ken Berry punched a single to right. 1-0, Chicago.

Stanky brought in veteran John Buzhardt, who easily retired Yastrzemski and Scott. One out away from a crushing defeat, the Red Sox remained alive as Joe Foy poked a single to left.

That brought up Tony Conigliaro, a local hero who had not been able to regain his batting eye and stroke following a two-week Army Reserve stint (These were different times).

He swung and missed at two Buzhardt curves, and, frankly, he looked helpless and totally overmatched. But Buzhardt next missed

In 1967 Gary Waslewski was a rookie right-hander for the Red Sox, while catcher Elston Howard was a 38-year-old veteran picked up in a trade earlier in the year. (Photo©Dick Raphael)

the strike zone with two curves and a fastball, and now the count was full. Buzhardt went to his bread and butter, the overhand curve.

Tony C swung and from the instant it left the bat there was no doubt. It was net-bound. In those days even a big home run was normally handled with restraint. A man could expect a greeting at home plate from the man, or men, on base, and no one else. But this time Tony Conigliaro was greeted by every man who had been on the bench. The Red Sox were starting to believe that something special was happening — and so was the city of Boston.

Tony Conigliaro was a hometown hero who hit a home run in his first at bat at Fenway Park. He was hit in the face by a pitch during the 1967 season and missed all of the 1968 season. His career was never the same after that. (Photo©Dick Raphael)

Tony Conigliaro was then 22 years old, and not merely on top of the world, but also the universe. He was a hometown boy then in his fourth season in the major leagues. How great was *that*? He broke into the majors at age 18, still living at home, and hit a home run in his first Fenway Park at bat. The next year he led the league in home runs. At age 19. Can you spell C-o-o-p-e-r-s-t-o-w-n? It was easy to assume he would become a 500-homer guy if he were to spend his career in a Red Sox uniform. And surely 600 wasn't out of the question if you allow for some reasonable year-to-year technical improvement right into his 30s.

He was a right-handed hitter with a classic Fenway stroke, and right from the start he had a flair for the dramatic. They always speak in the dugouts about the special guys you'd like to see up with men on base and the game on the line. Tony C was one of those guys.

He might have been in a little slump when he came up to the plate to face John Buzhardt, but that was transitory. No one was worried about Tony C. He was going to hit.

Tony was special to Boston fans, because he truly was one of them. He had an eye for the ladies and he also had some entertainment sense. He had even stepped into the recording studio to record *Playing The Field*, *Little Red Scooter* and *Why Don't They Understand?* He was way ahead of his time.

One week after the big Conigliaro blast, the Red Sox officially rekindled the ancient rivalry with the New York Yankees. Taking center stage was Jim Lonborg, who, in his new self-appointed role as the team's policeman, touched off a small-scale riot.

The story had begun the night before, when Bronx-born Joe Foy had delivered a grand slam home run in a 7-1 Boston victory. In the second inning of this game, Yankee starter Thad Tillotson hit Foy with a pitch. Message delivered.

This was before the designated hitter was inflicted on the American public. Tillotson had to bat in the bottom of the inning. Lonborg wasted no time, drilling the Yankee pitcher between the shoulder blades. The two exchanged words, with Foy chiming in from his perch on third base. That did it.

Benches emptied. It took 12 special policemen, one of whom was Brooklyn native Rico Petrocelli's brother, to break it up. An inning later Tillotson hit Lonborg with a pitch. You can imagine what happened next.

The fortunate thing was that when it was all over no one had gotten hurt. The Red Sox went on to win the game and Lonborg was being looked upon all around the American League as a guy you didn't fool around with.

June was just a so-so month (15-14), but when it was over the Red Sox were still in the unaccustomed position of being in the race, even with a mediocre 37-34 record. Chicago was up by 4½, but the first six teams were separated by just 7½ games with the season nearing the halfway point.

Yastrzemski's season totals were .331, 18 home runs and 53 runs batted in.

The Red Sox were still new to all this, and when they lost five games in a row early in July people had reason to believe the little run was over. On the Sunday before the All-Star break Lonborg went to the mound in Detroit and pitched a very important game, going the first seven innings in a 3-0 victory over the Tigers. Wyatt picked him up in the eighth and ninth. Rookie center fielder Reggie Smith (also the answer to the trivia question. "Who was the starting second baseman on Opening Day for the 1967 Red Sox?") hit a two-run homer.

There is no question this was a big game, not only for the Red Sox themselves, but for the fans, as well. Everyone needed reassurance that the Red Sox really were a team of substance.

The All-Star break may have come just in time to save the Red Sox from themselves. They were not used to this kind of intensive play, and they really needed a break, both mentally and physically.

On Friday, July 14, the Red Sox spanked the Orioles, 11-5. Conigliaro hit a home run which had everyone talking. One of the things about putting one out in Fenway's left field is that once it leaves the park it is difficult to know for sure just how far it may have gone. According to the eye witnesses to this particular first-inning blast off Oriole rookie Mike Anderson, this one might have come down in Canada.

Two days later Dick O'Connell was heard from again, shipping veteran George Smith, an infielder who hadn't played all season after tearing up his knee in the spring, to San Francisco for Norm Siebern, a left-handed hitter whose best years had come as a member of the New York Yankees.

Siebern had even been a contributing factor to my absolute favorite of all Yogi Berra lines. After watching Siebern struggle with the treacherous late-afternoon shadows in Yankee Stadium's left field, Yogi observed, "It gets late early out there."

The Red Sox were now winning as a matter of course, so much so that when they arrived in Cleveland on Saturday, July 22, they had a seven-game winning streak and were in sole possession of second place. Lee Stange beat the Indians on Saturday, and when the Red Sox swept a Sunday doubleheader they had a 10-game streak, and now it was official.

Boston was convinced. There were no more doubters, no more skeptics. The people had seen and heard and read enough. They had given their precious *imprimatur* to the 1967 Red Sox.

What I am saying is that for the remainder of July, and for all of August and September, Boston and New England were totally captivated by the Red Sox, and I mean completely.

We were still living in an age of innocence. Though the Red Sox were annually among baseball's leaders in televising games, it was nothing like it would be today, when they televise every one of the 162 games. Radio was still king.

You may have heard people claim they recall circumstances in which you could make your way around City X in the middle of a pennant race and not lose touch with the local baseball team because everyone seemed to have a radio tuned to the broadcast, and you may have dismissed this as pure hyperbole.

I am here to tell you that this is precisely what was going on, each and every night in Greater Boston during the summer of 1967.

I vividly recall visiting a friend in Cambridge, right across the Charles River. Driving over, I heard nothing but either Ken Coleman's or Ned Martin's voice at every red light. As we walked the streets of Cambridge, there was a radio carrying their voices on every porch. It was a complete revival of baseball interest in Greater Boston, and indeed all of New England.

And it wasn't just the basic idea that the team was winning, either. It had something to do with who the players were and how they were winning. Carl Yastrzemski had been reborn as a slugger without losing his other skills. Always acknowledged to be a superior defensive player, he was now submitting his finest defensive year, to complement his finest offensive year. In everyone's mind's eye all baseballs in all key situations were being directed toward Yaz when he was in the field. And when the Red Sox needed a big hit, Yastrsemski always seemed to be at the plate. It was, everyone maintained, a classic MVP performance.

Lonborg was the obvious Cy Young Award leader. There was no more dominating or majestic pitcher in the league. Tony C was once again Tony C. George Scott was knocking out homers while playing the most wide-ranging and sure-handed first base in the league. Jose Santiago, a pitcher whose right elbow was said to be held together by a surgical staple, was winning games, as was Cutty Sark's owner, the colorful Gary Bell.

Rico Petrocelli was supplying surprising power at short while making every play in the field. Jerry Adair was making Dick O'Connell look like a very prescient fellow. He was playing well in the field and delivering the type of hits that keep rallies going. John Wyatt was a reliable closer.

And always there was the prickly Williams, pushing, prodding, probing, agitating and intimidating friend and foe alike. He had brought a new, dicey edge to a team that had been ridiculed for the better part of 20 years as a team of utter dilettantes.

When the Red Sox returned to Boston after sweeping the Indians they were greeted by a delirious crowd at Logan Airport. There hadn't been such an outpouring of civic support for a Red Sox team since Nuf Ced and his boys were in their prime.

A crowd in excess of 32,000 came to see the first game back home after the winning streak. They went away disappointed, as California won, 6-4. But the Sox rebounded the following evening, although it took them a while to get rolling. Ancient California lefty George Brunet took a 4-1 lead into the seventh, but the Red Sox erupted for seven runs and the victory.

It was impossible not to become swept up in the excitement. Fenway Park now had an entirely new personality. It was no longer the frowning grandma, warning you not to put your feet up on the sofa. Now it was an amusement park. People were falling in love with both the park and the game all over again. Folks who hadn't come to the park since Ted Williams retired were dusting off their lingo once again and buying tickets. Suddenly, *everybody* in town just happened to be there when player-manager Joe Cronin pinch-hit himself for game-winning homers in both ends of a 1943 Sunday doubleheader. Suddenly, *everybody* in town happened to be in the crowd when the Red Sox beat the St. Louis Browns, 29-4, in 1950. And suddenly *everybody* in town just happened to be in Fenway Park on June 18, 1953, when the Red Sox established a major-league record that still stands by scoring 17 runs in the seventh inning of a 23-3 victory over Detroit. And, of course *everybody* in Boston just happened to be in Fenway eight years later to the day when Jim Pagliaroni's grand slam gave the Red Sox a 13-12 victory to cap a Red Sox rally that had begun with the team trailing, 12-5, two outs and nobody on in the ninth.

And is it necessary to mention that *everybody* in Boston happened to be in Fenway Park on September 28, 1960, when Ted Williams hit a home run off Baltimore's Jack Fischer in his final at bat?

Like most of the baseball-loving public, the Red Sox had taken over my life. On one lunch hour I took advantage of a fresh paycheck to buy some tickets for the remainder of the season. After spending the months of June and July sitting in the bleachers, I did not want to take any chances on being shut out in the heat of a pennant race. I was going to buy two tickets for six games, which was as many games as I could afford. Gazing up at the giant schedule posted above the ticket windows, I noticed that Minnesota was coming in for the final two games of the season on Saturday, September 30 and Sunday, October 1. I knew I'd be going to a Boston College-Army football game on Saturday, but Sunday sounded pretty good to me. I scooped up two choice box seats. In case the final game meant anything, Elaine and I would be sitting right behind the home plate screen, a little up the third-base line, in section 22, box 122E, seats 9 and 10. $3 apiece. Such innocence. This really *was* a long time ago.

◆　◆　◆

241

The Red Sox hit August with a 56-44 record. They were two games behind Chicago. Five games separated Chicago, Boston, Detroit, Minnesota and California.

On August 3 O'Connell bolstered a soft spot on the roster by picking up catcher Elston Howard from the Yankees.

August 1967. I remember the same thing everyone else does. I remember the last two weekends. Most of all, I remember the night of Friday, August 18. Yes, I was there when Tony C was hit in the face.

I didn't have a ticket. Elaine was visiting a friend on Cape Cod, and I was planning on sitting in the bleachers by myself. A couple of blocks from the ballpark, a guy offered me a box seat along the third-base line for face value. Great.

In the first inning California's Jimmy Hall lifted a soft pop foul down the first-base line. The ball bounced a few times and rolled under my seat. I reached down and picked up the only foul ball I have ever gotten while attending a baseball game, minus one I retrieved when it flew through an open window in the Tiger Stadium press box. I put the Jimmy Hall foul ball in a special case and it sits in my office today.

It was a strange evening. Bell looked great, but Jack Hamilton was matching zeroes through three. Scott led off the fourth with a single but was thrown out trying for two. Then someone threw a smoke bomb out of the left-field stands, holding up the game for a good 10 minutes. When play resumed, Reggie Smith flied out. That brought up Conigliaro.

Tony was notorious for hanging over the plate, but no matter what anyone told him, he wasn't going to change. He was Tony C, and he owned Boston. This time his general good luck ran out. A Hamilton fast-ball crashed into his face.

Tony Conigliaro was seriously injured. He would miss the rest of the season and all of 1968. The rest of his amazing life was a soap opera, culminating in a combination heart attack/stroke which incapacitated him completely and resulted in a horribly premature death at the age of 45 in 1990.

The Red Sox won the game, 3-2. Bell took a no-hitter into the seventh before Jimmy Hall — *my* Jimmy Hall — hit a home run into the center-field bleachers. Hall hit another one into the same spot in the ninth, but Bell held on.

Shortstop Rico Petrocelli makes the putout at second base after taking a throw from second baseman Mike Andrews. (Photo©Dick Raphael)

I was back in the bleachers the next day. Before the game, California reliever Jim Coates, a guy with the classic grizzled vet look, delighted in taunting the bleacherites by acting as if he would toss them a ball, but he never did. He really thought this was funny.

A couple of hours later, the laughs were on him. He was on the mound with his team trailing by two at 9-7 with the bases loaded. Williams sent up Norm Siebern, and the ex-Yankee delivered a ringing triple to right-center. No one appreciated the hit more than those of us in the bleachers.

Trailing 12-7, going into the ninth, the Angels staged a rally. They got the lead down to 12-11 and had the bases loaded with two outs. Bob Rodgers came up and hit a Baltimore chop behind the mound. It had been a 3-2 count and that meant the runners were all going. If someone didn't make the play, two runs, not one, would have scored. But Rico Petrocelli came charging in to make a sure-handed pickup and then throw out Rodgers at first. Whew.

George Scott was not only "the best fielding first baseman in Red Sox history," but also batted for a .303 average in 1967. (Photo©Dick Raphael)

That left a Sunday doubleheader. The first game was a snap. Smith switch-hit homers for the first time in his career. It was also the first time it had ever been done by a Red Sox player.

Game 2 was a pennant race classic. The Angels led it after three, 8-0. Can't win 'em all, right?

But you can try. The Red Sox began chipping away. 8-1. 8-4. 8-7. 8-8. And then Jerry Adair hit an eighth-inning home run off Minnie Rojas to win it. I remember exactly where I was: standing in front of the refrigerator in Elaine's kitchen at 39 Glenmont Road in Brighton, Mass. That's what a pennant race does to you. Or should I say *for* you?

Isn't that what being a sports fan means? Remembering where you were when this happened, or when that happened, or perhaps even remembering what song was playing, or what was number 1 on the charts when you did this or that or went here or there?

For example, I was in Mirror Lake, New Hampshire, when Jose Tartabull made The Throw. I sure remember *that*. This was a week later. The Red Sox were in Chicago, and the race tension was now becoming unbearable. It was Sunday afternoon. The Red Sox started the day in first place by a percentage point. They were leading the White Sox, 4-3, with Ken Berry on third and one out. John Wyatt was facing Duane Josephson.

The Chicago catcher hit a fly ball. It looked deep enough to score on Tartabull, a speedy guy not noted for his arm. Berry could scurry. This run was a Chicago gimme. But wait a minute.

As Tartabull's surprisingly strong throw arrived at the plate, 38-year-old Elston Howard demonstrated the wisdom that comes with age, even as he was summoning an athleticism he was no longer supposed to have. He somehow kept his left leg between Berry's sliding leg and the plate while one-handing the throw and slapping on the tag to end the game.

That's what umpire Marty Springstead said, anyway, and his was the only opinion which counted. Stanky howled, of course. Who wouldn't? No one could do what Howard had just done, especially a 38-year old catcher.

What most people forget was that this was the first game of a doubleheader, and that the Red Sox lost the second game. I never forget, because the Red Sox lost the game by a 1-0 score in 11 innings because Darrell (Bucky) Brandon, Boston's most continually ineffective pitcher all season long, spoiled a brilliant starting effort by Jose Santiago by walking four men in the 11th. With the full fury only youthful emotion can bring, I swore vengeance on Darrell Brandon and all future Brandons. Here I was, this disinterested college kid from New Jersey at the start of the season, and now I was prepared to order a hit on relievers who couldn't get the ball over the plate.

You have a certified pennant race if two teams are battling for the prize. Three teams involved spice the plot. Four make it historic.

As we hit September in 1967 we had four, and there was even a fifth, lurking in the weeds.

The American League standings at the conclusion of August:

Team	W	L	Pct.	GB
Boston	76	59	.563	—
Minnesota	74	58	.561	½
Detroit	74	59	.556	1
Chicago	73	59	.553	1½
California	66	65	.504	8

The Red Sox had a very trying week, culminating in a Eugene O'Neil doubleheader in Yankee Stadium on August 29. This extraordinary twin bill consumed 29 innings and resulted in a split.

The Red Sox won the first game, as Lonborg won his 18th with a three-hitter, 2-1.

Game 2 took 20 innings and 6 hours and 15 minutes to play, concluding at 1:57 in the morning. The Red Sox sure thought they were going to come away with an uplifting sweep after going ahead 3-2 with a run in the top of the 11th. But with two outs and two strikes on Steve Whitaker in the bottom of the 11th, rookie left-handed reliever Sparky Lyle couldn't get a call from plate umpire Ed Runge. Whitaker hit the next pitch for a game-tying homer. Nine tedious innings later Horace Clarke singled home the game-winner off Jose Santiago.

The teams were back on the field several hours later for a scheduled day game. Indulge me for another official Fan Experience. I was standing in the shower, gulping a refreshing can of beer (one of life's sweet little pleasures, to my way of thinking), listening to Ken and Ned on WHDH radio (850 on the dial) when Carl Yastrzemski, bogged down in an 0-for-18 dip, hit the game-winning home run right over the famed auxiliary scoreboard in right-center off southpaw Al Downing. Yaz was so exhausted after playing the full 29 the night before he hadn't even started the game. He entered as a defensive replacement in the ninth and popped up meekly against Downing on his first at bat.

Noting that Yaz was still a very average-sized guy and that he had been carrying an extraordinary physical and mental load for five months, people began to wonder if he weren't wearing down. His average had dropped to .308. He had 35 homers — 15 more than his previous career high — and he had already exceeded his 1962 career high of 94 runs batted in. The basic question was what, if anything, he had left?

Yaz had become more than just a very good baseball player. He had become an idol. Baseball was enjoying a rebirth in Boston thanks to this team, and people were thirsting for a true baseball hero, a void that had been filled to only a small degree by the pitching heroics of Dick Radatz. What Boston people really wanted was a *daily* hero. You know, someone like Ted. Yaz might not have been Ted, but in one significant way he was clearly better. Ted never won too many games for the Red Sox with his glove.

Carl Yastrzemski was dead, never to return. For the rest of his career, for better or worse, he was Yaz. The people of New England were now starting their day toasting up some "Big Yaz" bread, and they went on from there. It was Yaz-this, and Yaz-that, and there was even a song written by popular morning personality Jess Cain, who was regaling his many WHDH listeners with his rendition of *Carl Yastrzemski, The Man They Call Yaz.*

"A radio producer named John Connolly came to me with a little song he and his wife had written about Yaz," Cain explains. "I contributed something to it, and I sang it on the air. I did many song parodies involving Boston-area towns in those days, and I figured it would be one time and that would be it for this song. But Harold Clancy, the station owner, loved it. The next thing I knew I was in a limo heading to Fleetwood Records in Revere, Mass., to record *Carl Yastrzemski, The Man They Call Yaz.* People loved it."

At the end of the season, Fleetwood produced a season highlight album called "The Impossible Dream" with the Yaz song interspersed throughout. It sold in excess of 100,000 copies.

There is an interesting postscript to the song.

A few years ago Cain received a call from a representative of the television program *Chicago Hope*, who said that executive producer David Kelley (a Brookline, Mass., native) was looking for permission to use the Carl Yastrzemski song.

"I explained that I really had no call on the song, that the person who should benefit would be John Connolly's widow," says Cain. "John had been dead for quite some time."

With the aid of *Boston Globe* writer Susan Bickelhaupt, they were able to track down Connolly's widow, who was now living in the Washington, D.C., area.

"I forget exactly how much money they paid her," Cain says. "It was something like $1,000 or $1,500. But here's the kicker: she used the money to buy a headstone for John Connolly's grave."

One moral of the story: Ballplayers have absolutely no idea what effect they can have on people's lives.

Understand that the 1967 Red Sox were not a great team. Happily, neither were any of the other contenders. Each team wished it had a bit more of *something*. In Chicago's case, that something was hitting. The White Sox were doing it with sound pitching (four regular pitchers would finish with earned run averages below 2.50) and Stanky's moxie. They would also finish next-to-last in runs scored. But they were perhaps the most-feared team of the four, among the other three. Baseball people are nothing if not orthodox, and they were all afraid of Chicago's pitching. The ancient baseball axiom that good pitching will beat good hitting was uppermost in everyone's mind.

Following every pitch of every Red Sox game in the month of September was something Red Sox fans hadn't been called upon to do in 17 years, or ever since the rollicking 1950 crew — the last major-league baseball team to hit .300, by the way — finished four games behind the New York Yankees. Perhaps there would not have been quite this much excitement had anyone seen this coming. Suppose the Red Sox had been identified as an up-and-coming team for at least a few years. Suppose they had finished, say, seventh in 1964, a creditable fourth in 1965 and either a solid second or third in '66 after perhaps hanging around the race until at least the end of school, if not the Fourth of July. Then the Red Sox would have been fulfilling expectations, and that creates a totally different mind set. The town would have been appreciative, I am sure, but perhaps not so totally captivated.

But this was a complete gift from the entertainment gods. A seventh-place team would have represented improvement. A fifth-place team would have been embraced. But *this*? Actually being in an honest-to-God pennant race with Labor Day approaching? Almost too bleepin' good to be true. The town was galvanized. Nothing else mattered in Boston, and in much of New England, except what happened in yesterday's game. And totally unlike any other sport, a baseball pennant race is a *daily* enterprise. To compare any other sports race to a legitimate baseball pennant race is to wallow in ignorance.

Somewhere along the way, this entire quest had been named "The Impossible Dream." And it certainly wasn't difficult to conjure up the long-ignored Red Sox as a gang of Don Quixotes, tilting against the AL pennant windmill.

As for Yaz? What's to worry? He just had a little slump at the end of August, that's all. The Senators discovered this when he hit home runs number 37 and 38 on September 5. The race was excruciating on a daily basis. Three foes is a lot to keep track of.

One of the September highlights came on the night of the 12th. Lonnie was going for number 20 against Kansas City. I was sitting far down the right-field line, which happens to be the Siberia of Fenway. Lonborg was in and out of trouble all night, but the unquestioned apex of this game occurred in the bottom of the eighth. Lonborg was at the plate in a 1-1 game with catcher Mike Ryan on first. It was a classic sacrifice situation. But after starting to square around as if to bunt, Lonborg drew the bat back and lashed a liner past startled Kansas City right fielder Mike Hershberger. Good God, a triple! There have been many better teams than the 1967 Red Sox, even in Boston, but few which brought the endless possibilities of baseball more alive than the 1967 Red Sox. Lonborgs's fake bunt/three-bagger is Exhibit A.

With 14 games left, the four were separated by a game and a half. Boston, Minnesota and Detroit were tied for first at 84-64. Chicago was slightly in arrears. There was little doubt that the whole thing would be going down to the final weekend. I was selfishly salivating. Those October 1 tickets behind the screen were starting to have the importance of those letters of transit in *Casablanca*.

Yaz was now officially transcendent. He was in the midst of a concluding month in which he would hit .417, with nine home runs, 26 runs batted in and 24 runs scored, all of it augmented by some serious Gold Gloving in left field. He was acting like a leader in every respect. It is small wonder that Williams had always maintained that he has never seen a man have a better individual season than the one Carl Yastrzemski had in 1967.

It was hardly a smooth-sailing month for any of the would-be champions. The Red Sox, for example, lost three straight to Baltimore on September 15-16-17, but were fortunate not to lose any significant ground in the standings. As they arrived in Detroit on Monday, September 18, the four were now separated by just one game! Detroit was in first at 85-65. Chicago was a half-game behind at 85-66. The Red Sox and Tigers were tied at 84-66. It was now a major redundancy to observe that this game or that game was a Big Game. At this point of the season, in this crazy race, they were *all* Big Games.

The Red Sox came to bat in the top of the ninth trailing by a 5-4 score. Yaz came up with one out and none on. Now here was one thing he definitely shared with the great Theodore Samuel Williams. Each man loved batting in Detroit.

It makes sense. The distance to the right-field foul pole is 325 feet. The fence is not too high. The fence creeps away gradually, making the power alley in right-center quite reachable. The double deck stands make for an inviting target.

Williams always raved about Briggs Stadium (it would not be renamed Tiger Stadium until 1960). He had hit his single favorite home run in 1941, when he stepped up to the plate with two on, two out and the American League All-Stars trailing by two runs and had deposited a Claude Pausseau pitch into the stands. There can be little doubt that had he spent his career playing 77 home games a year in Briggs Stadium, rather than Fenway Park, he would have hit 575-600 home runs, as opposed to his career total of 521.

Yaz liked the ballpark for all the same reasons. In addition to everything else, the park was then painted a brilliant green-on-green-on-green all the way around, thus providing the single best hitting background in all of baseball.

Yaz was up there against Fred Lasher thinking one thing, and it wasn't, "Gee, if I can only get on base..." That would have been Carl Yastrzemski's way of thinking, but Carl Yastrzemski no longer existed. Now he was Yaz and Yaz was a long-ball kind of guy.

Lasher was a pretty good reliever. He challenged Yaz with a fastball and Yaz turned it around, drilling the ball into the upper deck. Tie game. One inning later Dalton Jones, a soft-spoken Louisianian with a nice, controlled left-handed stroke, hit the seminal home run of his nine-year major-league career. He only hit three homers all season, but he picked the best possible time to hit one of them, knocking a Mike Marshall pitch into the upper deck that ended the three-game losing streak.

There was more high drama the following evening. The key moment in the game occurred when Dick Williams, a riverboat gambler type of manager all year long, elected to allow rookie left-hander Bill Landis to face veteran slugger Eddie Mathews with the game hanging in the balance. Landis had been a very small cog in the machine. He was one of the team's Army Reservists (Conigliaro and Lonborg were among them), and thus he had missed some time fulfilling his military obligation (Kiddies: ask your dad what this was all about). He had only pitched 29 innings all season and he hadn't worked in 21 days.

So naturally Dick Williams decided that with the Red Sox protecting a 4-2 ninth-inning lead and two men on with one out, this was an ideal time to give Bill Landis some work. Mathews was nearing the end of his Hall of Fame career, but this was a man who would finish with 512 home runs. He was left-handed, and this meant that in Tiger Stadium he was indeed a threat to win the ballgame.

As usual that year, Dick Williams knew what he was doing. Landis fanned Eddie Mathews on a 1-2 pitch, whereupon the skipper said thank you very much and brought in Gary Bell (using a starter in short relief was not such an unthinkable concept in 1967) to retire Al Kaline and thus win the game.

Schedules were different then. Yes, it was a 162-game schedule, the same as it has been since the expansion years of 1961-62, when baseball said goodbye forever to the 16-team concept, but scheduled doubleheaders had not become anathema and there were far more days off in the course of a season than there are today, or ever will be again.

Thus the curious final week of the 1967 season for the Boston Red Sox:

■ Sunday, September 24 — at Baltimore
■ Monday, September 25 — Off
■ Tuesday, September 26 — Cleveland
■ Wednesday, September 27 — Cleveland

■ Thursday, September 28 — Off
■ Friday, September 29 — Off
■ Saturday, September 30 — Minnesota
■ Sunday, October 1 — Minnesota

The Sox finished up their season's work on the road with an 11-7 dispatch of the Orioles. Jones, Adair and Scott had four hits apiece, and Jones' were good for five runs batted in. Lonborg went six scoreless innings to pick up victory number 21 before the bullpen tried to give the game away.

Four games to go. Boston and Minnesota were tied for first at 90-68. Then came Chicago at 89-68, followed by Detroit at 88-69.

There is only one appropriate way to describe the quality of baseball the Red Sox played in Games 159 and 160 against Cleveland on those crisp late summer afternoons, but it wouldn't be particularly tasteful. Let's just say they stunk out the joint.

Bell lost to the Indians by a 6-3 score on Tuesday as the defense fell apart. Yaz did hit number 43, but the score was 6-0 when he did. Lonborg, starting on two days rest, was starched by a four-run second on Wednesday. The final was 6-0.

I was in the bleachers for both games. The ballpark was eerily quiet. It was almost as if the fans were choking, unable to handle true pennant pressure. The mathematics of it all were still manageable, of course, but when I walked out of Fenway that Wednesday I was one of many who believed the gallant run for a miracle pennant was over. The zombie-like play of the Red Sox was an unmistakable sign that they just weren't ready for all this.

But things were never static in 1967. The Red Sox awoke the following morning to discover that the lowly Kansas City A's had taken two from Stanky's White Sox. That finished them emotionally. On Friday night Chicago lost a 1-0 decision to Washington and was eliminated.

So here is the way it stood on the morning of September 30: In order for the Red Sox to be assured of the American League pennant they had to win two from Minnesota while the Tigers were doing no better than a split in the pair of doubleheaders they had remaining. And the Red Sox would rather have been playing anybody but Minnesota, a team against whom they were only 5-11.

Never let anyone tell you that the best team always wins, or that luck is an insignificant variable in matters of sport. The truth is that the best team, that being defined as either a) the team with the most good players, or b) the team which knows how to play the particular game in question better than anyone else, may or may not win. To this day the people involved with the 1967 Minnesota Twins believe they really were the best team that year, and I am inclined to agree with them.

I don't doubt for even half a second, for example, that had Minnesota starter Jim Kaat not blown out his elbow in the third inning of that game the Twins would have won. Kaat continues to believe it, and Kaat is a man who has never been self-delusionary. He had his good stuff that day. It was the biggest game of his life, and he was *ready*.

Luck was a lady for the Red Sox that Saturday afternoon. She wasn't going around blowing on some other guy's dice; she was blowing on theirs. She stayed right by the side of her escort, and her escort was the Boston Red Sox. She got rid of Kaat, who had that three-hit shutout gleam in his eye. She steered a routine grounder to Rod Carew off his shoulder in the fifth to set up Adair's game-tying single. She caused brain-lock in reliever Jim Perry's mind so that he would forget to cover first base and set up the second Red Sox run. And she snapped her fingers to distract shortstop Zoilo Versalles so that he would drop the throw on a potential inning-ending 1-6-3 double play in the eighth.

The big blows in the game were home runs. George Scott led off the seventh inning of a 2-2 game by knocking a Ron Kline pitch into the dead center-field bleachers. And Yaz put the game away with a three-run homer off lefty reliever Jim Merritt in the eighth. It was homer number 44 and it made the score 6-2. Harmon Killebrew hit *his* 44th with a man on in the ninth, but the Twins got no closer.

Detroit did indeed split the Saturday doubleheader with California. Everyone in Boston knew this as soon as it happened because WHDH, the Red Sox flagship radio station, had been picking up relevant broadcasts that did not conflict with its own. Everyone in Boston knew *everything* about what was going on, because radios were being carried all over the city. When Yaz hit the home run off Merritt, people cheered in restaurants, department stores, gas stations, hospitals, even, presumably, in confessional booths. It was like a Triple A V-J Day.

Here's how it looked on the morning of October 1:

Team	W	L	Pct.	GB
Boston	91	70	.565	—
Minnesota	91	70	.565	—
Detroit	90	70	.563	½

161 down, one to go, and each team ready with its best pitcher. It would be Jim Lonborg, 22-9, vs. Dean Chance, 20-13. At times like this I honestly wonder exactly what it is that people who aren't sports fans do for genuine excitement.

The Red Sox found themselves down, 2-0, after three innings and there was more blame for Yastrzemski than Lonborg. Yaz couldn't find a Tony Oliva liner on his personal radar screen in the first, and he made a foolish try to be a hero on a sinking shot by Killebrew in the third.

Chance was a certified American Original. He had won 20 games for the Angels in 1964, but the Angels had tired of his eccentricity and had shipped him to Minnesota in December of 1966. He could throw hard, and he delivered the ball with a peek-a-boo motion, giving the batter more shoulder than arm. The Red Sox did not like batting against Dean Chance.

He took that 2-0 lead into the sixth. The crowd was torn between its inbred Yankee pessimism and an enthusiasm borne out of the many comebacks they had seen from a collection of players officially carrying the nickname of the "Cardiac Kids." But as Jim Lonborg himself strode to the plate in the home half of the sixth there was more of an air of resignation and apprehension in the air than anything else. How could anyone expect a pennant, really, and especially from *this* team? After all, the Boston Red Sox had only won a pennant once in 48 years.

And then Jim Lonborg laid a textbook-perfect bunt down the third-base line. A snoozing Cesar Tovar had no play. Now there was noise, serious n-o-i-s-e, in Fenway Park. Jim Lonborg. People with associative memories immediately thought of the fake bunt/triple against Kansas City the night of his 20th victory. He wasn't just a pitcher, this Jim Lonborg. He was a *ballplayer*.

Jerry Adair singled up the middle. As long as I live, I will always see Rod Carew diving for the ball and missing it by inches, not that he would have had a play. Dalton Jones, after failing to bunt, poked a seeing-eye single to left between Tovar and Versalles. The noise had gotten louder with each base hit, and now Guess Who was walking briskly to the plate.

Yaz was already 5-for-6 in the two games. He had hit the killer home run the day before. He was having one of the great pennant-race Septembers of all time. How much more could we ask of him?

But he was Yaz, and this was Yaz's year. I know it's easy to rewrite history, given the benefit of 30 years hindsight. I know there is no way to document anything I now say on the subject. But I'm saying that I was more sure that Yaz would get *some* kind of base hit during that one at bat as I have ever been certain of any comparable thing in sport, and that includes Larry Bird making a clutch free throw.

Yaz hit Chance's first pitch on a sharp line to center, driving in Lonborg and Adair. 2-2.

The game was over. Truly. Minnesota just wasn't going to win, and Zoilo Versalles proved it with a bonehead play on a grounder hit by Ken Harrelson, the cleanup hitter brought into the mix by Dick O'Connell after Tony C went down. It was a high chopper, and Versalles had zero chance of getting Jones at the plate. But that's where he threw it.

Minnesota manager Cal Ermer, an early-season replacement for Quincy, Mass., native (and future Boston scout) Sam Mele, removed a shaken Chance, but it didn't matter. Lady Luck was back for another day's duty, blowing hard on that Boston set of dice. Before the inning was over, reliever Al Worthington would throw two wild pitches and Killebrew would boot a Reggie Smith one-hopper, and the Red Sox would have five runs.

And it had all begun with a smartly executed play by a Stanford man. No wonder they call Harvard the "Stanford of the East" where Lonborg comes from.

The remaining drama took place in the Minnesota eighth. With a man on first and no one out, Tovar grounded to Adair at second. The taciturn Oklahoman tagged pinch-runner Rich Reese and threw to first for a 4-3 double play, incurring a seven-stitch spike wound in so doing. Killebrew and Oliva extended the inning with singles, bringing up powerful Bob Allison, a right-handed batter who could check-swing a homer in Fenway.

Allison ripped a ball to the left corner, scoring Killebrew. But Lady Luck had one more duty to perform. She scrambled Allison's brain, making him forget that the man picking up the ball not only had the best arm of any left fielder in the league, but was also finishing a season of such personal magnitude there were already people wondering if Carl Yastrzemski had made some kind of off-season Joe Hardy-like pact with the devil. Yaz fired to second, and Mike Andrews slapped on the tag.

Running on Yaz, and doing it when you absolutely, positively could not afford to get thrown out?

One image remains frozen in my mind. Tony Oliva, refusing to believe anyone could be *that* stupid, stood on top of third base, staring at Bob Allison and, no doubt, uttering Cuban curses that would make the little hairs stand up on the back of your head. He continued to stare at Bob Allison as he trotted back to his position in left field. After someone brought his glove to him, he was still staring at Allison. As Jim Grant took his warm-up throws, Oliva was *still* staring at him. After what must have been two minutes, a disgusted Tony Oliva assumed his place in right field.

Lonborg had no trouble in the ninth, not, at least until Rich Rollins hit a little hump-backed liner to Rico Petrocelli for the final out.

We are all used to seeing people rush onto fields and arena floors now, but it wasn't necessarily the norm in those days, and there was no precedent at all in Fenway, at least not since Nuf Ced's last regular customer went to his grave. When the Red Sox clinched in '46 they were ahead by about 437 games, so there was no big deal. Now the emotions of the entire season were being unleashed. The fans came from everywhere, clutching at Lonborg, tearing off his hat, grabbing his jersey, and just plain endangering the good health of this fine Stanford biology major who now liked to throw inside and who could also do some sneaky things with a baseball bat in his hands.

Over in section 133, box 22, I couldn't believe what I was seeing. There were two or three kids actually climbing up the screen behind the plate, a screen which was never intended to carry any human body eight. It was just some cheesy chicken wire designed to protect the customers from being hit by some foul balls. And there, leaning out of the open broadcast window, was none other than Sandy Koufax, one year into his retirement and then a member of that year's NBC broadcast team. He was frantically waving his arms at the kids in a field-goal's-no-good manner while screaming, "Get back! Get back!" Which, thank God, they did.

Of course, the Red Sox hadn't actually won anything yet. All they knew at that moment was that Detroit had won the first game of its doubleheader at Tiger Stadium and that should there be a playoff game right here the following day the pitcher would be clever right-hander Lee Stange, who had pitched better than his 8-12 record all year, as his 2.77 ERA would lead one to believe.

The Red Sox celebrated in the locker room, but only to a point. The issue now was the goings-on in Detroit, and now WHDH had picked up the game. God bless WHDH, was all anyone could say.

Elaine and I were riding back to her house on the streetcar. Someone had a portable radio, and it wasn't tuned to the crop reports. And when Don Mincher hit a home run to put California ahead by an 8-5 score, the entire population of that street car let out a tremendous roar. Suddenly, we were all lifetime friends.

It came down to the bottom of the ninth in Tiger Stadium, which should have surprised no one. It was the Mother of All Pennant Races, not even over for the Red Sox when it was over. And the ending? Impossible. The Tigers had two on and just one out for Dick McAuliffe, a feisty left-handed hitting second baseman who was the personification of the phrase "tough out." McAuliffe *never* hit into double plays. Well, OK, almost never. In 556 at bats he had hit into one double play. And now? Ground ball to Bobby Knoop. Over to Fregosi for one. Back to first...Why don't we make that *two*?

Now the celebration could begin. The Red Sox, 100-1 shots at the beginning of the season, were champions of the American League. Tom Yawkey had stopped drinking four years earlier. But now he acknowledged that it was time for a little sip of champagne.

12
The
World Series

The Red Sox lost the 1967 World Series. Let's start with that. They lost the 1967 World Series to a better baseball team.

There was one great coulda-woulda attached to the Series. When the climactic Game 7 was played on Thursday, October 12, Bob Gibson went to the mound for St. Louis with three days rest, whereas Jim Lonborg went to the mound for the Red Sox with two days rest. This was a direct result of the fact that the Cardinals won the National League pennant by 10 games. St. Louis manager Red Schoendienst was able to set his pitching rotation. Gibson started Game 1 on October 4, Game 4 on October 8 and Game 7 on October 12. He had all the rest he needed heading into the Series and a full three days rest in between starts during the Series.

The Red Sox didn't clinch until the last day of the season. As you know, Lonborg pitched on Sunday, October 1. He came back in Game 2 on October 5 and Game 5 on October 9 with a full three days rest. He started Game 7 because Dick Williams had more faith in a not-so-rested Lonborg than he did in any other pitcher on his staff. Was this more of an indictment of his other starters, or more of an endorsement of Lonborg? I'm voting with the former.

If Williams truly believed he had a decent second starter, he would have put that man on the mound in Game 7. He was asking Lonborg, a man who on the morning of October 12 had already pitched 291 pressure-packed innings (110 more than he had ever thrown before) to perform a miracle, and he couldn't do it. Simple as that.

It was not a great World Series, but it did have its moments. Lou Brock absolutely tormented the Red Sox. The great leadoff man batted .414. He scored eight runs. He had a home run, two doubles and a triple. He stole seven bases, including three in Game 7. The Red Sox have never in their existence had a player like this, although there are early indications that Nomar Garciaparra might come close.

Yaz hit .400. He hit three home runs. There was nothing wrong with Yaz. There was nothing really *wrong* with the Red Sox, who showed some spunk by forcing a seventh game after being down, 3-1. The Cardinals were just better; that's all.

Lonborg was magnificent. He threw $7^2/_3$ innings of no-hit baseball in Game 2 before Julian Javier hit a double. He wound up facing just 29 batters in his 5-0 masterpiece. He was sensational once again in Game 5. This time he tossed a three-hitter. The Red Sox won it, 3-1.

In those two games Lonnie was even better than Bob Gibson. He was better, in fact, than *anybody*. But Gibson was still Gibson, and when it was over he won three games in the seven-game series to insure his legendary status.

Gibson was only 13-7 that year because he had suffered a broken leg in midsummer when Roberto Clemente hit him with a line

Carl Yastrzemski is greeted at the dugout steps after hitting a home run in the 1967 World Series. Note the old-style TV camera at the end of the dugoug. (Photo©Dick Raphael)

drive. True to his image, he finished the inning before he would limp off the field.

He won the opener, 2-1, the only Boston run coming from an improbable source: Jose Santiago hit a home run. He shut the Red Sox out, 6-0, in Game 4. And he was as good as he had to be in Game 7, allowing three hits and two runs in St. Louis' 7-2 victory.

Could a rested Lonborg have won Game 7? Well, sure, he *could* have. No one in World Series history had ever given up just four hits and one run in his first 18 innings of World Series competition.

He tried to gut it out in Game 7, but he clearly tired. The crusher was a three-run homer by Javier in the sixth. The Red Sox had no more fight left after that.

Since 1918 the Red Sox have been in four World Series and have lost four seventh games. This one was the only which didn't end in a bitter loss, and that is one reason why people look back on the 1967 Series with such fondness. It really was fun just to be in it. The Cardinals were a great team, the Red Sox gave them a tough fight and it was all a new, exhilarating experience for everyone concerned.

13

Altering the

Course of History

The 1967 Red Sox altered the course of Boston baseball history.

Baseball had been in, to borrow a Jimmy Carter phrase, a profound malaise. Ted Williams was gone and was never coming back. It had been so long since the Red Sox had been legitimately competitive that only the diehards were taking them seriously. In the mind of the public, Tom Yawkey was regarded as a foolish old man who didn't really care whether the Red Sox won or lost as long as he could play pepper with the bat boys and take his own batting practice when the team was on the road.

When Dick Williams declared during spring training that the team would win more games than it would lose people smirked. A decade and a half of mediocrity, capped off by back-to-back ninth-place finishes, had left a deep impression.

Early in the 1967 season, Yawkey was even talking openly about getting a new ballpark! There weren't enough seats. Where can you park? The damn wall is more trouble than it's worth. It gets our right-handed hitters out of their rhythm and it terrifies our pitchers. We're usually OK at home, but we can't play worth a damn on the road. We're the only team in the league who needs two completely different teams, one for home games and one for road games.

Yawkey believed all these things, and more. Other cities were getting new ballparks, or talking about getting new ballparks, and he wanted one, too.

That talk ceased when the 1967 Red Sox started winning baseball games. By June of 1967, Fenway Park was starting to become chic again. The Red Sox benefitted from excellent media coverage. They were blanketed by the print media, they had an excellent radio duo in Ken Coleman and Ned Martin, and, perhaps most important of all, they had an excellent television package by the standards of the day. The word spread rapidly.

People who hadn't come to the park in years came to see this team and came away re-enchanted with the ballpark. The grumbling about the new parks had already begun. They added nothing to the game. The old parks were invariably on top of the action. Even Yankee Stadium, with a peak capacity of more than 70,000 in its original configuration (it was renovated into its current shape following the 1973 season), put the customers close to the action. Like Fenway, Yankee Stadium was distinguished by its lack of foul territory down the lines. They mocked cavernous Municipal Stadium for many years, but I am here to say it wasn't a bad place to see a game. The good seats were fabulous.

I can go on and on, and, by God, I will. Comiskey Park, built in 1910, had very cozy upper-deck seating. Wrigley Field is justifiably beloved for its charm and proximity to the action. And then there is my personal favorite, Tiger Stadium.

The best seats in baseball are in the low rows of the upper deck at Tiger Stadium. In down moments, you can hear conversations on the field. And ask any announcer who has ever worked in the American League about the broadcast booth. Forget about conversations. You are so close that if the batter should burp the announcer can say "Excuse me." The broadcast booth in Tiger Stadium is so close to the field, in fact, that some announcers say it is downright dangerous.

Fenway has no upper deck, as such, although there are now luxury boxes and so-called roof boxes, which serve the same purpose. The seats sit low and they are as close to the action as any park, except, once again, those in the amazingly underrated park in Detroit. The 7,000 bleacher seats include some of the best cheap seats in baseball. The people sitting in the first row in straightaway center field are lucky people.

Fenway was a neglected treasure until the 1967 Red Sox came along. The people began coming in 1967, and they really haven't stopped.

The '67 Sox Red Sox drew 1,727,832, which broke the existing Red Sox record set in 1949 by 131,182. This means that more people came to see this team play than had ever come to see any Ted Williams team. Of course, they didn't play as many night games in The Thumper's day, but baseball had less competition for the entertainment dollar in his time, and you might logically think that teams featuring Ted Williams, Bobby Doerr, Johnny Pesky and Dominic DiMaggio would pull in crowds approaching 2 million, even with the Braves in town.

The '67 Red Sox touched New England's baseball soul, reminding people of the game's intricacy and inherent drama. It was as if an entire six-state region had become Born Again Baseball Fans.

It is a sports axiom that a team will draw even better the year following a title year because tickets are bought in anticipation of great things, and so it was that the 1968 Red Sox drew 1,940,788 despite finishing in fourth place, 17 games behind the champion Tigers. The 1969 team was a complete non-factor, but even then attendance didn't fall off much. That club drew 1,833,246, and by then it was obvious it wasn't going to matter all that much how good the team was any longer. Something was going on that was bigger than any given Red Sox team.

Dick Williams didn't make it out of the 1969 season. He was fired in the final week. The Red Sox were not able to recapture the

'67 magic. Problems started the following winter when Lonborg injured his knee in a ski accident and fell to 6-10 in 1968. Yastrzemski, whose 1967 season was, of course, unmatchable, fell to .301 with 23 homers and 74 runs batted in. His small consolation was that he was the only .300 hitter in the entire league during the ultimate Year of the Pitcher.

There were whispers that Williams had switched gears and was no longer the Big Meanie who had terrorized the team on a daily basis in 1967. What good was a Dick Williams who wanted to be loved? (If this charge was true, he never made *that* mistake again.) When the end came for Williams in Boston, he said that his proudest accomplishment was that his team had brought people back to Fenway Park.

The New England baseball genie was out of the bottle. The worst any subsequent Red Sox team has drawn in a non-strike season was 1,441,718 in 1972. Nowadays, anything under 2,400,000 is considered an off year. In other words, the Boston Red Sox fully expect every season to fill the ballpark to somewhere between 86 and 90 percent capacity.

It became clear in the early '70s that the new star of the Red Sox franchise was Fenway Park itself. Red Sox management caught on, and each subsequent ruling body has made ballpark upkeep and maintenance the number one priority. And as one old park after another began to disappear, Fenway Park and Wrigley Field each attained more and more cachet, becoming ends in themselves.

The Red Sox and the Cubs are, in fact, spiritual brothers. There are only two established teams which have gone longer without a World Series title than the Red Sox (1918), and both are in Chicago. The White Sox last won it all in 1917. And the Cubs won their second and final championship in 1908.

But the White Sox do not have a mystique. They have always been the "other" team in Chicago. The late Steve Goodman never wrote anything on the subject of the White Sox. But he did write *A Dying Cub Fan's Lament*, and you can hear it on well-stocked juke boxes in the Windy City.

The Red Sox and the Cubs have a few important things in common. They each have teams with tradition piled on tradition, each has developed fans who lived long lives without ever seeing the squad win it all and each plays in a baseball museum, not merely a ballpark. But that's where it stops.

The people of Chicago, even those who deeply love the Cubs, never really forget that all this passion has to do with a game. There are those — and I happen to be one of them — who think it is the best game that has ever sprung from the mind of mortal man, but in Chicago they have managed to keep it all in perspective.

They want to win, but they don't *lust* to win. They regard the Cubbies as you would a charmingly incorrigible child. A typical Cubs fans has a beer or two on the way to the game, has another beer or two at the game and then, win or lose, another beer or two on the way home. He cheers, he boos, he offers his opinion to one and all, but he always sleeps soundly and he never proposes taking up a collection to hire a hit man when he doesn't like the manager.

Cubs fans know their baseball, and they have their rituals. It is in Wrigley Field, and only in Wrigley Field, where it is *expected* that whichever bleacherite catches a home run off the bat of a rival batter will throw the ball back onto the field in disdain. There are no allowable exceptions, as far as I can tell. You've got to love that.

They are not so benign in Fenway. Unhappy Fenway fans are cruel, vicious and basically irrational. They are always ready to believe the worst, anyway, and so it was that when some disgruntled Red Sox players began referring to manager Don Zimmer as "The Gerbil" in 1977-78, the skipper was doomed. The level of vilification directed toward this man was almost beyond belief — unless you lived in Boston, where many people thought it entirely appropriate. In their view, if a man couldn't handle a pitching staff, what right did he have to live?

Somehow, some way, the people in Boston may care *too* much. There is no other sports franchise in America so haunted by history. No one gets involved in Boston baseball for very long without being confronted by the year 1918. You can spend a year in Chicago among legitimate sports fans without once hearing anyone refer to 1908, let alone 1917. You can't spend five minutes in a Boston sports bar without hearing someone talking about "the friggin' Sox" and "friggin' 1918."

Now to that we can add the year 1986. The Red Sox own the dubious distinction of coming closer to winning a World Series title, without actually doing so, than any team in the history of baseball. Who in New England doesn't know that the team came within one strike of beating the Mets in six games in the 1986 World Series?

The fans were inclined toward self-pity even before 1986. They had been continually reminded that the 1946 team lost the seventh game to the Cardinals when Enos Slaughter scored from first base while shortstop Johnny Pesky supposedly held the ball too long before making the relay throw to the plate. They had been continually reminded that the Red Sox lost the playoff game to Cleveland in 1948 when manager Joe McCarthy inexplicably selected Denny Galehouse to pitch. They were continually reminded that the Red Sox had only needed one win in the final two games at Yankee Stadium in order to win the 1949 pennant and had been unable to win any. They had been continually reminded that the 1975 team should have won Game 2 of the World Series and couldn't hold a 3-0 lead at home in Game 7. And they had continually been reminded that the 1978 team lost a playoff game to the Yankees when Bucky Dent hit a ball which would have been an out in every other American League park, but which was long enough to be a game-winning three-run home run in Fenway.

And who was doing all this reminding? Who wasn't? Fathers, grandfathers, uncles, priests, judges, delivery men...most of all, the media. People take turns telling the stories, and it gets worse by the year. You never heard all that much about 1946, 1948 and 1949 when I first came to Boston in the mid-60s. But when Dick Williams rekindled baseball interest in the town, suddenly everybody was a historian.

Red Sox fans have become, over the last three decades, the most self-absorbed, narcissistic followers of any team in America. Everyone else is tied for second place. In their eyes, no one else has ever suffered. No other team has ever let anyone down. Nobody knows the troubles I've seen. Please.

The Red Sox won pennants in 1967, 1975 and 1986. They won division titles in 1988 and 1990. Three times the Red Sox went to the seventh game of the World Series. Those seasons provided people with great moments and great memories.

Measure that against the situation in Cleveland. The Indians finished second to Chicago in 1959 and then spent the next 34 years without once being in a race past the end of June. That would be something to whine about. Is it not better to have loved and lost than never to have loved at all?

The Red Sox first broke the 2 million barrier in 1977, when 2,074,549 poured into Updike's "lyric little bandbox of a ballpark." That was a fascinating team which smacked 213 home runs, 33 of which came in a 10-game span in June. They blasted 16 home runs in one weekend sweep of the hated Yankees, and then went down to Baltimore and hit five more off Jim Palmer.

For all their vaunted sophistication and appreciation for the nuances of the game, New England baseball fans have always responded favorably to good old-fashioned sock. The ballpark has done it to them. Fenway is a hitter's paradise. Few Red Sox players, right-handed, left-handed or in between, have ever hit better on the road than they have at Fenway, and in some cases the home-road discrepancy has been embarrassingly large. Fans have been bred on offense, and they love their home runs.

The 1977 and 1978 seasons may have been the last time people regularly came to Fenway strictly in order to have fun. Their daily impresarios were radio broadcasters Ned Martin and Jim Woods (Ken Coleman had left for Cincinnati, although he would return in time to handle the pennant-winning season of 1986).

Ned Martin was the Thinking Man's Broadcaster, a cerebral Duke graduate who could quote Keats and Shelley, and who was famous for making people smile during the wee small hours of West Coast games. He was not really a man of his times because he had little interest in the increasingly important *business* of broadcasting. It had now become necessary to indulge sponsors, and Martin would have none of that. He wasn't good at making small talk at some dumb cocktail party with the Northeast Regional vice president of a brewery company. He was only interested in the game.

He had his own terminology. A pitch was "peeled" back to the screen. A frustrated batter "carved" at a low and outside breaking ball. His big expression of enthusiasm was "Mercy!" Like all true originals, what he did could only work for him.

Jim Woods was the reigning second banana of baseball broadcasters. He had worked in New York behind Mel Allen, in St. Louis behind Harry Caray and, for a raucous decade or so, as the resident yuk-it-up partner and nightly drinking buddy of the ultra-legendary Bob Prince, the colorful Pittsburgh sage known in the business as "The Gunner." Woods loathed authority even more than Martin did, and he was more direct about it. There wasn't a pretentious bone in his skinny body. He smoked three to four packs of cigarettes a day, and he closed up every bar in the league, many times over. He was just a home-spun guy from Missour-ah who believed there were only three important sports in the world: baseball, college football and horse racing. He was a railbird of the first order. He was thoroughly convinced Seattle Slew would win the 1977 Triple Crown after seeing the Preakness because "He came flying across that finish line with his ears up!"

Martin and Woods hit it off like peanut butter and jelly, and the audience loved them. Woods was the absolutely perfect complement to the sometimes ethereal Martin. Just when you've had a couple of innings done for you by an English professor, here came Woodsy, purring in that tobacco and alcohol-tinged baritone, shifting the broadcast gears entirely.

They were the broadcast duo for the pennant-winning season of 1975, but they reached their peak in 1977, the year of the Home Run. One of the Red Sox radio sponsors that year was Dodge, specifically the Dodge dealers of New England. Some bright young fellow had gotten the idea for a promotion. There would one "Home Run Inning" each game. For every Red Sox home run hit during that inning, a lucky listener would win a car.

Messrs. Martin and Woods, never comfortable with executive types of any stripe, were particularly vexed that year. They loathed the execs at Dodge, at the ad agency and at their own flagship radio station, a cheesy thing at the far end of the dial (WITS, 1510). Gone were the nice-'n-easy days of WHDH. Now, in their judgment, they were dealing with nothing but schmucks. Despite their overwhelming public popularity, the lunkheads at the station had actually tried to dump them after the '75 season, preferring to foist some generic yes-man toadies on the New England fandom.

Come June of 1977, the Red Sox began hitting home runs to all reaches of this land of ours, and they weren't skipping the Home Run Inning, either. The Dodge people figured they'd have to give out a car or two, but *this*? Martin and Woods were ecstatic. They loved the Home Run Inning. It was their favorite point in the game. Woods called the homers gleefully. "And Yaz has just parked a new Dodge in the driveway of Edward O'Malley of Somerville, Mass!" he would shriek. And if it happened to be a Fenway game, he would then lean out of his broadcast window, contort his body, look up at his friends in the press box (in other words, everybody) and pump his fist with a big grin on his face. He had just had the pleasure of giving away another one of those bastards' cars, and he was the happiest man in the world.

You will never hear anything like Martin and Woods again. Anywhere. Iconoclasts are not welcome any longer. Baseball broadcasting enthusiasm and expertise are now secondary to the ability to get every little so-called "drop-in" placed, even if the insipid sales pitch must take place between ball one and strike two.

Martin and Woods were the happy face on Boston Red Sox baseball. Their presence reminded you that the entire world could be both meaningful and fun at the same time.

Once the 1978 team blew a 14-game lead over New York in a little more than five weeks, the atmosphere changed forever. Henceforth, it wasn't just a matter of winning or losing a baseball game. From that point on it was an ongoing Passion Play in which the fans blended narcissism with masochism.

The 1986 World Series debacle was a self-fulfilling prophecy. Deep in their heart of hearts, many Red Sox fans never expected to win. And they wouldn't have known how to act if the team *had* won. They had long ago lost the capacity to have fun.

If you believe Dan Shaughnessy, they already know they aren't *supposed* to have fun. It's all in the fates.

Shaughnessy is the *Boston Globe* columnist and author of *The Curse of the Bambino*, a book which catalogues the litany of Red Sox woes which have followed the single stupidest transaction in American sports history; namely, the sale of Babe Ruth to the Yankees on January 5, 1920.

One of Ruth's nicknames was "Bambino," which, of course, is Italian for "baby." The premise is that the trading of Babe Ruth was such a heinous act that it actually entered into the realm of an Origi-

271

nal Sin which can *never* be forgiven. Never. If you subscribe to The Curse, you buy into the notion that the Red Sox are forever doomed to frustration.

Having been idiotic and uncaring enough to trade The Bambino, they will pay for it by never again winning a World Series.

Exhibit A is the 1986 World Series, starting with two outs and nobody on in the Mets' half of the ninth inning. The Red Sox led by two runs. There was nobody on base. Calvin Schiraldi only had to retire one more man and the Red Sox would win.

He couldn't. And neither could Bob Stanley. Gary Carter, Kevin Mitchell and Ray Knight (he, with two strikes) singled. Stanley threw either a wild pitch or catcher Rich Gedman allowed a passed ball, depending on your point of view (I'm a passed ball man, all the way). And then Mookie Wilson hit the most famous ground ball in Red Sox history.

It was hit in the direction of Bill Buckner, the first baseman. He wasn't all that bad a fielder, actually, but throughout the postseason it had been the custom of manager John McNamara to insert Dave Stapleton as a defensive replacement in these types of late-inning, protect-the-lead situations.

The ball rolled under Buckner's glove. Both runs scored. Mets win.

The Red Sox led Game 7 by a 3-0 score, but they couldn't hold the lead. For the fourth time since 1918 they had reached the seventh game of the World Series, and for the fourth time they had lost. There were many tales of people having roused sleeping babies and toddlers from the cribs and/or beds with two away in that fateful Game 6 ninth, just so they could some day tell *their* grandchildren they had actually seen the Red Sox win a championship. Some of these people really *do* take all this a bit too seriously, wouldn't you say?

Shaughnessy is a native of Groton, Mass., a sleepy town northwest of Boston. He grew up as a staunch Red Sox fan. He was all-too-well aware of the tortured history of the team, but it wasn't until he received a letter from Margaret Blackstone, an executive editor at E.P. Dutton Publishers, suggesting that there might be some literary merit to putting all the somewhat bizarre history of the post-Ruth Red Sox down on paper.

Shaughnessy was the perfect vessel. He is a passionate New England. He had an affinity for the team and the ballpark. He likes Old and he is inherently suspicious of New. He really did believe there was something about the Red Sox which set them apart from the ordinary baseball franchise.

Thus was born *The Curse of the Bambino*, a book which came out in 1990 and which has served as vindication for all the boundless self-pity which so thoroughly infuses the typical Red Sox fan.

First of all, whose idea was the title?

"To tell you the truth, I had never really seen it in those words anywhere else," he says. "I remembered that George Vecsey of the *New York Times* had once written the phrase, 'The Curse of Babe Ruth,' but the Bambino thing was just kind of hanging out there. I've got no copyright on that. I don't claim to have invented it."

I remember hearing that exact phrase uttered some 15 years ago by Darrell Berger, a Unitarian-Universalist minister and baseball buff who had been introduced to me by our mutual friend Henry Hecht, then a writer for the *New York Post*. In a sense, it is so obvious a connection that it is entirely possible it was conceived of simultaneously by a score of Great Baseball Minds.

But now, for better or worse, it really does belong to Dan Shaughnessy.

"The Curse" gives every self-absorbed Red Sox fan an opportunity to say I-told-ya'-so. It gives him the ammunition to proclaim that indeed *Nobody* really does know the trouble I've seen. There was a lot of negative energy bubbling up inside the dedicated Red Sox narcissist, and *The Curse of the Bambino* is his *Mein Kampf.*

Shaughnessy knew he was on to *something*, but even he was surprised at the breadth and depth of the response. For many of these pitiable narcissists (my description, not his) "The Curse" was a vindication of everything they believed to be true about the Red Sox.

The book sold some 25,000 in hardback, and it lives on in both paperback and audio tape. It will continue to have enormous appeal, at least until the Red Sox finally break The Curse, an event which right now appears to be tied in with the first sighting of a Tyrannosaurus rex strolling across the Boston Common.

"It's like religion," Shaughnessy reasons. "When you can't explain something rationally, we look to a larger force. It gives people a chance to explain the unexplainable.

"There are some incredible circumstances," he points out. "Starting with the ball rolling through Buckner's legs, the Red Sox have lost 13 consecutive postseason games. Thirteen! Is that just coincidence? Who can explain *that*? And the Bruce Hurst thing (Hurst was the winner in Games 2 and 5 in '86, and the loser in Game 7). If you rearrange the letters of Bruce Hurst, you get 'B. Ruth Curse.' "

Only a Red Sox fan would sit down and rearrange the letters of Bruce Hurst's name in the first place, which, according to Shaughnessy, is precisely the point.

Just so we'll be reassured, Shaughnessy sums up his *true* feeling on the matter. "It's silly and frivolous," he admits "and do I *really* believe it? Probably not. But there is *no way* they can lose Game 6. No Way. I've got a tape and once in a while I pull it out. It's like the Zapruder tape. I see the first two outs of the inning — easy fly balls to (Jim) Rice and (Dave) Henderson. It's over."

He relishes his role as the official prophet of Doom & Gloom. "The book will probably be in the first paragraph of my obituary," he says. But he also feels a bit guilty. He knows what he has done. "I plead guilty to all charges," he says, "but I feel I have provided a service. I've given these people some order in their lives."

Six years after writing *The Curse of the Bambino*, Shaughnessy went back to the well with a sequel of sorts entitled *At Fenway*. Sure, Dan, open up the wound *again*. Pass the salt, please. How about a little tabasco?

"I look at it as a reporter's love letter to Fenway Park," Shaughnessy says. "And this one is very personalized."

Like *The Curse of the Bambino*, *At Fenway* is a great read. But if Shaughnessy writes one more of these "Woe-Is-Us" things, they'll be jumping off the top of the Prudential Center. Is Dan Shaughnessy ready for that?

Much of *At Fenway* is indeed devoted to a lovemaking session with the ballpark. Hey, I love the ballpark, too. In the right seat — and I am a season ticket holder with four wonderful reserved seats behind the screen — and on the right day Fenway can be a superb baseball experience. The angles and contours referred to by Updike make the park an active participant in any given game. Things either do or don't happen in Fenway that either do or don't happen anywhere else, even in Wrigley Field or Tiger Stadium, both of which I would place above Fenway in the overall scheme of things. The Wall, the Ladder, The Door, the dangerous curve in right when the fence juts out sharply (mishandle a ball here and you may be creating an inside-the-park home run), the so-called "Triangle" area in right-center — these are all unique to Fenway.

Ever since 1967, people in Boston and New England have become very proprietary toward Fenway. It is a historic Boston tourist attraction that takes its place alongside Symphony Hall, The Museum of Fine Arts, Old Ironsides, Faneuil Hall, Old North Church and the Boston Common as must-see stops for the tourist. It is utterly and totally Boston.

Because it only seats 33,000-plus, it is necessary for people to purchase tickets in advance for the big series. And by "in advance," I mean December. Fenway is therefore insulated to a degree by the vagaries of weather. If it happens to be raining on the morning of August 15, management at least has the comfort of knowing that 30,000 people have already bought tickets. If some guy from Bellows Falls, Vt., doesn't want to sit in a drizzle, there's always next year for him.

The size of the ballpark definitely works in Fenway's favor. But Fenway has one big problem from a management viewpoint. A whopping 19 percent of the seats are located in the bleachers. That's a lot of lost dollars.

Fenway is small and cramped. I am 6-foot-1 and I cannot sit comfortably without angling myself. This is a baseball park built in 1912 for people born in the 19th century. They have added spiffy private boxes in order to accommodate the needs and whims of the high-rollers, but the average fan must contend with a facility lacking in comfort.

Fenway will go some day, and when it does there will be a weeping and wailing unmatched in American annals. Boston is very good at celebrating nostalgia. There was a great civic cry when the Boston

Garden closed at the end of 1995, but that was the junior varsity squad compared to Fenway. I can see Shaughnessy in the Che Gueverra role, several rounds of bullets crisscrossed over his shoulders, rifle in hand, waving his hardy followers into place as the crane with the first wrecking ball rolls toward the ballpark.

And it *will* be a sad day. Fenway Park is the happiest accident the city of Boston has ever had. No one would set out to construct such a bizarre ballpark. It began life serving a physical need and it will be heartbreaking to replace because it now serves a psychic one.

But far too many of those who come to Fenway Park are not really happy people. It's sport's answer to Sunday Mass. You come because you've conditioned yourself to think you're *supposed* to come. It's a duty. The father still brings the kid, but he makes sure to inform the youngster not to get too excited because "The Red Sox will always break your heart." If it's *joie de vivre* you're looking for, head to Wrigley, where people still know how to have fun. In comparison, Fenway is a heavy therapy session.

There are still reasonable fans left. Not every Red Sox follower is a candidate for the psychiatrist's couch. "They're clever," says Shaughnessy, who hears from lots of them because they assume he shares their pain. "They keep you on your toes. They send you letters and faxes. They put together their own stats. It's hard to stay a step ahead of them."

The modern Fenway fan knows he is the heir to a tradition, and when you combine that with the fact that he thinks he knows more about the game than people elsewhere, it all adds up to one conclusion: he is *entitled*. When people in Toronto get to watch two World Series winners, and when people in Denver and Miami wind up with playoff teams, he is not merely agitated or outraged. It is much deeper than that.

It is the same feeling he has when Mo Vaughn strikes out with the bases loaded. It is something personal. He is truly *offended*.

Where are Martin and Woods when we need them?

What
Makes
Boston Boston

One of the more reliable premises in the world of televised sport is the following: almost any event not involving a Boston team will result in Boston drawing one of the lowest audiences among the Top 25 major markets.

As one who has lived in Boston for 33 years, I always find this difficult to believe. I must travel in limited circles, because I never find a lack of interest in the national sports stories of the day. The local newspapers detect no such lack of interest, either, because they spend a great deal of money dispatching writers to all corners of the globe in order enlighten and perhaps even amuse readers presumably eager to soak up every scrap of information.

But when it comes to watching events not involving Boston teams, the TV experts insist that the average Greater Bostonian fights vainly the old *ennui*. Or so the almighty ratings say.

The only conspicuous exception to the rule is hockey, where Boston lives up to its reputation as the best hockey city in America.

One indisputable example of Boston's fierce television parochialism is its peculiar allegiance to candlepin bowling, a perverse offshoot of tenpin bowling unknown to most other Americans. Candlepin bowling is fiendishly difficult, giving lie to the pompous assertion of baseball people that the "single hardest thing to do in sport" is to hit a baseball thrown at 90 miles per hour. Sorry. I know of nothing harder than trying to throw a strike in candlepin bowling. It is a sport only a Puritan or a masochist could love, and over the years it has drawn absolutely astonishing TV ratings in Boston. Boston likes what it likes, and it really doesn't give a damn what anyone else does.

As apparently indifferent as the fans are when it comes to neutral competition, that's how fanatical they are about protecting their own institutions. In Boston it is tradition *uber alles*, and there are no apologies.

Boston is, for example, the only city on record known to have booed a scoreboard.

When Red Sox management decided to attach a modern, newfangled electronic scoreboard to the top of the center-field wall behind the bleachers prior to the 1976 season, fans were not pleased. The manual scoreboard in the left-field wall was good enough for them. Getting a new scoreboard meant that management was committing a cardinal Boston sin; namely, placing Boston in the position of being just like everybody else. An electronic scoreboard is what heathens had in ignorant cities, not enlightened enclaves such as Boston.

In time, people came to an accommodation with the scoreboard. But the old manual scoreboard, complete with the morse code designation for the initials "TAY," (for Thomas Austin Yawkey), is still in use, and is considered the main source of necessary information by serious Fenway patrons.

Change does not come easily in Boston. The Celtics once thought it would be a good idea to dress a young lady up as a leprechaun and have her mingle with the customers. She was so mocked and harassed that the idea was abandoned after one night and never reintroduced. The Red Sox discovered in the spring of 1997 that nothing had changed. They introduced a mascot — their first ever — called "Wally the Green Monster," and the poor guy was laughed at and booed when he went on the field. The Red Sox never risked another on-field appearance for Wally, preferring to keep him in front of children, rather than their tradition-bound elders.

Going into the 1997-98 season, 28 of the 29 NBA teams were employing either a dance team or cheerleaders of some sort. Care to guess the identity of the 29th? After going through 51 seasons with old-fashioned public address announcers who were not a thorough screamers bellowing out such fingernails-on-the-blackboard banalities, the Celtics have now hired a prototypical modern NBA PA man. They could be making a huge mistake.

The Bruins and Celtics were in the unique position of alienating their constituency in an attempt to make them more comfortable. For every person interested in the amenities available in the new downtown Fleet Center, I would wager there were two who would have been just as happy to remain in the Boston Garden, which, to them, was Grandma's house, shabby furniture and all.

The Garden, built in 1928 as a replica of New York's Madison Square Garden, had unbeatable sightlines for both basketball and hockey. As an areal building dependent on poles, however, it also had some laughable seats. I once purchased a midcourt stadium seat for a Celtics-76er game, only to discover that the only way I could actually see the baskets was to bend sideways from the waist. The Garden didn't just have poles; it had pillars. But it also had the greatest proximity to the court and ice from its wonderful balcony seats, and it also had an unmatched feel and sound. The great players in each succeeding generation always fell in love with it. Bobby Orr and Larry Bird practically wept when it closed down in 1995.

The closing of the Boston Garden was cause for great civic weeping, but it was only the warm-up act for the hysteria which will reign when the inevitable day comes that the Red Sox will play their final game in Fenway Park. People would prefer to be more comfortable, but when the end of the park comes the fans will know it will be due to economics and not altruism, and they will be angry because they will know that something very special and irreplaceable will have been lost.

The simple truth is that Boston is a snobby sports town. A further truth is that it has a thorough right to its snobbery.

There is no other city in America able to make the following statement: since 1926, when Eddie Shore joined the Boston Bruins, until the present day, with Raymond Bourque still very much a viable player, Boston, Massachusetts, has never once seen a single day without a top-of-the-line, no-dissent, superstar in at least one sport.

Are you ready?

■ Eddie Shore, 1926-39

■ Jimmie Foxx, 1936-42

■ Ted Williams, 1939-60

■ Bob Cousy, 1950-63

■ Bill Russell, 1956-69

■ John Havlicek, 1962-78

■ Bobby Orr, 1966-76

■ Phil Esposito, 1967-75

■ John Hannah, 1973-85

■ Larry Bird, 1979-92

■ Raymond Bourque, 1979-present

That's without even mentioning such great stars as Dit Clapper, Milt Schmidt, Frankie Brimsek, Johnny Bucyk, Cam Neely, Lefty Grove, Bobby Doerr, Johnny Pesky, Carl Yastrzemski, Jim Rice, Fred Lynn, Luis Tiant, Wade Boggs, Roger Clemens, Mo Vaughn, Bill Sharman, Tom Heinsohn, Sam Jones, Dave Cowens, Jo Jo White, Kevin McHale, Robert Parish, Dennis Johnson, Gino Cappelletti, Steve Nelson, Ben Coates and Drew Bledsoe.

So, yeah, they're a little spoiled.

In dramatic contrast to the way sport is perceived on the West Coast, the Boston sports scene is very much in tune with the rhythm of the seasons. In the winter, when it is cold and snowy, people like to congregate indoors. Good Celtics and Bruins teams benefit from a passionate fandom. Baseball is important because it takes place outdoors. Spring training has long been an important Boston ritual because it is inextricably bound up with the change of seasons. One of the time-honored Boston February journalistic rituals is a story concerning the van which takes the Red Sox equipment south to spring training. This, in the mind of some people, is the first indication that this damn snow will melt and we will actually have a spring. And to people in Boston, spring and baseball are feel-good concepts.

And long before spring training became corporate and chic, it was a very big deal to the people in New England, who were among the very first to recognize the special nature and innocence of what was going on down there in Florida during the month of March. The Red Sox were attracting the so-called "snowbirds" to Florida in staggering numbers during the '60s, '70s and '80s while their rivals were playing before a few hundred people in their own spring training venues.

As to where the Patriots fit into all this, the answer is that until very recently, they didn't. For more than 30 years, they were the "other" franchise in town. People with pro football as a sports priority were regarded as bizarre Dallas wannabes. That's all changed now. Recent surveys place the Patriots at the top of the Boston fan heap, especially among young people.

School teachers are a good gauge, since they monitor all fashion changes. They report that Red Sox hats and jackets have been replaced by Patriots paraphernalia. This dramatic change has all taken place in the past four years, and it is directly attributable to the electric presence of Bill Parcells, who simply *made* people care, even if they didn't particularly want to.

Boston is undergoing an identity crisis. There is no other town where people more fervently wish they could reproduce the Good Old Days, not only because teams such as the '67 Red Sox, '72 Bruins and '86 Celtics were such eminently rootable clubs, but also because the town is starting to feel it has been placed on the back burner of the American sports lab.

Not too long ago the Red Sox were regarded as a rich franchise. No longer. Because Fenway is not an income-generating ballpark along the lines of Oriole Park at Camden Yards in Baltimore or Jacobs Field in Cleveland or Coors Field in — ugh — *Denver*, the people are being told by management that they now reside in a "medium" market, at best.

Their steady 2 million-plus attendance at Fenway isn't enough to sustain a viable franchise. It is difficult for New England baseball fans to accept the idea that their support is no longer quite worthy enough.

The Patriots likewise need a new stadium, and they will have one. They have now spent a quarter-century outside the Boston city limits. They are true citizens of New England. As popular as they have become, they are far behind in this tradition business. They have successfully weaned themselves away from Boston proper. They can move about without fear of disrupting either their supporters' emotional well-being or memories. Few football stadiums evince emotional reactions. A trip to a professional football game is an outing, anyway. It has to do with pregame barbecues, tossing down a few beers and, frankly, male bonding. This is a universal football truth. The game is only part of the experience.

It seems to me that the reason Boston sports fans reserve a disproportionate amount of their interest for their own teams, in contrast to the more varied "patron-of-the-art" viewpoint of people in other locales, is that the Boston fan has a more distinct inherent attachment to the idea of rooting as a valuable human experience.

He has been bred to appreciate the ins and outs of the game so he will know not only the good from the bad but also the great from the good, but that is merely the starting point. He needs that team connection to make it all worthwhile. He is willing to endure the pain of losing in order to better appreciate the exquisite high of winning.

Though he has only on occasion actually lived in Boston, Jonathan Schwartz is intimately *connected* to the city by his intense devotion to the Red Sox and Celtics. "Even in the depths of the 1996-97 Celtics' season," he reports, "I seldom went to bed without knowing how the team had done that evening." That is precisely what rooting is all about. Rooting is, all too often, bleeding. The Boston sports fan is very good at this.

"I cannot conceive of following sports without rooting," says Schwartz. "It is just not possible for me. To follow the progress of the team with one's heart is so worthy and intimate. It puts me in constant day-to-day basis with a concern that is outside myself, even though it is, to me, about myself. Of course, this is somewhat irrational. I am not one of the 25, or one of the 12. I am not on a roster. I am completely unknown to them.

"No matter who's on first base that particular year, or who's on the pitching staff, the opportunity is afforded to me on a daily level to participate in this thing outside my little territory," he says.

Part of the fun of rooting is hating. Any good sports fan knows that. No true sports fan lacks a villainous foe. "I dislike the New York Giants," Schwartz reports, "and I hope they go 0 and 16 in perpetuity. The reason is that included among those 70,000-some odd people at Giants Stadium are many Yankee fans — at least 39,000 of them. I like the sports atmosphere in New York to be morose. I really hate the Knicks and what happened to them last year against Miami (when suspensions stemming from a fight may have cost them a chance to play in the Eastern Conference Finals) couldn't have been finer in my eyes."

For Schwartz, to root is to live. "I'm not interested in hanging out with people who are incapable of rooting," he says. "That carries over into every aspect of my life, from food to films to *anything*. I want people who love or hate, as opposed to people who say, 'Oh, that's nice.'"

Peter Shankman grew up in Worcester, and he can never recall a time when he wasn't interested in the Boston Celtics. "My brother and I would lie in bed, listening on a transistor radio to the Celtics playing the Lakers on the West Coast," he says. "My mother and father knew what we were doing, and, while they really weren't happy about it, they figured it was harmless compared to other interests we could have."

He sat home and recorded the "Bob Cousy Day" ceremony on a reel-to-reel tape recorder. And when he was old enough, he bought his own tickets.

"I can't imagine not having this in my life," he says. "What else would I get into, computers? I've been lucky enough to see some of the greatest games that have, by everyone's account, ever been played anywhere. I can't imagine growing up somewhere — I don't know, Fargo? — where you couldn't have an experience like this. It's really all I've ever known. Going to all these games has always brought out the child in me. The Celtics are kind of like my 'Rosebud.' "

This allusion to one's childhood is apropos when it comes to the way Bostonians look at their Big Four sports teams. The teams *are*, in fact, their children. The Red Sox, Bruins and Celtics are the older children.

The Red Sox, without a championship in anyone's lifetime, are spoiled underachievers who tease you and then ultimately break your heart. They can be charming, but they invariably lack true substance. If they're in town, they'll come around and take mom out to dinner. But if there is a family crisis, they are nowhere in sight. The other children just don't understand what mom sees in them.

The Bruins want desperately to please, but they just don't know how anymore. There was a brief shining moment a quarter-century ago when they had it all figured out, but somehow they lost the formula and have not been able to get it back. But they try, and for this fact alone the parents still love them.

The Celtics, once the Golden Boys who could do absolutely no wrong, frittered away an entire fortune. They don't understand why everyone thinks they're arrogant. They revel in their past glories, but they haven't done anything the family can be proud of in years.

The Patriots are the talented little brother. They have watched all their siblings disappoint people, and now they are ready to make a name for themselves. They are the family's last hope. They are desperate to make mom and dad proud.

And there you have Boston, Mass. There is no other city quite like it.

Bibliography

Appel, Marty. *Slide, Kelly, Slide*. Latham, Md.: The Scarecrow Press, 1996

Benson, Michael. *Ballparks of North America*. Jefferson, N.C.: McFarland & Co., 1989

Boston Globe newspaper articles, 1912, 1967, 1971, 1972, 1986, 1996 and 1997

Carroll, Bob; Gershman, Michael; Neff, David; and Thorn, John. *Total Football, The Official Encyclopedia of the National Football League*. New York: HarperCollins Publishers, 1997

Clark, Ellery H., Jr. *Boston Red Sox, 75th Anniversary*. Hicksville, N.Y.: Exposition Press, 1975

Coleman, Ken and Valenti, Dan. *The Impossible Dream Remembered*. Lexington, Ma.,: Stephen Greene Press, 1987

Fischler, Stan and Fischler, Shirley. *Fischler's Hockey Encyclopedia*. New York: Thomas Y. Crowell Company, 1975

Fitzgerald, Ed (editor). *Sport Magazine's Book of Major League Baseball Clubs, the National League*. New York: Grosset & Dunlap Publishers, 1955

Hardy, Stephen. *How Boston Played*. Boston: Northeastern Press, 1982

Lazenby, Roland. *The NBA Finals*. Dallas: Taylor Publishing Company, 1990

Lowry, Philip J. *Green Cathedrals*. Woburn, Ma.: Addison-Wesley, 1986

McSweeney, Bill. *The Impossible Dream*. New York: Coward-McCann, Inc., 1968

Roberts, Howard. *The Story of Pro Football*. New York, Chicago, San Francisco: Rand McNally & Company, 1953

Russell, John. *Between Games, Between Halves*. Washington, D.C. and San Francisco, 1986

Shaughnessy, Dan. *Evergreen*. New York: St. Martin's Press, 1990

Updyke, John. Reprinted from *Assorted Prose* by John Updike by permission of Alfred A. Knopf Inc. First appeared in the *New Yorker*. Hub Fans Bid Kid Adieu. New York, 1960

Portions of this book have previously appeared in Ryan, Bob, *The Road To The Super Bowl* Indianapolis: Masters Press, 1997

BUNKER HILL COMMUNITY COLLEGE
The four seasons
GV 584.5 B6 R93 1997

3 6189 00300260 6